C000136931

WHAT HAPPE
ARK OF THE COVENANT?

AND OTHER BIBLE MYSTERIES

WHAT HAPPENED TO THE ARK OF THE COVENANT?

AND OTHER BIBLE MYSTERIES

NICK PAGE

Authentic

MILTON KEYNES • COLORADO SPRINGS • HYDERABAD

Copyright © 2007 Nick Page

Reprinted 2009

15 14 13 12 11 10 09   8 7 6 5 4 3 2

First published 2007 by Authentic Media
9 Holdom Avenue, Bletchley, Milton Keynes, Bucks, MK1 1QR, UK

1820 Jet Stream Drive, Colorado Springs, CO 80921, USA

OM Authentic Media, Medchal Road, Jeedimetla Village,
Secunderabad 500 055, A.P., India

www.authenticmedia.co.uk

Authentic Media is a division of IBS-STL U.K., limited by guarantee, with its Registered Office
at Kingstown Broadway, Carlisle, Cumbria CA3 0HA. Registered in England & Wales No.
1216232. Registered charity 270162

British Library Cataloguing in Publication Data

A catalogue record for this book is available from the British Library

ISBN-13: 978-1-85078-751-8

Unless otherwise stated all Scripture quotations are from the
New Revised Standard Version, copyright © 1989, by the Division of Christian Education of
the National Council of the Churches of Christ in the USA, and are used by permission.
All rights reserved.

Book Design by Nick Page

Cover Design by fourninezero design.

Print Management by Adare

Printed and bound in the UK by J F Print Ltd., Sparkford, Somerset

CONTENTS

Introduction	7
How tall was Zacchaeus?	13
Who danced for Herod?	19
Why are there pagan idols in David's house?	27
Why does Jesus organize a procession?	35
Where did Peter go?	41
Just how strong was Samson?	53
Did Jesus visit the theater?	61
What do cherubim look like?	69
Where was Jesus born?	77
Why does Rachel want mandrakes?	83
Were Jesus' family ashamed of him?	89
What happened to the Ark of the Covenant?	99
Why did Judas kiss Jesus?	113
Who killed Goliath?	117
Where did Jesus live?	123
Why did the Israelites hate the Philistines?	129
Why did Barnabas go and fetch Paul?	135
How did Jesus die?	145
What did Uzziah's machines do?	153
How old was Joseph?	159
What books did Paul want brought to him in Rome?	165
What was so special about Joseph's coat?	171
How did Peter get in the courtyard?	177
Why do the bears kill the boys?	189
How did Luke get on board the ship?	193
Bibliography	201
Index	213

ILLUSTRATIONS

The Machaerus fortress	22
Jesus enters Jerusalem on a donkey	34
Appearances of Peter in the book of Acts	41
The death of Peter	50
Samson carrying away the gates of Gaza	54
First-century builder's workshop	60
Græco-Roman theatrical masks	66
Ivory carving from Assyria	74
An Assyrian winged bull	75
The Church of the Nativity in Bethlehem	76
First-century synagogue	88
Family of Jesus	97
Travels of the Ark of the Covenant	102
Mentions of the Ark of the Covenant in the Old Testament	104
The Ark of the Covenant	107
"Peter's house" in Capernaum	127
Map: Syria and Cilicia	140
The Church of the Holy Sepulchre, Jerusalem	144
Map: Judah under King Uzziah	152
Defensive platform with shields	157
St. Joseph and the Infant Christ	160
The Appian Way in Rome	164
Scroll and codex	167
Roman steps, St Peter Gallicantu	178
Ancient boats from Herculaneum	196

INTRODUCTION

Reading the Bible often throws up intriguing questions.

Sometimes these are big questions – questions about theology and doctrine and the big ethical issues. But more and more I seem to be focusing on the questions at the other end of the scale. Where did Jesus live? Why was Paul so worried about his parchments? How tall was Zacchaeus? Exactly how much could Samson lift?

That's what this book is all about. It's about the little alleyways of the Bible, rather than the main motorways. Alleyways don't look very important, but they can lead you to some really exciting places.

It reminds me of the city of York. It's a beautiful city, full of wonderful buildings and with a rich Christian heritage.[1] Towering over the city is the Minster, one of the greatest churches in the world; it is that which sucks in the crowds. All the main routes seem to draw you towards the Minster. But York also has a wonderful network of alleyways and passages known locally as "Snickleways." If you duck down one of these – an unprepossessing alley off Goodramgate – you find Holy Trinity church, one of the most perfect little churches in England. The floors are uneven and the riotously ramshackle box-pews look like they were laid out by a one-eyed interior designer, with a squint. It's been described as a "wonderfully wonky kind of place" and that's a perfect description.[2] Not only is it a wonderful place in its own right, but from the churchyard you can look up and see the Minster from an angle and a perspective that most of the tourists don't see.

That's the great thing about unexplored alleyways or little-known by-roads. They not only lead you to some fascinating destinations, they allow you to see the familiar places from an entirely new angle.

---

[1] For example, Constantine, the first Christian emperor of Rome, was born in York. That the man who changed the face of the Western world was qualified to play cricket for Yorkshire is a little known historical fact.

[2] Here: http://www.yorkstories.co.uk/churches/holy_trinity_goodramgate_york.php And there are some fantastic photos as well.

WELCOME TO THE WONKY PLACES

So this is a book of snickleways, a book about some of the deeply "wonky" places of the Bible; an unashamed, enthusiastic plunge into the pool of biblical history. This is an aspect of Bible study that is often missing from sermons or Bible studies, but increasingly I'm convinced of two things: firstly, that the historical and social background to the Bible can really enhance our understanding of God's message, and secondly, that people really love the history anyway.

When I've led Bible studies that talk about how tall Jesus was, or what it really meant for Paul to travel by ship, the response has been fascinating; there's been a real thirst to find out more. Partly this is because the historical background – as I hope this book shows – can sweep away some of the clutter and misconceptions. Partly it's because it's just fun to find out these things. But partly it's because all of a sudden the events seem more real, more grounded.

When you understand that Jesus' procession into Jerusalem on Palm Sunday was not the only procession of the week, you begin to see Jesus' actions and ministry in a whole new light; when you explore just why the Israelites were at war with the Philistines, you begin to see the relevance; when you explore Paul's request for parchments, you begin to grasp something of the innovative passion of the Early Church.

These are lessons that require us to enter a different world. As L.P. Hartley so memorably put it: "The past is a foreign country: they do things differently there." In many ways, the world of the first Christians, let alone the world of the Old Testament, was hugely different to ours; but in many ways it was very similar. The tensions, needs, desires and conflicts that are involved in being human have not changed much over the centuries.

So this book is an attempt to explore this different country in a way that is imaginative, open and just, well, fun.

ANYONE FOR FUN?

This book is unashamedly imaginative. It's full of "I wonders" and "What ifs?" History is all about those kind of questions. People often talk about imagination as if it were nothing to do with science or history; but the truth is that all scientific breakthroughs and all historic insights need a little bit of imagination. The role of imagination in history is crucial. To reconstruct the past, to piece together a chain of events: these are imaginative acts. It has to be based on building-bricks of real, solid data, of course, and I've sought to base these reconstructions on solid historical foundations but even when you have the bricks, it still takes imagination to put the house together.[3]

For me, it's a huge learning curve. I've written books of history and books about the Bible, but I'm keenly aware that out there are scholars with brains the size of a planet. But in many ways that makes me slightly less worried. Scholars and academics, for entirely understandable reasons, speak in a certain kind of language and live in terror of over-simplifying; me, I can say what I like.

Still, it's been quite a challenge. All I can say is that I have drawn heavily on the immensely detailed and thorough scholarship of others. The blinding insights are mostly theirs; but the mistakes are all my own.

OTHER VIEWPOINTS ARE AVAILABLE

If there is one thing that dipping a toe in this area has taught me, it is this: there is always another viewpoint. In the world of academia, and particularly in the worlds of archeology and biblical history, for every opinion there is a counter-opinion. Or seven. For every assertion about the meaning of a word, there is someone else

---

[3] A good example is the document known as Q (from the German *quelle* or source), which is the hypothetical collection of Jesus' sayings used in the gospels of Matthew and Luke. The existence of Q has now become so widely accepted that it's sometimes forgotten that Q is an imaginative construct. No actual copy exists. When I read of scholars confidently subdividing Q into different versions, I do start to wonder whether everybody ought to take a deep breath and calm down. Interestingly, more scholars are now coming to challenge the theory; see Mark Goodacre's *The Case Against Q* (http://NTGateway.com/Q)

working on a paper proving that it couldn't possibly mean that; and that the person who suggested it meant that in the first place is an ignoramus with deep personal hygiene problems. So I await a correspondence with these people with interest.

One area where I am sure I will be challenged is that, in this book, I've chosen to take the text at face value. I've chosen to start from the position that the writers were trying to tell the truth. Virtually any of the questions in this book could be answered, should you so wish, by saying "Well, they made the whole thing up in the first place", "There never was an Ark of the Covenant", "Jesus did hardly any of the things ascribed to him" and "Luke invented the boat journey."

There is no answer to that, except to say (a) that if we go down that route we get a very short book and (b) such confident assertions by people living at least two thousand years after the events may be arrogant. I can't help feeling that sometimes we have a colonial attitude to our ancestors. Today, we wouldn't dream of talking about "inferior races", yet, when dealing with the authors of the gospels or the people of Bible times, that seems to be the attitude. Bless them, they just didn't know any better... They were such primitive people, they didn't know what we know now.

Well, I think that they knew some things a lot better than we do. They knew what crucifixion was like, for example, so you'd have thought they would have been able to spot any obvious contradictions. They knew their world better than we do, for all our archeological and historical reconstructions. They knew the difference between the extraordinary and the impossible.

And the extraordinary is what this book is all about. Jesus, it seems to me, has to have been an extraordinary person. There has been, over recent years, an attempt to get back to the "historical" Jesus, to strip away the miracles and the speeches and the alleged layers of later myth-making. The trouble with this approach is that, in the attempt to strip away all that people consider historically impossible, all you get left with is the historically unremarkable. Take away, for example, Jesus' miracles, prayers, birth, resurrection, prophecies, most of his stories, and you're left with someone so dull you wonder how anyone ever took it into their heads to follow him. In seeking to get back to the real Jesus, the quest for the so-called historical Jesus only manages to remove any reason why he should be remembered in the first place.

If nothing else, I hope that through examining the ordinary background of the times, the daily life and routine, the geography, sociology and culture of the world around them, this book will shine a little light on some truly extraordinary people.

A FEW THANKS ARE IN ORDER

I'd like to thank a few people, most notably my wife, Claire, and the many friends here in Eynsham who have patiently endured my obsession with trivia and my tendency to bore them for hours with details of first century plumbing and ancient Mesopotamian leisurewear. My thanks are due to the staff of Wycliffe Hall, especially to Dr. Peter Walker, who is partly responsible for setting me off on this kind of thing and, in particular, getting me excited about Paul. The Department of Assyrian antiquities at the British Museum were very kind in bothering with my queries about the Balawat gates. Lastly, my thanks are due to the staff of various libraries for helping me in my quest, notably Wycliffe Hall, the London Library, the Bodleian Library, the Radcliffe Science Library and the Sackler Library, Oxford.

AD AND BC

A minor note. A lot of histories now prefer to use the designation CE (Common Era) and BCE (Before Common Era) instead of Anno Domini and Before Christ. I have stuck with the old designation not because I am an old fogey (well, not *just* because of that) but because I've yet to meet anyone outside of the world of academia who understands what CE and BCE mean. There's a thin line between being politically correct and just plain baffling.

AND FINALLY...

I've arranged this book so that Old Testament and New Testament topics alternate. (Sort of.) It just felt more fun and varied that way. My otherwise saintly editor, however, thought that they should be in chronological order. Despite many hours of what is termed in politics "full and frank discussion" we couldn't decide either way. So we thought we'd let you choose.

If you are logical, anal-retentive type, you may find reading the chapters in this order will keep your blood pressure at a healthier level.

What happened to the Ark of the Covenant?
Why does Rachel want mandrakes?
What was so special about Joseph's coat?
Just how strong was Samson?
Who killed Goliath?
Why did the Israelites hate the Philistines?
Why are there pagan idols in David's house?
What did Uzziah's machines do?
Why do the bears kill the boys?
What do cherubim look like?
Where was Jesus born?
How old was Joseph?
Who danced for Herod?
How tall was Zaccheus?
Did Jesus visit the theater?
Where did Jesus live?
Were Jesus' family ashamed of him?
Why does Jesus organise a procession?
Why did Judas kiss Jesus?
How did Peter get into the courtyard?
How did Jesus die?
Why did Barnabas go and fetch Paul?
Where did Peter go?
How did Luke get on board the ship?
What books did Paul want brought to him in Rome?

HOW TALL WAS ZACCHAEUS?

"Zacchaeus was a very little man, And a very little man was he..."

The story of Zacchaeus has become a staple of children's talks and songs. The tale of the tiny tree-climbing tax-collector has a kind of fairy tale quality about it, which naturally lends itself to children's talks. A lot of debate focuses on the form of the story: is it a legend? Is it a conversion story? Is it Jesus saying it's OK to be a tax-collector? Or is it simply a biographical story in which the final saying of Jesus comes at the end?

But the thing I really want to know is: just how tall was Zacchaeus?

Here's the story

> He [Jesus] entered Jericho and was passing through it. A man was there named Zacchaeus; he was a chief tax collector and was rich. He was trying to see who Jesus was, but on account of the crowd he could not, because he was short in stature. So he ran ahead and climbed a sycamore tree to see him, because he was going to pass that way. When Jesus came to the place, he looked up and said to him, "Zacchaeus, hurry and come down; for I must stay at your house today." So he hurried down and was happy to welcome him. All who saw it began to grumble and said, "He has gone to be the guest of one who is a sinner." Zacchaeus stood there and said to the Lord, "Look, half of my possessions, Lord, I will give to the poor; and if I have defrauded anyone of anything, I will pay back four times as much." Then Jesus said to him, "Today salvation has come to this house, because he too is a son of Abraham. For the Son of Man came to seek out and to save the lost."(Luke 19.1–10)

So Luke tells us three basic things about Zacchaeus: he's small, he's wealthy, he's a chief tax-collector. We get information on his physical, economic and social status. Immediately we conjure up a picture: a small man with a power complex.[1] A man who makes

---

[1] The Napoleon complex – the idea of short men becoming dictators – is a bit of a myth. At 5'6" tall Napoleon was slightly taller than average for his time, as was Adolf Hitler (5'8"). Stalin, however, was only 5'5".

up in wealth what he lacks in stature. We all "know" people like Zacchaeus. We make up our mind quickly. Which, maybe, is the point.

HOW TALL WAS HE?

Reading the gospels can be incredibly frustrating to modern readers, because they leave out a lot of what we would find interesting. In particular, they tend not to give a great deal of physical description. In Luke, for example, we see a man "covered in leprosy" (Luke 5.12), a man with a withered hand (Luke 6.6), a woman who was bent over and could not stand (Luke 13.11) and that's about it. And all those are just descriptions of physical problems which were about to be healed. Luke's description of Zacchaeus is the only purely physical description in his gospel.

But how tall was he? What did it mean to be short in Jesus' day? To find out how tall he was, we need to find out what the normal height for his time was. The information for this comes, basically, from measuring skeletons, particularly the long bones such as the femur.[2] A report on a forensic reconstruction of the face of a first century Palestinian peasant was featured in – bizarrely – *Popular Mechanics* magazine. The reconstruction, done for a BBC programme, claimed that "From an analysis of skeletal remains, archeologists had firmly established that the average build of a Semite male at the time of Jesus was 5'1", with an average weight of about 110 pounds."[3]

This has quite a few implications for the way we view Jesus. I mean, most of us wouldn't see Jesus as a short man. We'd see him as tall, often with long blond hair, a nice white nightie, pale skin and blue eyes, but if Jesus was representative of the people

---

[2] See Ubelaker, D.H., *Human Skeletal Remains: Excavation, Analysis, Interpretation*, (Washington: Taraxacum, 1978), 44ff.

[3] Fillon, M. "The Real Face of Jesus," *Popular Mechanics*, (2002). I've not been able to trace the source for these statistics, but it's in the right area. The male skeletons of the fifteen ossuaries found near Jerusalem were an average of 167cm, or 5 foot 5 inches – see Haas, N. "Anthropological Observations on the Skeletal Remains from Gi'vat ha-Mivtar," *Israel Exploration Journal* 20 (1970), 38–59. However, these were reasonably well off people (as they had a family grave). Poorer people would have been shorter because of their less nutritious diet.

of his time, he'd have been somewhere around 5'1" tall, dark-skinned, with short-cropped black hair and deep brown eyes.[4] And Zacchaeus must have been considerably shorter. We're looking at someone well below 5 foot tall; maybe 4'7" to 4'10".

A SMALL-MINDED INDIVIDUAL

The point is that in the Græco-Roman society in which Luke lived and worked, people believed that your physical appearance was directly related to your inner character: what you looked like reflected who you *were*. This is called "physiognomics" and it was widely practised by philosophers and physicians. A writer known only as "Pseudo-Aristotle" shows only too well the way in which small people were viewed in the first century world: "These are the marks of a small-minded person: he is small-limbed, small and round, dry, with small eyes and a small face, like a Corinthian or a Leucadian."[5]

The same attitudes would have been shared not only by the other people in Luke's tale – the crowd and the Pharisees – but also by those who first listened to or read the tale. They, too, would have been part of a world which viewed physical appearance as reflective of character.

The Romans operated their tax-collecting on a franchise basis: individuals "bid" for tax-collecting rights. They promised the Romans they would deliver a certain amount of tax income; once they delivered that amount – hit the target, as it were – anything above that was theirs to keep. So the job was an invitation to exploitation, bribery and cheating. Jericho would have been a good location for a tax-collector, since much of their money was made by collecting the duty owed on the transport of goods across boundaries and borders. The city was on several major trade routes

---

4   Paul writes, in 1 Corinthians that long-hair is "degrading" to a man (1 Cor. 11.14–15). Experts believe he may have been reflecting orthodox Jewish teaching of the time and the prevailing culture of his day. So Jesus may not have been as hairy as he is customarily portrayed.

5   Quoted in Parsons, M.C. "Short in Stature: Luke's Physical Description of Zacchaeus," *New Testament Studies* 47 (2001), 50–57.

– including the route from the lands beyond the Jordan to the east
– and it would have been a lucrative post.

To the crowd in Jericho, therefore, the "message" given out
by Zacchaeus's appearance is backed up by his profession. As a
tax-collector – indeed, the chief tax-collector – he was part of an
unclean profession. In the *Mishnah* it says "If a tax-gatherer enter
a house, [all that is within] the house becomes unclean."[6] Tax-
collectors were outcasts in Jewish society at the time of Jesus. It
was not just that they were collaborators, it was that they were
seen as extortioners.[7] It has been suggested that the accusation
that Jesus was a "friend of tax-collectors" is similar to the use of
the phrase "nigger-lover" in the southern states of the USA during
the 1950s and 1960s.[8] It was challenging the accepted order,
fraternizing with the enemy, not something that a "respectable"
person would do.

Zacchaeus was sinful by association: he was a tax-collector and
he was exceptionally short. What more evidence do you need?
This attitude was rejected by Jesus, time and time again. When
his disciples ask him "Who sinned, this man or his parents, that
he was born blind?" (John 9.2–3) he rejects the basis of their
question. He rejects, in short, the idea that physical abnormalities
have anything to do with inner qualities. Indeed, throughout
the story, we should remember that there is no indication that
Zacchaeus had cheated anyone. "Half of my possessions I will give
away," he says, "and *if* I have cheated anyone of anything I'll pay
back four times as much."[9]

Zacchaeus is a figure of fun, a foolish, ridiculous character so
short he can't even see over the crowd. He is not only an outcast
by virtue of his profession and his stature, he is physically excluded
from the inner circle. Luke is almost deliberately painting Zacchaeus

---

6   Tohoroth 7.6, Danby, H., *The Mishnah, Translated From the Hebrew*, (London: Oxford
    University Press, 1933), 726. The *Mishnah* is a written collection of the oral Jewish law and the
    first document of rabbinic Judaism. Although it reached its final form around 200AD, it reflects
    the earlier oral law championed by sects such as the Pharisees.

7   Ironically the name "Zacchaeus" comes from the Hebrew *Zakay*, meaning "pure, innocent."

8   Walker Jr., W.O. "Jesus and the Tax Collectors," *Journal of Biblical Literature* 97 (1978), 230.

9   Hamm, D. "Luke 19:8 Once Again: Does Zacchaeus Defend or Resolve?" *Journal of Biblical
    Literature* 107 (1988), 431–437.

as a tiny, despicable creature. What this tale is about, therefore, is the kingdom of God embracing all those whom society rejects. The kingdom's open-minded approach to people is in direct contrast to the close-minded approach of society. What happens is that Luke turns this whole thing around; the small man has a great heart. The outcast becomes the host of the feast. The person everyone avoids is the one person to whom Jesus speaks.

PHYSIOGNOMICS RULES

A happy ending, then. And a big sigh of relief that physiognomics is dead and buried.

Except, well, it isn't actually. A recent survey of CEOs in Fortune 500 companies showed that they were, on average, six feet tall; a full three inches taller than the average American man. Thirty per cent of the CEOs were six foot two or above, compared to only 3.9% of the overall United States population. Other surveys have revealed that 90% of CEOs are of above average height and less than 3% were below 5'7".[10]

In other words, we still, albeit subconsciously, feel that tall people are superior. We still engage in physiognomics, although we might not admit to it. But one look at the movies confirms that these attitudes still run deep; think how many cinematic villains are deformed in some way. James Bond is routinely pitted against villains with facial disfigurements, artificial limbs or metal teeth. Never one to ignore a good cliché, Dan Brown's *The DaVinci Code* features two "disabled" characters and – guess what – they're both villains!

It's clear that physiognomics is alive and well. We still judge inner qualities by outer appearance. Tall, good-looking with nice teeth? That'll be a successful businessman, then. Thin, pale with red eyes? Ah, that'll be the psychotic, albino monk. Life is so simple when you stick to the surface.

It works in reverse, as well, with many, many people believing that transforming the outside of the body will change their character.

---

[10] Rauch, J. "Short guys finish last," *Economist* (23 December 1995).

But the sad truth is that if a nasty git puts on an expensive suit, he'll just be a well-dressed nasty git.

At least Zacchaeus had no illusions about himself. He saw himself for who he really was. And unlike so many in that crowd, he knew he needed Jesus. He knew that he had to see this man. He sacrificed what little dignity he had to see Jesus. He knew that most people in Jericho thought him despicable, but he went one better: he made himself look ridiculous.

And the final irony in Luke's deliciously ironic tale is that, while all the spiritually and physically perfectly proportioned people rage and grumble, this small man, this man about whom everyone had made up their minds, is welcomed into the kingdom of God.[11] He responded to Jesus, changed his life and revealed that he was, in fact, the biggest man in town.

---

[11] A legend from a few hundred years later tells the tale of Zacchaeus being made – much against his will – Bishop of Caesarea. The story is obviously fiction, but the reasons Zacchaeus gives for not wanting to be a Bishop would probably be echoed by many a modern incumbent: "...only grant me not to have this name," he says, "for it teems with bitter envy and danger." Pseudo-Clement. *Homilies* 3.63.

WHO DANCED FOR HEROD?

What prize would you give to a twelve-year-old girl for a dancing display? Some gift vouchers? A rosette or cup? The severed head of a rebellious preacher?

> For it was Herod who had sent and seized John and bound him in prison for the sake of Herodias, his brother Philip's wife, because he had married her. For John had been saying to Herod, "It is not lawful for you to have your brother's wife." And Herodias had a grudge against him and wanted to put him to death. But she could not, for Herod feared John, knowing that he was a righteous and holy man, and he kept him safe. When he heard him, he was greatly perplexed, and yet he heard him gladly. But an opportunity came when Herod on his birthday gave a banquet for his nobles and military commanders and the leading men of Galilee. For when Herodias's daughter came in and danced, she pleased Herod and his guests. And the king said to the girl, "Ask me for whatever you wish, and I will give it to you." And he vowed to her, "Whatever you ask me, I will give you, up to half of my kingdom." And she went out and said to her mother, "For what should I ask?" And she said, "The head of John the Baptist." And she came in immediately with haste to the king and asked, saying, "I want you to give me at once the head of John the Baptist on a platter." And the king was exceedingly sorry, but because of his oaths and his guests he did not want to break his word to her. And immediately the king sent an executioner with orders to bring John's head. He went and beheaded him in the prison and brought his head on a platter and gave it to the girl, and the girl gave it to her mother. When his disciples heard of it, they came and took his body and laid it in a tomb." (Mark 6.17–29 ESV)

The death of John the Baptist is a weird story. At its climax is the famous dance of Salome, a dance which has given licence to thousands of writers, artists, playwrights and film-makers to be quite salacious, while smugly claiming they were just showing what was in the Bible. Here's a good example

What the young princess danced was the exciting, voluptuous dance of the Egyptians and the Greeks... One after another the veils came away, shaking like foam, and dropped to the floor. The purple hem of the byssus skirt with its many folds, worn under the veils, jerked and twisted in the dance like a blood-red snake round the slender legs of the dancer above her delicate ankles.

Salome was dancing now with shoulders and breasts bared... There was such silence in the hall that all the intent spectators could hear the jingle of the gold bracelets and anklets at every step the dancer gave. Now she threw back her shoulders and with her right hand suddenly pulled off her last garment, the white byssus skirt, from her hips, and at that moment with her light brown body shimmering like sandalwood in the soft light, dropped to the floor.[1]

Crikey. I bet the author had to go and have a lie down after that. Despite the rather fevered nature of the description, this passage encapsulates so much of the received wisdom about the event. Salome has become a byword for lewd dancing and malevolent, bitter hatred. She's been the subject of numerous paintings; she's been danced by Rita Hayworth and immortalized in an opera by Richard Strauss. She is synonymous in popular folklore with the dance of the seven veils.

But the Bible doesn't say anything about what type of dance it was. Nor, in fact, does it mention the dancing girl's name. And, far from depicting Salome as a kind of buxom stripper, we're left with a picture of a girl, maybe only twelve or so; uncertain, unsure, and used as a pawn in a game of power between husband and wife.

A BIT ABOUT ANTIPAS

First a bit of background. The Herod in question is Herod Antipas, son of Herod the Great and ruler of Galilee. Antipas was married to the daughter of Aretas, King of Arabia. While on a visit to Rome,

---

[1]   Busch, F., *The Five Herods*, (London: Robert Hale, 1958), 115–116.

he stayed with a half-brother of his – confusingly also named Herod – who had a wife called Herodias.[2] Herod Antipas fell in love with Herodias and she agreed to elope with him, provided he divorce his first wife. She, however, got wind of what was happening and fled to her own country.

John the Baptist, meanwhile, heard of this behavior and started preaching publicly against it. The issue was that Leviticus prohibits marrying the wife of one's brother (Lev. 18.16), so Antipas – a ruler of a kingdom the major part of whose subjects were Jews – was ritually impure (Lev. 20.21). This was not the only transgression of the purity laws with which Herod Antipas was associated; he built Tiberias, his grand new city on the western shore of Galilee, over a pagan graveyard, which meant that any Jew settling in the city would be impure for seven days (Num. 19.11–16). Antipas had to settle the city with slaves and freed prisoners, whom he provided with houses on condition they never leave the city.[3]

John's main message called for personal repentance and prophesied the imminent removal of the wicked and the arrival of the Messiah. When you combine this with personal attacks on the current ruler, it's easy to see why Antipas would have been angry. However, his anger would also have been exacerbated by the fact that John was active in the desert region near Nabatea – where Antipas' first wife came from. This would have been the last place where Antipas wanted unrest.[4]

So, Antipas arrested John and incarcerated him in the Machaerus, a hill-top fortress built originally by Herod the Great on the east side of the Dead Sea. Excavations at the Machaerus have revealed that the palace fits the story well: there was a prison and, crucially

---

[2] Herodias was a relative, the grand-daughter of Herod the Great. The Herodian family tree is *incredibly* confusing. See Connolly, P., *Living in the Time of Jesus of Nazareth*, (Oxford: Oxford University Press, 1983), 39.

[3] Taylor, J.E., *John the Baptist Within Second Temple Judaism*, (London: SPCK, 1997), 244. Witherington III, B., *The Gospel of Mark: Socio-Rhetorical Commentary*, (Grand Rapids: Eerdmans, 2001), 213.

[4] See Webb, R.L., *John the Baptiser and Prophet: A Socio-Historical Study*, (Sheffield: JSOT Press, 1991), 366–67. Indeed, after John's death, Aretas did avenge the insult to his daughter by soundly defeating Antipas's army; see Scobie, C.H.H., *John the Baptist*, (London: SCM Press, 1964), 180.

The site of the Machaerus fortress (now in Jordan), where John the Baptist was imprisoned and killed. The picture looks west, across the Dead Sea and into modern Israel.

for the way the tale is presented in the gospels, two dining rooms, one large and one small.[5]

However, the arrest was not entirely Antipas's decision. It was Herodias who burned with rage at the words of John, who wanted him dead and buried. In the Gospels, Herod Antipas is depicted as weak and vacillating. He was content to put John out of action, to lock him up, remove him from the desert, but, once he had John incarcerated, he used to go and listen to him (Mark 6.20). He was scared of John, but also fascinated by this wild preacher, this throwback to the great days of Israel's prophets.

So we come to the climactic evening: Herod's birthday. Herod knew how to throw a party. He may not have been very good at observing the Jewish law, but when it came to Roman parties, he was in his element. Josephus tells us of a banquet he threw to celebrate

---

[5]   Gundry, R.H., *Mark: A Commentary on his Apology for the Cross*, (Grand Rapids: Eerdmans, 1993), 314. The other Herodian palaces such as Masada, the Herodion and Jericho all appear to lack separate dining rooms – a strong argument for the historical reliability of this story. On these fortresses, see Murphy-O'Connor, J., *The Holy Land: An Archaeological Guide From Earliest Times to 1700*, (Oxford: Oxford University Press, 1986), 237–241, 283–6.

the signing of a treaty between Tiberius' representative Vitellus and Artabanus of Parthia. The party involved the construction of a magnificent pavilion in the middle of the river for the occasion.[6]

In the large dining room, we can imagine the men dining together, while the women gather in the small dining room. When everyone had eaten (a lot) and drunk (a lot), then the stage was set. Herodias's daughter came forward to dance.

ENTER SALOME, DANCING

But who was she? And how old was she? The gospel accounts do not give her name. However, we know from Josephus that Herodias had a daughter called Salome from her first marriage. Salome was later to marry Philip the Tetrarch and after him, Aristobulus.[7]

Since this is the only daughter we know of from Herodias's first marriage, it seems likely that Salome was, indeed, the dancer. As to her age, the gospels use a particular word to describe her: *korasion.* The exact meaning is unknown, but it appears to be a diminutive of the Greek word for girl or maiden. It probably means a girl who is not quite of marriageable age; the same word is used of Jairus' daughter who is twelve years old (Mark 5.42). We don't know when Salome was born, but she was old enough to marry Philip before he died in 34AD. So, if John was beheaded some time between 29AD and 32AD, Salome would have been around twelve or thirteen.[8]

The probability that Salome was only twelve puts a different perspective on the dance we imagine she performed. The dance need not have been the erotic frenzy that is often portrayed. Some scholars have seen in this scene an atmosphere of a stag party, but the dance could have been very tame by our standards. It's something of a shock that a high-ranking girl such as Salome should have danced before a group of men at all; dancing was not a respectable

---

[6] Taylor, *John the Baptist Within Second Temple Judaism*, 247. Roller, D.W., *The Building Program of Herod the Great*, (Berkeley: University of California Press,1998), 244.

[7] Philip was her uncle and Aristobulus her cousin. I *told* you the family tree was confusing. See Connolly, *Living in the Time of Jesus of Nazareth*, 39. Busch, *The Five Herods*, 120.

[8] Hoehner, H.W., *Herod Antipas*, (Cambridge: Cambridge University Press, 1972), 155–56.

occupation. However, it's not impossible. Jewish literature records several kinds of dancing, and it is not necessary to believe that every kind of dancing is immoral or disrespectful. Salome could have entertained the guests without any loss of dignity – or clothing. We have to remember that this was a banquet. Herod was probably drinking heavily, and in that atmosphere, a young girl dancing for her elders would be warmly received. And that's the tone of the whole scene. A graceful, elegant dance would have been enough to push a drunken Herod into his boastful promise.[9]

Of course, it may be that Herod Antipas fancied his step-daughter, but even that, in the context of the time, is not quite as creepy as it seems today. In the Roman society where Herod had been brought up (not to mention Salome herself), twelve was a perfectly normal marriageable age. Roman girls married young, often before they'd even reached puberty. Roman law set the minimum age of marriage as twelve, but the law seems to have been frequently flouted.[10]

Whether it was lust, affection, or just drunken high spirits, one thing is certain: Herodias knew exactly what effect the dance would have. The scheming, brooding presence of Herodias hovers over this tale. It was she who set the dance up. She sent Salome in to dance before the men. And when Herod made his drunken offer – "Whatever you ask me, I will give you, even half of my kingdom" – the first thing Salome did was to run into the next dining room and ask her mother what she should ask for. It was her mother's idea, her mother's plan.

This is the true grubbiness of the tale. It's not about some nubile stripper getting men all hot and bothered; it's about a vengeful woman using her own daughter as a lure. Salome was told to go and dance and secure the promise of a reward; and then to come back for further instructions. So that's what she does.

And the reward she was told to ask for is the head of John the Baptist. On a plate.

---

[9]   Hoehner, *Herod Antipas*, 156.

[10] Stark, R., *The Rise of Christianity: How the Obscure, Marginal Jesus Movement Became the Dominant Religious Force in the Western World in a few Centuries*, (San Francisco: HarperSanFrancisco, 1997), 106–107.

PROOF OF DEATH

Why would she want the head? Simply because the head was proof of death. Throughout the ages severed heads have been publicly displayed – stuck on poles, hung on trees – to prove to people that the person is actually dead. Herodias was taking no chances. She had seen the fascination that John the Baptist held for her husband. She did not want Herod spiriting the preacher away and claiming he was dead. She wanted to see the evidence. On a plate, right there before her.

Herod was in a corner and couldn't back out. So, John was executed. His followers retrieved his body and buried it, probably near the Machaerus, since it was the usual custom to bury the body on the same day. And Herod, it seems, never quite recovered from the enormity of his crime. When he first heard reports about Jesus, his fears and guilt came rushing back to the surface. Mark 6.16 says, "But when Herod heard this, he said, 'John, the man I beheaded, has been raised from the dead!'" On the night Jesus was arrested, Herod tried to talk to him, to recreate, perhaps, the conversations he had with John. But Jesus was not John, and he refused to talk (Luke 23.6–12).

THE STUFF OF LEGEND

So that's the story. A young girl dances before a drunken ineffective king, all to secure the death of a public nuisance.

Salome has since been changed by legend. Her age has increased and her clothing decreased. She has become the archetype of the woman who uses her erotic charms for an evil end. A fourteenth century legend had her walking over a frozen lake. When the ice broke, she sank to her neck in the water and her head was torn off by the ice floes.[11]

Salome was really a puppet; it was her mother who was pulling the strings. For Herodias, however, I am delighted to say it all ended badly. Having maneuvered herself into the arms of Herod

---

[11] Busch, *The Five Herods*, 120.

Antipas, she became envious when her brother, Herod Agrippa I, was given the title king. So she insisted that Antipas should go to Rome to ask for a similar advancement, which in the end brought about his downfall. The Emperor Gaius Caligula, unimpressed by this scheming couple, and believing that they were, in fact, traitors, gave their lands and their money to Agrippa, and banished them to Lyons, where they ended their lives in "perpetual" exile.

As Josephus puts it: "And thus did God punish Herodias for her envy at her brother, and Herod also for giving ear to the vain discourses of a woman."[12]

---

[12] Hoehner, *Herod Antipas*, 168. Roller, *The Building Program of Herod the Great*, 244. Taylor, *John the Baptist within Second Temple Judaism*, 247.

WHY ARE THERE PAGAN
IDOLS IN DAVID'S HOUSE?

It has all the elements of a thriller: a hero who survives numerous assassination attempts; an evil madman driven by hatred; a woman, close to the villain, who falls in love with the hero. And like all the best thrillers, the hero looks to be doomed, but tricks the villain and escapes.

1 Samuel chapters 18 and 19 tell of a series of threats to David's life by the increasingly paranoid King Saul. David has been successful against the Philistines (much to Saul's irritation); he has married the king's daughter (much to Saul's annoyance); he is friendly with Saul's son Jonathan (much to... well, you get the idea). The king hates him. Saul hurls a spear at David when he is playing the harp, then, in a final attempt to kill David, sends a band of soldiers to surround his house

> Saul sent messengers to David's house to keep watch over him, planning to kill him in the morning. David's wife Michal told him, "If you do not save your life tonight, tomorrow you will be killed." So Michal let David down through the window; he fled away and escaped. Michal took an idol and laid it on the bed; she put a net of goats' hair on its head, and covered it with the clothes. When Saul sent messengers to take David, she said, "He is sick." Then Saul sent the messengers to see David for themselves. He said, "Bring him up to me in the bed, that I may kill him." When the messengers came in, the idol was in the bed, with the covering of goats' hair on its head. Saul said to Michal, "Why have you deceived me like this, and let my enemy go, so that he has escaped?" Michal answered Saul, "He said to me, 'Let me go; why should I kill you?'" (1 Sam. 19.11–17).

It's a great story, and probably the earliest account in literature of the "decoy dummy in the bed" trick.[1] Michal lets David down through the window. Clearly their house backed onto the city wall, like that of Rahab the prostitute (Josh. 2.15). By letting David down through the window, he avoided the gate – which would have been

---

[1] It's a trick that you can find replicated in many stories, from Sherlock Holmes to the film *Albert RN*, where prisoners make a dummy to cover the absence of their escaping colleagues.

guarded. The life-size idol fools the soldiers into thinking David's ill. When Saul asks his daughter "Why have you let my enemy go?" Michal replies that she had to: he was threatening to kill her. It's a clever lie; it justifies her action, whilst at the same time preserving the fiction that she still respects her father.

But it does leave you with an interesting – and perhaps uncomfortable – question: what was a life-size, pagan idol doing in David's house? Psalm 59 is traditionally ascribed to this period in David's life; how can the poet who wrote "You, O God, are my fortress" (Ps. 59.9) possibly have a giant idol in his hallway?

MICHAL IN CHARGE

The first thing that strikes you about this story is how utterly wet David is. He gives the impression of simply not knowing what to do. It is Michal who takes the initiative and puts into practice a successful plan

- she finds out about the plot (1 Sam. 19.11a)
- she tells him to escape (1 Sam. 19.11b)
- she lowers him through the window (1 Sam. 19.12)
- she puts the idol in the bed (1 Sam. 19.13)
- she delays the investigation with stories of his illness (1 Sam. 19.14)
- she tricks her father into thinking her hand was forced (1 Sam. 19.17)

Indeed, in the few accounts we have of her, Michal's individuality is striking. She has a spark to her; a rebellious streak.

The fact is, Saul never planned on David marrying any of his daughters, let alone Michal. He intended it as a reward to lure David to his death. Initially he promises him his eldest daughter Merab, as long as David continues to fight the Philistines. David has the awestruck reaction of any "commoner" marrying into royalty: "Who am I and who are my kinsfolk, my father's family in Israel, that I should be son-in-law to the king?" (1 Sam. 18.18). Perhaps he'd have thought a bit harder had he substituted the phrase "psychotic madman" for "king", but he goes ahead and fights the Philistines, successfully. Saul responds in typical fashion: he marries his eldest daughter to someone else. Then he finds that another of his daughters, Michal, has fallen in love with David and this is something he can use to his advantage: "Now Saul's daughter Michal loved David. Saul was told, and the thing pleased him. Saul thought, 'Let me give her to him that she may be a snare for him and that the hand of the Philistines may be against him.' Therefore Saul said to David a second time, 'You shall now be my son-in-law'" (1 Sam. 18.20–21).

There's a catch, though. In order for David to marry Michal he has to bring back one hundred Philistine foreskins. Since most men, let alone Philistines, are not in the habit of donating their foreskins to a worthy cause, David has to go and kill them. Saul believes he will be killed in battle; but of course David achieves the task and Saul reluctantly agrees to let his daughter marry his enemy.

The tale reveals a lot about the characters of all three protagonists. Firstly, it shows a young David, proficient on the battlefield, but utterly naive when it comes to the machinations of court intrigue. He is awestruck by the whole situation and seems never to grasp that Saul might actually not like him very much. That is not to say that he goes into this marriage naively. He knows exactly why he's doing it: he wants to join the royal family. David might have been "a man of faith" but he was not against a bit of social climbing to serve his own ends. He didn't get to be king by merely strumming his harp and writing some neat lyrics about sheep.

Secondly, we see Michal declaring her love for David. The unusual nature of this is lost to us now, but 1 Samuel 18.20 has been described as "the only time in biblical Hebrew narrative when a woman is said to love a man."[2] For a woman in those times to declare such a thing, to take the initiative, was highly unusual; especially when we remember that she was the daughter of a king, bound by protocol and royal routine. She *loved* this man, and, unusually, she let it be known. Unlike Bathsheba and Abigail, two of David's other wives, Michal is not described as "beautiful", nor

[2] Clines, D.J.A., and T.C. Eskenazi, *Telling Queen Michal's Story: An Experiment in Comparative Interpretation*, (Sheffield: Sheffield Academic Press, 1991), 33.

does the text ever suggest that David loved Michal. He just wanted to be the king's son-in-law (1 Sam. 18.26).[3]

Third, we see a devious, unscrupulous king use that to his advantage. Saul's hatred of David has been likened to Lyndon B. Johnson's obsession with the Kennedys[4] and there is that sense of corrosive paranoia about it. Saul's hatred of David is certainly stronger than his love for his daughter, for he was planning to kill the man she loved, to make her a bride and a widow.[5] He didn't care that destroying David would also destroy her.

So we can build up a picture; a young woman, unloved by her father, is given away in marriage as a kind of trap. She is desperate to be loved by her new husband, but he has married her for his own ends. Her father cares nothing for her. Her husband cares nothing for her. She is, effectively, on her own.

WHAT ABOUT THE IDOLS?

Which brings us back to the story. Sometimes we don't really read the Bible. We see what we want to see, rather than what's there. In particular we build up significant Old Testament figures into quasi-Christian saints. Top of the list of these is David, the great shepherd king of Israel. "The writer of all those Psalms was surely a great man of God," goes the argument; "I mean, of course he had a bit of a lapse with Bathsheba, but other than that he was perfect." This idolization of David has led to rather anguished pleading from some commentators: "It is impossible to suppose that David could have either used, or countenanced the use of these images. God was too much a spiritual reality to him to allow such material media of worship to be even thought of."[6]

Well if David didn't "countenance the use" of them, what were they doing there? The idea that these idols, big enough to be mistaken for a man, could be hidden in David's house, is ludicrous.

[3] Brenner, A., *Samuel and Kings*, (Sheffield: Sheffield Academic Press, 2000), 38.

[4] Brueggemann, W., *First and Second Samuel*, (Louisville: John Knox Press, 1990), 143.

[5] Brenner, *Samuel and Kings*, 38.

[6] Blaikie, W.G., *The First Book of Samuel*, (London: Hodder & Stoughton, 1888), 307.

These were big, and very obvious.[7] Having said that, they clearly belonged to Michal: she used them and she knew where to find them. David must have known they were there, but there is no indication that he cared one way or the other. God certainly was, in the words of Blaikie, "a spiritual reality to him", but not so much that he was going to tell the king's daughter what to do; certainly not if it jeopardised his progression to the throne. David here is young, naive, passive; he has a lot of growing up to do, both mentally and spiritually. He has not yet learned to have full faith in God. There are idols in his house because, well, he isn't bothered about them.

Michal's father was, at least, on speaking terms with God, but Michal seems to have looked in the other direction. Michal clearly does not share her husband's faith: she worships the gods of the Canaanites. The story hints at a fact that we don't like to acknowledge about the golden years of Israel, under David and Solomon; they were never quite as golden as we think, because the other Canaanite gods never went away. This is a time when Jerusalem has not been conquered, when there are Canaanite city-states still spread across the land and their practices were a constant lure. Saul ends up consulting a necromancer (1 Sam 28.8–25), but even some of the great heroes of the Old Testament get involved with false gods. Gideon gives in to idolatry (Judg. 8.22–28). Solomon builds the Temple, but ends up worshipping foreign gods (1 Kgs. 11.4–8). Throughout the times described in the Old Testament there was a battle going on, a battle between the true worship of God and the false faith of Canaan.

Many houses must have been like David's, with the old idols still in the corner. The greatest struggle for the prophets, not to mention people like David, was to get people to commit fully to God. They would follow him when things were good; they would make their public profession, but there, hidden away in a cupboard or a box in their house, they would keep the household gods. Just in case.

---

[7] The Hebrew word used to describe the idols is *teraphim*. This is the same word used to describe the household gods stolen by Rachel from her father Laban. In Rachel's case the gods were small enough to be hidden in a trunk. These were obviously a lot bigger. See Klein, R.W., *1 Samuel*, (Waco: Word Books, 1983), 197–198.

WHAT HAPPENED NEXT

Michal's story is not, sadly, a romance, but more of a tragedy. She helps David escape, but there is no indication that he tried to take her with him. Of course, he could have realized that he was heading into danger, but the story doesn't say that he tried to persuade her or she tried to accompany him. There is already a distance between them.

For Michal it was the beginning of another strange twist in her story. David disappears and open conflict breaks out between him and her father. Saul gives her away to another man: "Palti, [or Paltiel, elsewhere] son of Laish, who was from Gallim" (1 Sam. 25.44). Maybe Saul has decided David won't come back. Maybe Michal has decided that he will not want her, even if he does. Once again, she is being traded like a piece of meat.

And here more irony piles in, because Palti clearly does love Michal. When, eventually, the civil war between the House of David and the House of Saul is ended, David agrees to end hostilities, but only if he can have Michal back (2 Sam. 3.14). It cannot be that he has any affection for her – in the intervening years he has married six more wives and fathered a son by each of them.[8] It's rather that he has learnt to be assertive; he is in charge now. It's a political move; David wants to strengthen his claim to the throne by reasserting his connection to the House of Saul.

Again, Michal changes hands. Sadly, Paltiel seems to have fallen in love with her; he accompanies her the whole way, weeping, and only leaves her when ordered to do so. She seems to have found a man, at last, who loved her, only to lose out once again.[9]

The final act in Michal's saga occurs when David brings the Ark of the Covenant to Jerusalem, the city he has conquered and the place that will be known as "the city of David." As the Ark enters the city, David, dressed only in a linen cloth, dances before it; a whirling,

---

[8] The wives are Ahinoam of Jezreel; Abigail the widow of Nabal of Carmel; Maacah, daughter of King Talmai of Geshur; Haggith; Abital, and Eglah (2 Sam. 3.1–5)

[9] There has been some debate about the legality of David's demand, but he seems to be following ancient law and custom. See Anderson, A.A., *2 Samuel*, (Dallas: Word Books, 1989), 57–58. Clines, and Eskenazi, *Telling Queen Michal's Story: An Experiment in Comparative Interpretation*, 81.

ecstatic figure. Once again, a window features in this story; Michal is standing at a window watching her husband, the king, dance, but now the position is changed. Once she loved him and rescued him; now she "despised him in her heart" (2 Sam. 6.16). Once she helped him escape death; now she sees him exposing himself in front of anyone who cares to look. As he returns home after this triumph, Michal comes to greet him: "And David returned to bless his household. But Michal the daughter of Saul came out to meet David and said, 'How the king of Israel honored himself today, uncovering himself today before the eyes of his servants' female servants, as one of the vulgar fellows shamelessly uncovers himself!'" (2 Sam. 6.20).

What changed Michal from an adoring into a bitter wife? Well, the intervening years can't have done much to confirm David as a loving husband. But maybe the clue lies back at that first escape, with the putting of idols in her bed. David has learnt, in the intervening years, the true power of the God he worshipped; that's why he is prepared to dance and whirl in an unselfconscious ecstasy. Michal, however, never learns to let go. She is still locked into a world of status, despite the fact that her status as daughter of one king and wife of another has never really done her much good.

She ends her life in a strange, lonely place. The daughter of a deposed, disgraced king; the unfavored wife of his successor. An in-between figure, Michal ends her life childless. Possibly this is because David never slept with her again after this final argument, but the Bible seems to link her barrenness with her lack of belief in Yahweh: she is portrayed, in the words of one commentator "as barren of belief in the God of Israel, the God who could open her womb."[10]

The idols were in David's house because Michal put them there. This young, independent, clever woman was always prone to idol worship: but not just idols of stone and clay. At the start of their marriage, she idolised a young, naive David who didn't really care about her. Later on, she idolised status, honor, dignity and "the correct way to behave." Both of her idols were to let her down.

Michal's tragedy is, in the end, startling modern. Like so many people today, she simply idolised the wrong things.

---

[10] Brenner, *Samuel and Kings*, 45.

Jesus enters Jerusalem on a donkey. A wonderful carving from the west façade of Strasbourg Cathedral (13th century). I am particularly fond of the donkey.

WHY DOES JESUS
ORGANIZE A PROCESSION?

Each year or so, the leaders of the biggest nations in the world make their way, with much pomp and ceremony, to a meeting where they make Very Important Decisions.[1] At least, that's what the press releases always say. What's interesting is that there is always a "counter-procession", as it were; an alternative gathering, where "anti-capitalist" campaigners stage their own marches and demonstrations, put on their own summits and organize events to make the points they want to make.

Fast rewind to 33AD[2] and you find Jesus doing exactly the same thing.

ORGANIZED SPONTANEITY

It's part of growing up in a church: Palm Sunday, the Sunday before Easter, and everyone's waving palm crosses, or big leaves they've made out of cardboard in Sunday school; and all to celebrate Jesus' triumphant entry into Jerusalem.

The impression given – the impression I grew up with at least – is that it was a spontaneous event; yet if you look at the text closely, you notice that the whole thing has the air of organization about it. Yes, it certainly has a kind of madcap, carnival atmosphere, but this has been staged. What spontaneity there was, was organized.

When they were approaching Jerusalem, at Bethphage and Bethany, near the Mount of Olives, he sent two of his disciples and said to them, "Go into the village ahead of you, and immediately as you enter it, you will find tied there a colt that has never been ridden; untie it and bring it. If anyone says to you, 'Why are you doing this?' just say this, 'The Lord needs it and will send it back here immediately.'" They went away and found a colt tied near a door, outside in the street. As they were

---

[1]   It's either the G7 or the G8. Sometimes it seems to be the G10. You'd have thought that the most powerful economies would have been able to count.

[2]   Or possibly 30AD depending on your preference. For alternative dates of the crucifixion, see Finegan, J., *Handbook of Biblical Chronology: Principles of Time Reckoning in the Ancient World and Problems of Chronology in the Bible*, (Peabody: Hendrickson Publishers, 1998), 353–369.

untying it, some of the bystanders said to them, "What are you doing, untying the colt?" They told them what Jesus had said; and they allowed them to take it. Then they brought the colt to Jesus and threw their cloaks on it; and he sat on it. Many people spread their cloaks on the road, and others spread leafy branches that they had cut in the fields. Then those who went ahead and those who followed were shouting, "Hosanna! Blessed is the one who comes in the name of the Lord! Blessed is the coming kingdom of our ancestor David! Hosanna in the highest heaven!" Then he entered Jerusalem and went into the Temple; and when he had looked around at everything, as it was already late, he went out to Bethany with the twelve (Mark 11.1–11).

Now that's a curious end to the event: after all the joy and acclamation of the procession, Jesus just has a look round and goes away again. After all the build-up, he goes home because it was getting a bit late. I don't know about you, but I'm looking for a bit more. It's as if Aragorn, in *The Lord of the Rings*, leads his forces to the gates of Mordor only to buy a postcard and go home again; it's like Luke Skywalker, flying into the Deathstar, just to get a pint of milk and some bread. Rocky Balboa climbs into the ring to face his opponent, then they climb back out again and go and have a coffee.

I'm looking for an explosion, a act of protest, a confrontation. So where is it? The answer is that it's already happened. The point of this story is in the journey. The protest is in the procession.

DONKEY RIDING FOR FUN AND PROPHET

This is an organized protest. This is deliberate fulfilment of prophecy. Jesus orders his disciples to go and fetch a colt from the village. He has the colt brought to him, probably near the crossroads, where the road to Bethphage went off to the south from the main Jericho-Jerusalem road.[3] He's doing this to echo the words of Zechariah: "Rejoice greatly, O daughter Zion!

---

[3] Wilkinson, J., *Jerusalem as Jesus Knew It: archaeology as evidence* (London: Thames and Hudson, 1978), 114–15.

Shout aloud, O daughter Jerusalem! Lo, your king comes to you; triumphant and victorious is he, humble and riding on a donkey, on a colt, the foal of a donkey" (Zech. 9.9).

Zechariah is not a prophet who features greatly in sermons these days (largely because he's so flipping difficult to understand) but few prophets of the Old Testament contain more predictions about the Messiah; the Anointed One, the forthcoming king of Israel. This is one of those predictions and, in choosing a colt, Jesus is making the point. "I'm the king" is the message, at least for those who know their Old Testament prophets.

Whether they spotted the reference or not, the people greet him with a custom usually associated with royalty; they throw their cloaks on the ground.[4]

But think about that colt for a moment. This is clearly a young animal; one that has never been ridden. It's probably quite small as well. There's something comic about this; something humble and unassuming, like a grown man riding a child's bike. Yes, he's making a visual quote from Zechariah, but there is also a sense of joy, a sense of fun.

So far, so Messianic, but there's still the problem of the ending. Why go to all that trouble just to point people to the Hebrew Scriptures? The answer lies, perhaps, in what is happening on the other side of the city.

MIRROR IMAGE

Mark is very clear about the direction of the procession: Jesus and his disciples came into the city from the east, over the Mount of Olives, picking up his transport from Bethphage on the way. Looking at the overall shape of Mark's account, he also implies that it happened on the start of the week of Passover, one of the most important, if not the most important week of the Jewish calendar.

---

[4] 2 Kings 9.13 shows Jehu being greeted in a similar way. Indeed, the practice of spreading garments before a beloved or celebrated figure was known in the Graeco-Roman world. Plutarch tells of troops spreading their clothes at the feet of Cato the Younger when he left the army. There is also a sarcophagus of Adelphia which shows a man laying some kind of garment beneath the hooves of the horse on which Adelphia is riding.

Jerusalem despite being a very small city in area, had some forty-five thousand inhabitants. But during the festivals that population could swell to as many as one hundred and eighty thousand.[5] The crowding, combined with the religious fervour of the occasion, made for a combustible mixture, which is why another procession entered the city on that day, or near to it. The tinderbox atmosphere of the festival meant that Pontius Pilate, the Roman prefect in charge of Idumaea, Judea and Samaria was in town.

Despite various Hollywood depictions, Jerusalem was not full of Roman soldiers. Pilate probably had at his disposal around three thousand troops. For most of the time, control of Jerusalem was delegated to the high priest and the council, who policed the city using the Temple guards. This force was several thousand strong, at least. During the first Jewish revolt, 8,500 Temple guards were killed defending Ananus, a former high priest.[6]

There was a small garrison of troops in the Antonia fortress, which the Romans built to the north of the Temple, specifically so that they could overlook the Temple Mount. Most of the time, they kept a low profile, but at festival time it was important that the Roman presence should be visible. Josephus records several major disturbances and wrote that the feasts were "the usual time for sedition to flare up."[7]

Most of the year Pilate lived in Caesarea Maritime, the city on the Mediterranean coast which Herod the Great had constructed along Græco-Roman lines. Caesarea was temperate, freshened by sea breezes; it was equipped with a hippodrome and theater and all the sophistication of a Roman city; it even had an alternative name, "Sebaste" which is the Greek form of the Roman name "Augustus": in every way it was a long way from Jerusalem. But during the festival, Pilate would have come into Jerusalem, entering the city with all the pomp and ceremony that the Roman army could muster. As we have seen, there weren't that many troops in

---

[5] See Jeremias, J., *Jerusalem in the time of Jesus: an investigation into economic and social conditions during the New Testament period* (London: SCM Press, 1974), 77–84, where he does some very complex calculations based on the area of the Temple courts.

[6] Sanders, E.P., *The Historical Figure of Jesus*, (London: Penguin, 1995), 23–26.

[7] Josephus, *The Jewish War*, (Harmondsworth: Penguin Classics, 1981), 40

the region – certainly not enough to quell a major disturbance. The purpose of Pilate entering Jerusalem was to make sure that the Jews remembered who was in charge; to remind them, perhaps, that even though the numbers of Roman troops in the city were small, there were a lot more if necessary.[8] So there would have been gleaming armor, polished leather, cavalrymen on horseback, armored foot soldiers and at the head of it all, the Imperial standard, the golden eagle; it was a physical demonstration of who was in charge. This was the emperor's representative, marching in to take charge of the city. The road from Caesarea probably took Pilate via Joppa on the coast, then up through the hills and into Jerusalem from the west. Not only that, but Pilate's headquarters would no doubt have been in the former palace of Herod the Great – the most impressive building in Jerusalem. (After all, the most powerful people always get the best accommodation.) And Herod's palace was on the western side.

Viewed in this light, therefore, Jesus' procession takes on a whole new meaning. This was not some random act or spontaneous outburst; it was a mirror image. On one side of the city – the west – a show of power and prestige, a deliberate display of economic, political and military authority; on the other side of the city an entirely different form of power and a deliberate display of prophetic authority. To the west of the city the emperor's representative comes riding on a horse, surrounded by soldiers; from the east, God's representative comes riding on a one-size-too-small donkey, surrounded by a rag-tag army of outcasts and oddballs. Coming through the western gate of the city is the kingdom of the world; while on the other side enters the kingdom of God.

This "political" aspect of this event is also picked up in Jesus' conscious embodiment of Zechariah. We have seen that he chose an animal to identify, as it were, with this passage. But the passage goes on: "He will cut off the chariot from Ephraim and the war horse from Jerusalem; and the battle bow shall be cut off, and he shall command peace to the nations; his dominion shall be from

---

[8]   If things got out of hand, troops would be brought in from Antioch, where around thirty thousand were stationed.

sea to sea, and from the River to the ends of the earth" (Zech. 9.10).

Jesus is coming as a king, it is true, but he is coming as a king of peace, in contrast with the armored troops, both those entering across the city and those in the Antonia fortress, who no doubt looked across the Kidron valley to see this bizarre procession winding its way down the Mount of Olives.

CARNIVAL TIME

This, then, is the point of the procession. This is why Jesus did nothing more than have a look round and go home. He'd done what he came to do. He'd made his point. His procession was a deliberate statement, a throwing down of the gauntlet. It could almost be seen as a kind of mockery of the Imperial procession. Pilate had his soldiers; Jesus has a rag-tag collection of outcasts. Pilate had, no doubt, a fine horse; Jesus has a donkey, and not even a fully grown donkey at that.

The procession was organized to make a theological point and also a political point. It was a polarizing procession: one that forced people to make a choice. Jesus was asking the onlookers and followers to literally choose sides.

And the choice remains today. All of us are faced with the same decision and the same choice. Which side of the city are we on? Which procession will we join? Are we going to march with the worldly kingdom, with its military might and financial muscle, with its golden standard gleaming and its trumpets blowing?

Or are we going to join the carnival on the other side of town?

WHERE DID PETER GO?

Peter dominates the first half of the book of Acts. He preaches at Pentecost and features in miraculous acts of healing; he confronts the Jewish leaders and shatters the religious conventions of the time by engaging with Gentiles. He's full of energy and passion, the "heart and soul" of the emerging Jesus movement. And then, suddenly, this driving force, apparently, drives away. He just drops out of the narrative completely.

Here's a graph which demonstrates the fact. It shows the percentage of each chapter of Acts where Peter is either mentioned or physically present and active.

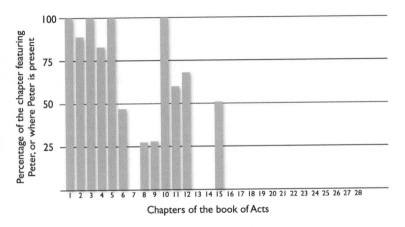

Chapters of the book of Acts

We can see that he features in the first five chapters (which include such famous events as Pentecost, the healing of the beggar and Peter and John's appearance before the council). Then he isn't mentioned during chapters six and seven (the stoning of Stephen), features in the next five chapters (especially chapter 10, where he is at the house of Cornelius), makes a brief appearance at the council of Jerusalem (Acts 15) and then disappears completely, never to be mentioned in Acts again. At the end of chapter fifteen he, along with other Apostles, agrees to send a letter to the church at Antioch... and that's it.

So the big question is, where did he go?

THE DISAPPEARING ACTS

First, we should note that it's not the first time Peter disappears in the book of Acts. In Acts 12, he is thrown into prison by Herod Agrippa I, the grandson of Herod the Great. This is part of a wave of persecution in 41AD which also sees James, the brother of John, beheaded (Acts 12.2).[1] Peter is miraculously released from prison and returns to a house-church run by Mary, the mother of John Mark (Acts 12.12). After being left waiting at the gate by mistake, he is eventually let in: "He motioned to them with his hand to be silent, and described for them how the Lord had brought him out of the prison. And he added, 'Tell this to James and to the believers.' Then he left and went to another place" (Acts 12.17).

Some scholars have argued that this is a euphemism; that Peter actually dies in prison and this "vision" of him becomes his last appearance on earth. In this reading, the "another place" is actually heaven; Peter has, as we would put it, "gone to a better place."[2] This theory doesn't hold water. It's not just that Peter reappears a few chapters later at the council of Jerusalem, it's also that, according to Paul, he's active in Antioch in between (Gal. 2.1–14). What the text implies is that Peter gets out of Judea – Herod Agrippa's territory – for his own protection. By 49AD, he's back, in attendance at the council of Jerusalem and after that he disappears, apparently for good.

NO PLACE LIKE ROME

There are several clues in the Bible as to where he went and what happened to him. The first clue is found in the end of 1 Peter, where he writes

[1]   Finegan, *Handbook of Biblical Chronology: Principles of Time Reckoning in the Ancient World and Problems of Chronology in the Bible*, 373–374.

[2]   For this theory see Robinson, D.F. "Where and When Did Peter Die?" *Journal of Biblical Literature* 64 (1945), 255–67. Smaltz, W.M. "Did Peter Die in Jerusalem?" *Journal of Biblical Literature* 71 (1952), 211–16.

Through Silvanus, whom I consider a faithful brother, I have written this short letter to encourage you and to testify that this is the true grace of God. Stand fast in it. Your sister church in Babylon, chosen together with you, sends you greetings; and so does my son Mark. Greet one another with a kiss of love. Peace to all of you who are in Christ (1 Pet. 5.12–14).

The reference to "Babylon" has been a bone of contention among scholars for a long time.[3] It is generally agreed that it doesn't literally mean Babylon; by this time the original Babylon was a small village on the banks of the Euphrates and the idea of Peter sitting there and writing to churches in Asia Minor doesn't make sense, since it's thousands of miles away from the people he's addressing.[4] Instead it's probably a code word, meaning Rome. Some have seen in this an indication that the letter is late; after the destruction of Jerusalem by the Romans in 70AD the Romans are being likened to the Babylonians, who also destroyed Jerusalem some six hundred years earlier. Revelation, which is certainly after this date, makes many references to Babylon, especially in 17.18, where it is termed "the great city that has dominion over the kings of the earth." [5]

However, the tone of the letter doesn't necessarily indicate this. There is no stinging criticism of Rome in the letter – indeed, the readers are admonished to obey the emperor and the authorities. So Babylon in this sense might not mean the "destroyers of Jerusalem" but merely "a place of exile." As Babylon was a place of exile for the Jews, so Peter is in "exile." His natural home is in Jerusalem, but he is exiled in Rome, the home of the emperor.

Another clue is the presence of Mark, who we know was summoned to Rome by Paul in the sixties (2 Tim. 4.11). There is further confirmation that Peter was in Rome from sources outside

---

[3] As has the authorship of the letter. For a good overview of the issues see Blomberg, C.L., *From Pentecost to Patmos: Acts to Revelation: An Introduction and Survey*, (Nottingham: Apollos, 2006), 441–443. However, even if you dismiss Petrine authorship, it still presupposes that Peter stayed in Rome, so at the very least it supports the traditional view.

[4] There was another Babylon – a Roman military camp near what is now Cairo, but Peter going there doesn't make much sense either. See Cullmann, O., *Peter: Disciple, Apostle, Martyr*, (London: SCM, 1953), 85.

[5] Blomberg, *From Pentecost to Patmos: Acts to Revelation: An Introduction and Survey*, 443.

the Bible. Ignatius, writing around 100AD, shows that there is a tradition of both Peter and Paul being "in charge" in Rome. Writing to the Roman church, he says: "I do not enjoin you, as Peter and Paul did."[6]

As to when he arrived, Peter certainly doesn't seem to be there when Paul arrives, and there's no mention of him in the last few verses of Acts which tell of Paul's stay in the city. Nor is there any mention of him in Paul's letter to the Romans, written around 57AD. Had Paul known him to be there, it's unlikely he would have been missed from the list of personal greetings.[7] So Peter must have arrived later in Rome, probably around 63–64AD.

THE TRAVELS OF PETER

So that's where he was, but where had he been in between?

For this, there isn't much information. We do know, both from Acts and from Paul's letters, that Peter went traveling. In Acts we see him venture north, first to Samaria (Acts 8.14–25), then to Lydda and Joppa (Acts 9.36–43), then to Caesarea (Acts 10). We know from Paul that he was in Antioch (Gal. 2.11–14). That takes us up to about 48AD. But one brief reference a bit later shows that Peter is still on the move into the mid-fifties. Paul's first letter to the Corinthians (written around 54AD) shows that Peter (here called Cephas) was accompanied by his wife when he went traveling: "Do we not have the right to be accompanied by a believing wife, as do the other apostles and the brothers of the Lord and Cephas?" (1 Cor. 9.5).

Indeed, we know from the same letter that he'd probably been to Corinth. In 1 Corinthians 1.12, Paul refers to Christians in the city who claimed to "belong to Cephas" [i.e. Peter]. This implies that he had been there and baptized. There's also a clue to some of the places he went in the opening of 1 Peter. He writes to Christians in five areas of Asia Minor: Pontus, Cappadocia, Galatia, Asia and Bithynia. A person traveling overland towards Rome from

---

[6] Ignatius, *Letter to Romans*, 4, in Lightfoot, J.B., *The Apostolic Fathers*, (London: Macmillan and Co, 1893), 151.

[7] Cullmann, *Peter: Disciple, Apostle, Martyr*, 79.

Antioch in Syria would naturally pass through these areas. So the possibility is that Peter has, over the years, made his way west, visiting established churches and planting new congregations, teaching, preaching, building up congregations, sharing stories of his experiences as an elder of the church and a "witness of Christ's suffering" (1 Pet. 5.1).[8]

Ah yes, the stories. Time to move back to Rome.

THE MEMOIRS OF PETER

It is often claimed that Peter was the first bishop of Rome, but this is unlikely – for one thing he didn't found the church there, for another the claim doesn't appear until the third century. [9] However, it is very likely that the tradition reflects a real involvement with the church in Rome. One can only imagine the excitement among the church when this man arrived in the city. Here, after all, was an *apostle*; a man who could link the church of Rome with the events of Jesus' life; a man who could look back thirty years to when it all started. A man with a lot of memories.

Which is where Mark comes in. Mark wasn't just visiting Peter in Rome, he was working alongside him. This comes from a writer called Papias: "This also the elder used to say. Mark, indeed, having been the interpreter of Peter, wrote accurately, howbeit not in order, all that he recalled of what was either said or done by the Lord. For he [Mark] neither heard the Lord, nor was he a follower of His, but at a later date (as I said), of Peter..." [10]

Mark, then, was acting as Peter's translator, and later wrote down Peter's reminiscences to form the core of the Gospel of Mark. Although some scholars doubt this account, recent work has shown the importance of eyewitness testimony in the transmission of the gospel stories and, particularly, the links between Peter and the

---

[8] Perhaps the fact that Peter is active in the area lies behind Paul's failure to go to Bithynia (Acts 16.7). Paul himself says that he does not like to work where others have already been (Rom. 15.20)

[9] Brown, R.E., and Meier, J.P., *Antioch and Rome: New Testament Cradles of Catholic Christianity*, (London: Geoffrey Chapman, 1983), 98.

[10] Eusebius, *The Ecclesiastical History and the Martyrs of Palestine*, trans. Lawlor, H.J., and Oulton, J.E.L., (London: SPCK, 1927), I, 101.

gospel of Mark.[11] Mark has more frequent references to Peter than any of the other gospels, and there is a strong probability that Peter was the eyewitness source. Mark's gospel reflects the perspective of "the twelve" but more than that, it is mediated through Peter's experiences and feelings.[12] There are times when Peter seems to be speaking to us, when he becomes clear and distinct as an individual. As Richard Bauckham puts it: "…in the Gospel of Mark, Peter is not only typical of the disciples to some degree, but also the most fully characterised individual in the Gospel, apart from Jesus."[13] Significantly, it shows Peter at his worst as well as his best. If one was creating a spin-doctored, air-brushed portrait of a leader, showing him as a failure at the crucial moment would not be a great idea; but if one were writing down the leader's own account, if one were recording the stories the leader himself told, then such honesty is much more understandable. Some scholars have argued that Peter would be unlikely to portray himself in a bad light.[14] Instead, what we find is that Peter seems to have been viewed with respect across all the varied factions of the Early Church. I believe that was, partly at least, because he had been so honest.

THE DEATH OF PETER

Peter, as we've seen, was probably not in Rome when Paul arrived in 62AD. But he must have arrived sometime in the next two years. We've seen also that Rome may have been the place where Mark wrote down the stories. As to Peter's other activities, nothing is known for sure.

One legend has imprinted itself on the Christian consciousness: the famous *Quo Vadis* story, but this story does not originate in what you would call "sober history." It comes from a book called The Acts of Peter (written sometime between 180–225AD). In Acts

---

[11] See especially Bauckham, R., *Jesus and the Eyewitnesses: The Gospels as Eyewitness Testimony*, (Grand Rapids: Eerdmans, 2006), 155ff.

[12] For example Mark 9.5–6, where Peter's babbling is put down to the fact that "he did not know what to say, for they were terrified."

[13] Bauckham, *Jesus and the Eyewitnesses: The Gospels as Eyewitness Testimony*, 175.

[14] Personally, I think that says more about the scholars than it does about Peter.

chapter 8, Peter has a confrontation in Samaria with a magician called Simon Magus; a later writer, rather in the manner of film producers, turned this into a sequel in which the two meet up again in Rome. It's a rather rambling, incoherent story which features, among other things, a talking dog, a miraculous repair job to a statue of Caesar and the amazing resurrection of a herring. At the end of it, Simon Magus tries to fly and gets quite a long way up before the prayers of Peter bring him crashing to earth, breaking his leg in three places.[15]

It also contains the *Quo Vadis* legend. The tale runs that Peter, to avoid death, is encouraged by "the brethren" to flee from Rome.

> And he obeyed the brethren's voice and went forth alone, saying: Let none of you come forth with me, but I will go forth alone, having changed the fashion of mine apparel. And as he went forth of the city, he saw the Lord entering into Rome. And when he saw him, he said: Lord, whither goest thou thus (or here)? And the Lord said unto him: I go into Rome to be crucified. And Peter said unto him: Lord, art thou (being) crucified again? He said unto him: Yea, Peter, I am (being) crucified again. And Peter came to himself: and having beheld the Lord ascending up into heaven, he returned to Rome, rejoicing, and glorifying the Lord, for that he said: I am being crucified: the which was about to befall Peter.[16]

Peter is crucified but, at his own insistence, with his head downwards.[17]

It's an interesting story, but, coming as it does at the end of such a ridiculously fantastic tale, it's hard to work out how much history

---

[15] See James, M.R., *The Apocryphal New Testament: Being the Apocryphal Gospels, Acts, Epistles and Apocalypses: With Other Narratives and Fragments*, (Oxford: Clarendon, 1924), 300–336. There is also an account in Brown and Meier, *Antioch and Rome: New Testament Cradles of Catholic Christianity*, 205ff.

[16] Acts of Peter 35, James, *The Apocryphal New Testament: Being the Apocryphal Gospels, Acts, Epistles and Apocalypses: With Other Narratives and Fragments*, 333.

[17] Crucifixion upside down is not impossible or even improbable. The Romans took a gruesome entertainment in such things. See pp.147–148.

there is among the legend. What it does confirm, perhaps, is that Peter did come to Rome and he did die there.

"WHERE YOU DO NOT WANT TO GO..."

In 64AD, beginning on July 19th, a fire broke out in Rome which burnt for nine days. Such was the unpopularity of Emperor Nero, that, even though he was out of the city at the time, many suspected that he was responsible for the fire. Nero did the only thing he could: he found someone else to blame. And he fixed on the Christians. Tacitus describes what happened next

> But all the endeavors of men, all the emperor's largess and the propitiations of the gods, did not suffice to allay the scandal or banish the belief that the fire had been ordered. And so, to get rid of this rumor, Nero set up as the culprits and punished with the utmost refinement of cruelty a class hated for their abominations, who are commonly called Christians... Accordingly, arrest was first made of those confessed [to being a Christian]; then, on their evidence, an immense multitude was convicted, not so much on the charge of arson as because of hatred of the human race. Beside being put to death they were made to serve as objects of amusement; they were clad in the hides of beasts and torn to death by dogs; others were crucified, others set on fire to serve to illuminate the night when daylight failed.

> Nero had thrown open his grounds for the display, and was putting on a show in the circus, where he mingled with the people in the dress of a charioteer or drove about in his chariot. All this gave rise to a feeling of pity, even towards men whose guilt merited the most exemplary punishment; for it was felt that they were being destroyed not for the public good but to gratify the cruelty of an individual.[18]

---

[18] Tacitus, Annals 15.44 in Bettenson, H.S., *Documents of the Christian Church*, (Oxford: Oxford University Press, 1986), 1–2.

This, according to the Early Church, is the wave of persecution in which both Peter and Paul met their ends. Already in 1 Peter we find a man encouraging a church facing persecution. So the likelihood is that it was written in the first wave of persecution that Nero unleashed on the church.

The tradition that Peter died in Rome is supported by Clement, writing in the last decade of the first century AD. He tells of the martyrdom of Peter and Paul

> But, to pass from the examples of ancient days, let us come to those champions who lived nearest to our time... There was Peter who by reason of unrighteous jealousy endured not one but many labors, and thus having borne his testimony went to his appointed place of glory.

> By reason of jealousy and strife Paul by his example pointed out the prize of patient endurance... when he had borne his testimony before the rulers, so he departed from the world and went unto the holy place, having been found a notable pattern of patient endurance.[19]

Clement is writing from Rome, and seems to be reflecting a strong local tradition.[20] The story of Peter's crucifixion comes, as we've seen, from a much later source. But it is entirely plausible that he was crucified in Rome, in that wave of persecutions unleashed by the increasingly mad Nero. One last fragment of evidence points to this. On the shores of Galilee, the risen Jesus tells Peter: "Very truly, I tell you, when you were younger, you used to fasten your own belt and to go wherever you wished. But when you grow old, you will stretch out your hands, and someone else will fasten a belt around you and take you where you do not wish to go" (John 21.18).

---

[19] Clement of Rome, Letter to the Corinthians 5, Lightfoot, *The Apostolic Fathers*, 59.

[20] The reference to "jealousy and strife" may refer to disputes between the different churches in Rome. It may, indeed, refer to the situation described in Paul's letter to the Philippians, where he describes people proclaiming Christ out of envy and rivalry (Phil. 1.15). For a full treatment of this evidence, see Cullmann, *Peter: Disciple, Apostle, Martyr*, 89ff.

The death of Peter. Detail from the west front of Strasbourg
Cathedral (13th century).

John here includes in his gospel a prophecy which may have circulated independently in the church. That it refers to crucifixion seems undeniable: the victim's arms were first stretched out, and then the *patibulum* or cross-beam was bound to them.[21] Paul, being a Roman citizen, would have probably been beheaded, but Peter, an ageing Palestinian working man, an ex-fisherman, would have been one of the many ordinary Christians who met a gruesome death, killed for entertainment at the whim of a paranoid tyrant. Or maybe the paranoid tyrant's lieutenants. For Nero was absent from Rome from September 66 to March 68, leaving Rome under the command of Helius and Tigellinus. Since 1 Clement talks of Paul bearing witness "before the rulers", this may mean he died during this period. Since several of the later apocryphal Acts talk of the apostles being sentenced by "the prefect" rather than the emperor, this may reflect an earlier tradition. If that is the case, it means that Peter and Paul died sometime between late 66AD and early 68AD.[22]

Whatever the date, the Early Church believed that Peter died in Rome and they preserved a shrine in the area where they thought it had happened. Excavations beneath the main altar of St Peter's Basilica in Rome have revealed a *tropaeum*, a commemorative shrine which is probably that identified by a writer called Gaius around 200AD.[23] Whether the famous bones discovered beneath are those of the apostle is more doubtful, but it certainly marks the site of a very early shrine. So Peter was probably killed in the Circus Nero which stood just a little way south of Vatican Hill.[24]

So that is Peter's story. He leaves the pages of Acts and for some fifteen years, from 49AD to his death around 67AD, his movements and activities are largely unknown. He peeps out from the mists of history, fleeting, fragmentary.

Peter is a fascinating character. He was not the leader of the Jerusalem church: that went to James and the family of Jesus. He

---

[21] Beasley-Murray, G.R., *John*, (Waco: Word Books, 1987), 408–09.

[22] Finegan, *Handbook of Biblical Chronology*, 387–388.

[23] Eusebius, *The Ecclesiastical History and the Martyrs of Palestine*, I, 60. Cullmann, *Peter: Disciple, Apostle, Martyr*, 117–121.

[24] Brown, and Meier, *Antioch and Rome: New Testament Cradles of Catholic Christianity*, 97.

was out-muscled intellectually by Paul. Yet he remained the real soul and heart of Christianity. He embodied the humanity of it all; the great man, whose great failures had been turned round by Christ. Maybe he was doing what he always did best; moving forward, doggedly following Jesus and telling everyone his stories.

JUST HOW STRONG WAS SAMSON?

When I was growing up, I was an avid reader of comic books. (I still have several thousand in my loft – every now and then I go on a binge of comic book reading and gorge myself on Batman, Daredevil and Spiderman, *et al*). Each week I would go up the road to the newsagent and blow my entire pocket money allowance on as many of the latest Marvel comics as I could afford. Each comic book had a letters page and each month these pages would become a battleground of conflicting opinions about the relative merits of the various superheroes. And one of the commonest questions was "Who is the strongest?" "Who is the strongest – Hulk or Thor?" "If Daredevil fought Spiderman, who would win?"

Samson, of course, was never mentioned.[1] But I can't help wondering, how strong was he? The Bible depicts him as a kind of superman, but just how "super" was Samson?

One event that might give us a clue is his stealing of the city gates of Gaza. The story is told in Judges

> Once Samson went to Gaza, where he saw a prostitute and went in to her. The Gazites were told, "Samson has come here." So they circled around and lay in wait for him all night at the city gate. They kept quiet all night, thinking, "Let us wait until the light of the morning; then we will kill him." But Samson lay only until midnight. Then at midnight he rose up, took hold of the doors of the city gate and the two posts, pulled them up, bar and all, put them on his shoulders, and carried them to the top of the hill that is in front of Hebron. (Judg. 16.1–3)

The event has featured in numerous pieces of art. One of the most famous is Doré's illustration, in which we see Samson, staggering up the hill, the gates on his shoulders, while in the distance the dawn breaks over a suddenly open-plan Gaza.

---

[1] Although there was a comic book character I recall called Doc Samson. He had long green hair and was a psychiatrist who had tried to cure the Hulk. Instead he got caught in gamma rays: his hair turned green and he developed superhuman strength. This is a professional hazard that is rarely mentioned in the psychiatric journals.

*Samson carrying
away the gates
of Gaza. A
nineteenth
century
engraving by
Gustav Doré*

Anyway, the illustration gave me an idea. I could find out how strong Samson was by finding out how heavy the gates of Gaza were.

All I had to do was work out how much the gates weigh and then we'll know just how strong he was.

What could be easier?

THE PHILISTIA WEIGHT-LIFTING CHAMPION

Quite a lot of things, actually. Because archeologists haven't retrieved, as far as I can tell, many ancient gates. Gatehouses, yes, since those were made of stone, so they've been excavated. But the actual doors, the gates themselves, have long gone.

The nearest thing we have are the Balawat gates, reconstructed in the British Museum. These gates, from the palace of the Assyrian emperor Shalmaneser III (858–824BC), were discovered in 1878. They consisted of two poles about fifteen feet high, out of each of which were projecting brass "scrolls" measuring some six feet in length. These were more ornamental, being temple gates, but they might at least give us an idea of what a city gate might weigh.

Which is when I hit the second problem: no-one's ever weighed them. However, inquiries at the British Museum revealed that while they didn't know the weight of the gates, they knew the dimensions. Each gate is 7.92m high, 1.45m wide and 7.95cm thick. The gates are made of cedar, as the gates of Gaza probably would have been. Cedar is rot-resistant and extremely durable. It was the most used wood for monumental doors in Egypt, so it's likely that Gaza, just up the coast, would follow suit.[2] Cedar has a density of 380kg/cubic meter. A quick thrash on a calculator reveals that each gate contains 0.91 cubic meters of wood, giving us a weight of 347kg.[3]

So all we have to do is double that and we've got our answer.

Almost. Because the gates would have been plated with metal, to give them some form of fire-proofing. The Balawat gates had

---

[2] Meiggs, R., *Trees and Timber in the Ancient Mediterranean World*, (Oxford: Clarendon Press, 1982), 55, 293.

[3] All densities taken from http://www.simetric.co.uk

sixteen bronze bands the width of the door, each 26cm high and 3mm thick. Assuming the gates of Gath had the same (and if anything they would have had more) that gives us 0.011 cubic meters of bronze. At approximately 8000kg per cubic meter, the bronze strips would have weighed around 88kg.

So we have each door weighing 435kg (around 960lb). Job done.

Except we haven't taken into account the doorposts. Doors in the ancient near-east did not have hinges as we have them today. Instead, each leaf of the door was attached to a pole. The pole would fit into sockets at the top and the bottom of the gateway. The base of the door pole would be protected with a metal or leather "shoe", to stop it wearing away.[4] They would have been huge double doors and plated with metal to repel burning arrows or torches. Each night they would have been barred by a huge beam which went across them horizontally and slotted into recesses on the door post. Stealing the gates, therefore, would be simply a case of lifting them out of their sockets. So, to find the true weight of each door, we have to add a pole. Now, I would have done this as well, but by this time I was losing the will to live.

Anyway, I think we've got enough to work with. Leaving aside the doorposts (which Samson didn't) we're already looking at someone capable of lifting at least 870kg of doors; someone who could lift more than three times the current world record.[5]

Someone who could lift three grand pianos.

And then carry them to Hebron. Thirty-seven miles away. Up a hill.

---

[4]   See Wright, G.R.H., *Ancient Building in South Syria and Palestine*, (Leiden: Brill, 1985), 446–448. King, P.J., and Stager, L.E., *Life in Biblical Israel*, (Louisville: Westminster John Knox Press, 2001), 234–236.

[5]   The official world record for weightlifting is currently 263.5kg, set in the men's +105 kg class by Hossein Reza Zadeh of Iran, who lifted 263.5 kg (580.9 lb) at the 2004 Athens Summer Olympics in the "clean and jerk" event. It should be noted that competitors only have to hold the bar above their heads until they are judged to be stationary. One imagines that if the rules required them to carry the weight for 37 miles, the sale of steroids would skyrocket. Powerlifting records are, I believe, greater, but the multiplicity of federations and rules makes it hard to work out.

PHILISTINE KRYPTONITE

All of which is why Samson is often depicted as a legendary superhero. Indeed the Jewish legends about him grew even greater. Jewish folklore depicted him as measuring "60 ells" between his shoulders, but maimed in both legs.[6] Also, curiously, they claimed that "whenever the Holy Spirit rested on him, he emitted a bell-like sound which could be heard from afar."[7] This conjures up a lovely image of Israelites listening to the distant "bonging" of Samson murdering another truckload of Philistines.

It's easy to see why such legends grew, because his feats are those of a superhero. And like all superheroes, he has a flaw, a secret vulnerability. Achilles had his heel, Superman has his kryptonite; Samson had his hair. And women; Philistine women.

Before he stole the gates, Samson had been visiting a prostitute. Many commentators down the centuries have had real problems with Samson's sexual behavior (although not perhaps as many problems as Samson had). Occasionally there have been attempts to clean him up a bit. The American Sunday School Union, for example, obviously felt that the tender minds of their charges weren't going to be sullied with details of a Philistine brothel: "Samson fearlessly went to the Philistine stronghold and took up lodgings for the night."[8]

Samson's story is full of these encounters. There was obviously something about foreign women that got to him. Scholars have seen in this an attempt by the writers of Judges to address a perennially difficult issue for Israelite society: their attraction to women from the nations around them. Foreign women were exotic, mysterious and laden, apparently, with sex appeal, but the Samson story underlines the dangers and compromises involved.[9]

---

[6] An ell is 45 inches making his back approximately 225 feet wide. Must have cost him a fortune in T-shirts.

[7] *Encyclopedia Judaica*, (Jerusalem: Encyclopedia Judaica, 1971), 774.

[8] American Sunday School Union Biographical Dictionary (1883), quoted in Gunn, D.M., *Judges*, (Oxford: Blackwell, 2005), 210.

[9] *The Anchor Bible Dictionary*, V, 950–54.

Even after the exile, the issue of marrying foreigners is still a live issue for the inhabitants of Jerusalem (Neh. 13.23–29).

There was something in Samson's psyche, however, that constantly drew him to these situations. It has been suggested that Samson was suffering from a personality disorder. According to Dr. Eric Altschuler of the University of California, San Diego, Samson exhibits many of the classic signs of antisocial personality disorder, including lying, bullying, repeated involvement in fights, cruelty to animals, and fire-starting.[10]

Others have speculated that his attraction to Philistine women was bound up with the danger. It wasn't just the woman he was after, it was all the tension and excitement that came with being in the heart of Philistine territory. Perhaps the best insight into Samson's character has come not from a theologian but from a psychologist. In a case study written in 1989, Ilan Kutz wrote: "Samson has the compulsion to re-enact unwanted or unhealthy behavior, without the capacity to learn from the mistake, pain or damage."[11]

Samson is compulsively drawn to untrustworthy women, even enemies. He makes an attachment to them and when it goes wrong, as unconsciously he knows it will, he explodes in an orgy of rage and bitter resentment.

This episode is typical. He walks into the stronghold of an enemy, to a woman that he knows will betray him. Throughout his life he courts disloyalty, finally deluding himself that Delilah loves him. He is "actively, though unconsciously, seeking and planning his own suicide."[12]

There was something in Samson, then, that urged him to place himself in positions of danger; that urged him to seek out sex with Philistine women. It was this, as much as the hair, which caused his downfall. Little by little, bit by bit, we see him compromise, give more away, until finally he is captured. In the end his strength

---

[10] Altschuler, E.L., *et al* "Did Samson Have Antisocial Personality Disorder?" *Arch Gen Psychiatry* 58 (2001), 202–203.

[11] Kutz, I., "Samson's complex: the compulsion to re-enact betrayal and rage." *British Journal of Medical Psychology* 62 (1989), 123.

[12] Kutz, "Samson's complex: the compulsion to re-enact betrayal and rage.", 129.

returned for one final, suicidal effort, but by then it was too late to save himself. Or perhaps he was too tired to fight his own nature any more.

Samson, physically, is depicted as the mightiest warrior; a man of prodigious strength, the stuff of legends. His story, however, is largely about the loss of that supernatural power: a loss caused because there were powers greater than his, powers which he could not subdue and fights which he could not win. It wasn't the strength of his enemies that defeated him in the end; it was the voices inside his head.

How strong was Samson? Not strong enough.

The tools of the tekton's trade. A recreation of a first-century builder's workshop in Nazareth.

DID JESUS VISIT THE THEATER?

Mark chapter 4 contains a curious little detail about Jesus' crowd management during his Galilean ministry: "Again he began to teach beside the sea. Such a very large crowd gathered around him that he got into a boat on the sea and sat there, while the whole crowd was beside the sea on the land. He began to teach them many things in parables…" (Mark 4.1–2a).

There are coves around the north shore of Galilee that form natural amphitheaters, curved bowls which are perfect for hearing anyone down on the water's edge. So what Jesus did here is obvious: he created a kind of water-borne stage, which meant that, with the crowd sitting on the banks of the hill, a large crowd could hear him perfectly. It's a great trick. But the thing that interests me is, where did he learn it?

Amphitheaters were, of course, familiar to people in the Græco-Roman world. No town or city worthy of its name was without its theater, all built to the same design. Theaters were sophisticated in their use of acoustics. By placing the audience in a raised curve, the actors could be heard clearly, even at the back. It is this technology that Jesus is using here. Which begs the question, had he ever been to the theater?

Some people would dismiss such an idea out of hand. But then, how did he learn this trick? And why does he keep using the Greek word for actor? And, more to the point, why does the risen Lord Jesus, when confronting Paul, decide to quote the Greek playwright Aeschylus?

JOSEPH & SON, BUILDERS

To answer the question we have to look at Jesus' career – that is, the fifteen or sixteen years he spent at his trade. This is an area which is not often looked at by preachers and teachers in today's church, partly because it's not mentioned much in the gospels but also, one suspects, because it's not very glamorous.[1] The fact is, however,

---

[1] Which is why, centuries later, many fictional accounts of Jesus' early years grew up. Legendary writings such as the *Proto-Gospel of James* and the *Infancy Story of Thomas* are full of the child, and often the toddler Jesus, performing miraculous acts, such as causing his teacher to collapse in a faint and turning his classmates into birds.

Jesus spent around five times as long working as a tradesman and craftsman in Galilee as he did raising the dead, healing the sick, casting out demons and strolling across lakes. So I don't think we can dismiss it as easily as that. He wasn't just marking time. He was hard at work.

Jesus, as we know, spent the majority of his adult life as a builder. Not, you'll note, a carpenter. The word used to describe Jesus in Mark 6.3 is *tekton*, which does not mean just "carpenter", despite the fact that it is traditionally translated as such. *Tekton* was the Greek word for a general builder, a construction worker, including a stonemason and metalworker.[2] In fact, a person who was just a carpenter might have struggled to find full-time work in Nazareth. Wood was a scarce commodity in Israel generally, but especially so in the parts of Galilee where Jesus lived; that's why people built houses out of stone, or simply dug caves into the sides of hills. A *tekton* would have been able to turn his hand to a number of crafts, including stone masonry and basic metalwork. Jesus would have been skilled in woodworking, but also in working with stone and metal as well.[3]

Another reason why Jesus might have struggled to find enough work is the size of Nazareth. Today it's a bustling city but in Jesus' day it was a small settlement of maybe four to five hundred people. It was reached down a side road from the main highway.[4] So it may very well have been hard for "Joseph and Son" to find enough work in their small community.

However, just a few miles away, there was a big building project going on. Herod Antipas was rebuilding a magnificent new city, with baths and shops, a palace and a theater.

---

[2] Balz, H., and Schneider, G., *Exegetical Dictionary of the New Testament*, (Grand Rapids: Eerdmans, 1990), III, 342. Goodrick, E.W. , Kohlenberger III, J.R. & Swanson, J.A. , *Zondervan NIV Exhaustive Concordance* (Grand Rapids: Zondervan, 1999).

[3] Guelich, R.A., *Mark 1–8:26*, (Dallas: Word Books, 1989), 310. Gundry, *Mark: A Commentary on His Apology for the Cross*, 290, 296. Thiede, C.P., *The Cosmopolitan World of Jesus: New Findings From Archaeology*, (London: SPCK, 2004), 15.

[4] Horsley, R.A., *Archaeology, History, and Society in Galilee: The Social Context of Jesus and the Rabbis*, (Valley Forge: Trinity Press International, 1996), 109–111.

WELCOME TO SEPPHORIS

In 4BC, following the death of Herod the Great, there was an uprising in Galilee. A man called Judas the son of Ezekias took over the arsenal of weapons that Herod had stored at a place called Sepphoris – or Zippori as it was known in Hebrew – and challenged the might of Rome. The uprising was brutally and efficiently crushed by the Romans, aided by infantry and cavalry sent by Aretas, the Nabatean king of Arabia. They captured Sepphoris, set fire to it, and sold the inhabitants into slavery.[5]

A year later, when Herod Antipas, the son of Herod the Great, returned to take charge of the region, he obtained Roman permission to rebuild the city. Josephus describes how Antipas rebuilt the city on the model of a Roman capital. Antipas was a Græco-Roman ruler, not a devout Jew. He even renamed the city Sepphoris Autocratoris, in honor of the emperor, who in Greek might be called *autocrator.*[6]

Rebuilding Sepphoris was a major task, and the work would no doubt have drawn many craftsmen and laborers to the area. Which is interesting, because Sepphoris was only three miles northwest of Nazareth.

There is, of course, no proof that Jesus and Joseph (and maybe his brothers) worked at Sepphoris – the city isn't mentioned in the New Testament at all. But it seems hard to believe he never went near the place: a rider on horseback could have done the journey in fifteen minutes, for Jesus it would have been less than an hour's walk.[7] It's not unreasonable to imagine Jesus and his father

---

[5] Batey, R.A. "Sepphoris—An Urban Portrait of Jesus." *Biblical Archaeology Review* 18 (May/June 1992). Sepphoris learned from its mistake. During the Jewish revolt of 66AD, the Jews of Sepphoris refused to take up arms. Josephus described them as "the only people of that province who displayed pacific sentiments. For with an eye to their own security and a sense of the power of Rome they offered a cordial welcome to the commander-in-chief and promised their active support against their own countrymen." See Freyne, S., *Galilee, From Alexander the Great to Hadrian, 323 B.C.E. To 135 C.E.: A Study of Second Temple Judaism,* (Edinburgh: T&T Clark, 1998), 125–128.

[6] Arguments rage over just how Greek Sepphoris was. Recent research has indicated that it had a strong Jewish identity. See Chancey, M. & Meyers, E.M. "Spotlight on Sepphoris: How Jewish was Sepphoris in Jesus' Time?" *Biblical Archaeology Review* 26 (July/August 2000).

[7] Batey, R.A. "Is this not the carpenter?" *New Testament Studies* 30 (1984), 250.

making the short journey north, to a city where there was massive building going on, and money to be earned.

And one of the key building projects was a theater. This magnificent building was capable of seating three thousand people.[8] Archaeologists differ on whether the theater was built in the late first century, or during the time of Jesus, but there are a number of reasons for thinking that a theater would have been among the earliest of Herod's constructions.[9] Herod Antipas had been brought up in Rome, surrounded by the marvels of that huge city and, in particular, the extensive building programme of Augustus. Josephus says that Herod Antipas rebuilt Sepphoris so that it was "the ornament of all Galilee." It was Antipas' place of residence from around 2BC to the point where he started work on Tiberias some twenty years later.[10] As a Roman client-ruler, he would have been hugely influenced by imperial Roman ideology – in town planning as much as anything else.[11] He built an elaborate water supply, along Roman lines.[12] After all, his father was a great theater-builder; building theaters was in the blood. So it is hard to imagine Herod Antipas resisting the temptation.[13] The size of the theater suggests that there was a huge interest in drama in the city. Which is intriguing because, ethnically, the city remained Jewish.

The idea that Jews deplored the theater is not true, at least not at the time of Jesus. Although there may have been some resentment of it as a Greek import, the theater in the early years of the first century AD had not yet become the crude spectacular it was later to become. We know that Jews elsewhere in the Roman world went

[8] Jensen, M.H., *Herod Antipas in Galilee: The Literary and Archaeological Sources on the Reign of Herod Antipas and Its Socio-Economic Impact on Galilee*, (Tübingen: Mohr Siebeck, 2006), 155.

[9] Four teams have excavated Sepphoris in modern times with the aim of establishing a precise dating. So far they have reached no agreement. See Jensen, *Herod Antipas in Galilee: The Literary and Archaeological Sources on the Reign of Herod Antipas and Its Socio-Economic Impact on Galilee*, 151, 154.

[10] Hoehner, *Herod Antipas*, 84–87.

[11] Horsley, *Archaeology, History, and Society in Galilee: The Social Context of Jesus and the Rabbis*, 53. Roller, *The Building Program of Herod the Great*, 243.

[12] Freyne, *Galilee, From Alexander the Great to Hadrian, 323 B.C.E. To 135 C.E.: A Study of Second Temple Judaism*, 124.

[13] See Stanton, G., *The Gospels and Jesus*, (Oxford: Oxford University Press, 1989), 147.

to the theater; in Miletus, there is a row of seats with an inscription on them showing that they were expressly reserved for the Jews – an early version of the corporate box.[14]

Sepphoris was not the only theater in Palestine. There was one at Caesarea Maritime, where the Roman administration was based. There was one in Jericho and even one in Jerusalem, which Herod the Great built in 28BC to house games held in celebration of Octavius' victory over Anthony and Cleopatra. There were theaters in Samaria, and also in Sidon. There were also theaters in the cities of the Decapolis, the ten Greek cities east of Galilee.[15]

Even if Jesus did not visit the theater, he may have helped to build it. And even if he didn't help to build it, he knew what theaters were like. Which must be how, when faced with a huge crowd by Lake Galilee, he had the idea of turning the venue into a theater.

YOU LOAD OF ACTORS…

More than that, he knew some theater terminology.

One of the things that Jesus spoke most strongly about was lying; pretending to be something you're not. And the word that he used for this was "hypocrite." The word occurs some seventeen times in the gospels and it comes from the Greek word *hypokrites*, meaning "actor." Actors on the Greek stage frequently acted in large masks, designed to reflect the kind of characters they were playing. Behind the masks, of course, was the ordinary person, playing a role. Jesus took this concept and applied it to the religious leaders of the day, all dressed up in their religious costume and wearing their "masks" of piety.

> "So whenever you give alms, do not sound a trumpet before you, as the hypocrites do in the synagogues and in the streets, so that they may be praised by others. Truly I tell you, they have received their reward" (Matt. 6.2).

---

[14] There was even a famous Jewish playwright, the wonderfully named Ezekiel the Tragedian, who wrote in the second-century BC. Thiede, *The Cosmopolitan World of Jesus: New Findings From Archaeology*, 24.

[15] Jesus traveled to all these areas (Mark 10:46; John 4:3–6; Mark 7:24, 31; Matt. 15:21; Mark 7:31)

Images of Græco-Roman theatrical masks.

"And whenever you pray, do not be like the hypocrites; for they love to stand and pray in the synagogues and at the street corners, so that they may be seen by others. Truly I tell you, they have received their reward" (Matt. 6.5).

"And whenever you fast, do not look dismal, like the hypocrites, for they disfigure their faces so as to show others that they are fasting. Truly I tell you, they have received their reward" (Matt. 6.16).

These images of people acting a part may also draw on other stage techniques: the practice of announcing a dramatic entrance with a trumpet's fanfare, for example; or actors reciting their lines, with all the right gestures and actions. Or tragic actors, their faces sad but stoical, as they face the hardship of fasting.

A BIT OF AESCHYLUS

There is one final, intriguing snippet linking Jesus to the theater of his day. Here is a part of Paul's account of his encounter with Jesus on the Damascus road:

> With this in mind, I was traveling to Damascus with the authority and commission of the chief priests, when at midday along the road, your Excellency, I saw a light from heaven, brighter than the sun, shining around me and my companions. When we had all fallen to the ground, I heard a voice saying to me in the Hebrew language, "Saul, Saul, why are you persecuting me? It hurts you to kick against the goads" (Acts 26.12–14).

The final statement – which compares Paul's struggles to a horse hurting itself by fighting against the spurs of the rider – is a quotation from a play by Aeschylus. He used it in his play *Agamemnon*, also in *Prometheus*. It was also a phrase used in Euripides' *Bacchae*.[16]

Now this was obviously a Greek proverb, but the use of it is significant. Paul – who here is giving testimony at his hearing before the Governor Festus – may be using a phrase that the Governor would recognize. He, on his own admission, is translating the words from what he calls "the Hebrew language" which is Aramaic, not Hebrew (just to confuse you). But what if he's not paraphrasing? What if he's reporting exactly what was said? After all, this was the most important event in Paul's life. It was burned into his brain. Wouldn't he be likely to remember? If Jesus did use this phrase to Paul, maybe it's because he learnt it at the theater: the same theater where he saw all those play-actors, the hypocrites.

And the point of all this? Well, it's not to justify the attendance or non-attendance at theater. The real point of this little mystery lies in the *tekton* years, those years so often dismissed as irrelevant or unimportant. Because what was happening in that time was that Jesus was looking all around him, observing. He was picking up on words that people used, phrases they knew. He was looking at

---

[16] Aeschylus, *Agamemnon*, 1624; *Prometheus*, 325. Euripides, *Bacchae*, 795.

how buildings were made, and later he would be able to make use of that knowledge.

He would use the metaphor of the capstone; he would tell stories of people building towers without counting the cost, or of people putting their foundations in sand. He would liken the Pharisees to actors, playing a role, but being totally different out of costume. He would talk about people who pick grains of sawdust out of other peoples' eyes, while ignoring the huge plank of wood in their own.

And, in a small lakeside, when a crowd was desperate to hear his words of hope, he remembered his building techniques and created a makeshift theater. Why? Because, in the best sense of the word, he was being dramatic.

WHAT DO CHERUBIM LOOK LIKE?

They are the staple decoration of innumerable oil paintings; they peek out from the carved corners of thousands of rococo churches; they flutter around tombstones and memorials, those cute cherubs, rosy-cheeked babies with their tiny wings.

They are toddlers, these cherubs, the winged members of some heavenly playgroup. But the reality is different. It certainly involves wings, but also lions, oxen, and hooves. As we shall see, cherubs aren't really angels at all. And they're certainly not baby-like. Put a cherub in your playgroup and everyone would instantly need a change of nappies. Including the staff.

DO NOT BE AFRAID

Angels are big business these days. The bookshops are crammed with books about angels. Here's a typical book blurb

> Learn how to access angels and their wisdom through *The Angel Bible*, your definitive guide to angelic lore. This book features practical exercises, meditations and affirmations you can perform to help you reach out to the angels that surround you for guidance, healing and inspiration. Through *The Angel Bible*, you will learn to sense the presence of angels, communicate with your guardian angel and use crystals to alleviate common ailments. Complete with beautiful color illustrations, this is the ideal book for everyone who is interested in angels.[1]

I'm not sure what creatures this author is talking about, but what I do know is that they're not angels, at least not as the Bible understands them. Because a common response to angelic appearances in the Bible is fear. Angels nearly always have to preface the message they bring with the statement "Do not be afraid."

This should give us a clue that the depiction of angels as babies with chubby cheeks and tiny tinkerbell wings is not exactly accurate. Seeing a ten pound baby flying around would not scare you; it might repulse you, particularly if you are allergic to kitsch,

---

[1] Advert for Raven, H., *The Angel Bible: Everything You Ever Wanted to Know About Angels:* (London: Godsfield Press, 2006)

but it wouldn't frighten you. In fact, they're rarely described at all; they just "appear."[2] For example, here's the report that Samson's mother gives of the positive result to her angelic pregnancy test

> Then the woman came and told her husband, "A man of God came to me, and his appearance was like that of an angel of God, most awe-inspiring; I did not ask him where he came from, and he did not tell me his name; but he said to me, "You shall conceive and bear a son. So then drink no wine or strong drink, and eat nothing unclean, for the boy shall be a nazirite to God from birth to the day of his death"" (Judg. 13.6–7).

Angels are God's messengers, not heavenly creatures that we can command. They most commonly appear in human form, albeit slightly awesome humans. Their messages can certainly be comforting (e.g. 1 Kgs. 19.7), but they can also be dramatic and unsettling (e.g. 2 Kgs. 1.3–4). They can protect people in distress (e.g. Dan. 6.22–23), but they can also be fierce warriors with swords, capable of destroying armies (e.g. 1 Chr. 21.27; Is. 37.36).[3]

And they don't have wings. Nowhere in the Bible does it say that angels have wings. When Gabriel visits Mary there is no mention of either flying or wings; when the three angels appear to Abraham they appear like men; Jacob sees angels going up and down a staircase; wouldn't it have been easier to fly?[4]

So where did all these babies come from? In fact, that picture comes from classical statuary and art and it's called a *putto*. *Putto* is Italian for a young boy; in art, *putti* are pudgy, naked babies, predominantly male and with tiny wings. They often featured on the sarcophagi of children in classical times, but in the fifteenth and sixteenth centuries painters such as Donatello and Raphael

---

[2] One exception is Matthew 28.3, where the angel on the tomb is described as looking "like lightning" with clothing "white as snow."

[3] For a good overview of angels in the Bible, see *The Anchor Bible Dictionary*, I, 248.

[4] In Revelation, there is a description of an angel "flying" (Rev. 14.6) and in Daniel, Gabriel is described as arriving "in swift flight" (Dan. 9.21). But no wings are mentioned.

used them in paintings. From there they gradually morphed into angels.[5]

Yet there are some heavenly creatures in the Bible that definitely have wings: but they're not angels, they're cherubim.

REAL AND FAKE CHERUBIM

There are 92 mentions of cherubim in the Bible, spread among 67 verses, all but one in the Old Testament.[6] Of these mentions, by far the majority (around two-thirds) are descriptions of "fake" cherubim, as it were; statues, relief carvings or embroidered pictures. Such artworks were found in the following places

- Two cherubim stood on the lid of the Ark (Exod. 25.18–22). The cherubim on the Ark formed a kind of "throne" for God, an area from which he would speak to Moses (Exod. 25.20–22; Num. 7.89). So God is often called the Lord "the who is enthroned on the cherubim" (1 Sam. 4.4; 2 Sam. 6.2; 2 Kgs. 19.15; 1 Chr. 13.6; Ps. 80.1; 99.1; Is. 37.16).

- A number of cherubim were woven into the curtains of the Tabernacle (Exod. 26.1,31; 36.8,35).

- There were two huge cherubim on the back wall of the Holy of Holies (1 Kgs. 6.23–28). Each were ten cubits high and covered with gold. Opinion is divided over whether they were three-dimensional statues, or carved in relief on the real wall. Either way, their wings formed a kind of covering under which the Ark was placed (1 Kgs. 8.6–7).

- There were cherubim carved on the walls of the Temple (1 Kgs. 6.29), on the doors (1 Kgs 6.32); on the bronze stand for the huge basin (or "sea") in the court of the Temple (1 Kgs. 7.27–36).

- In Ezekiel's vision of the Temple there are also decorative pictures of cherubim in the inner room (Ezek. 41.18–20).

---

[5] Campbell, G., *The Oxford Dictionary of the Renaissance*, (Oxford: Oxford University Press, 2003), 641.

[6] The only mention in the New Testament is in Hebrews 9. 5, and that's describing an Old Testament building: the Holy of Holies.

So most of the mentions of cherubim in the Bible are not of real creatures, but of *pictures* of real creatures.

The only accounts we have of real cherubim are as follows

- A guardian figure at the gates of the garden in Eden (Gen. 3.24).

- A description in a psalm of God "riding" a cherub (2 Sam. 22.11).

- Descriptions of God being "enthroned" on the cherubim, which may draw on descriptions of the top of the Ark of the Covenant (Ps. 80.1; 99.1; Is. 37.16).

- Ezekiel's vision of cherubim (Ezek. 10.1–20; 11.22). Here, they are winged creatures (Ezek. 10.5) who appear to be pulling some kind of wheeled chariot (Ezek. 10.2,9) and supporting a sapphire throne (Ezek. 10.1). They also have hands beneath their wings (Ezek. 10.8). The creatures have four faces (a man, a lion, an ox, and an eagle), four wings and feet "like those of a calf."[7] These may be the same as the creatures seen in Revelation (Rev. 4.6–8) who are not called cherubim and only have one face each.

- Ezekiel describes a cherub "guarding" and then exiling the King of Tyre (Ezek. 28.14,16).

From this we can identify a number of distinct roles.

First and foremost, the cherubim appear to be kind of a transport corps for God. He "rides" upon them; probably the image that the writer has in mind is a chariot being drawn by cherubim.[8] This is brought out fully in Ezekiel's vision, where the cherubim throne has developed into a kind of bizarre cherubim chariot, with wheels whirring in all directions.[9] Their normal function, therefore, is to carry God's throne. Calling God "he who is enthroned on the cherubim" is like calling a jockey "he who sits on a fast horse"; or

---

[7]   We don't know whether Ezekiel actually saw creatures with four faces, or with one face that had the attributes of a human, lion, ox and eagle, but it doesn't much matter. We're not talking normal here. We're talking a creature of whom it could be said "only its mother could love it."

[8]   Chronicles speaks of the cherubim in relation to a chariot (1 Chr. 28.18); "the golden chariot of the cherubim."

[9]   Van der Toorn, K., Becking, B., & Van der Horst, P.W., *Dictionary of Deities and Demons in the Bible*, (Cambridge: Brill Eerdmans, 1999), 191

the Queen "she who rides in a great big gold coach that costs the taxpayers a fortune but which makes a great photo-opportunity." In this sense, the cherubim show God's majesty, they are a sign of his presence. He doesn't just come into a room, he rides in, as a monarch would in a coach.

The second distinct role of the cherubim is as guardians, either protecting someone or stopping people entering (e.g. in Genesis). In Genesis, cherubim are placed at the entrance of the garden of Eden to stop Adam and Eve returning. Although the verse mentions a flaming sword, it doesn't say that the cherubim were holding the sword. The sword just seems to hang there, going back and forth like some device out of Indiana Jones: "He drove out the man; and at the east of the garden of Eden he placed the cherubim, and a sword flaming and turning to guard the way to the tree of life" (Gen. 3.24). As already mentioned, Ezekiel also talks of God appointing a cherub as a kind of guard (Ezek. 28.14,16).

These functions allow us to differentiate between cherubim and angels. Angels are warriors and messengers; cherubim have more workmanlike functions. They are not messengers in the sense that the more human-resembling angels are. These are the transport battalion or the watchdogs.[10] They're both heavenly beings, but not the same kind.

WHAT'S IN A NAME?

But to return to the key question: what did they look like? Unlike angels, cherubim were part of the decoration of the Ark of the Covenant, the Tabernacle and the Temple. We know that they had wings. We know that they pulled a chariot, or carried God in some way. And there is clearly a lot of "animal" in there. Ezekiel describes them as having four faces: lion, eagle, ox and man; which probably refers to what are called the "excellencies" of the created order – the best of each type. So, the lion is the greatest of the wild beasts, the eagle the king of the birds, the ox the greatest domestic

---

[10] For the iconographic imagery, see Ryken, L, *et al., Dictionary of Biblical Imagery*, (Leicester: Inter-varsity Press, 1998)

Ivory carving from Assyria, showing a winged lion with a human head.

beast and man, the pinnacle and crown of creation.[11] Ezekiel is therefore painting a picture of a creature which combines the best of all creatures.[12]

Perhaps the clue comes from the name, because the word "cherubim" is probably connected with the Akkadian word *karibu* or *kuribu*.[13] *Karibu* were a kind of composite creature, like a sphinx, with the head of a human but the body of a lion. These kind of figures were common in the nearby ancient cultures. There are plenty of examples of ancient guardian figures, which often appear as lions or bulls, but with human faces and huge wings. In the British Museum, for example, are two huge guardian figures from Assyria, winged bulls with human faces. Elsewhere there are plenty of depictions; carved ivories of winged lions with human heads from Phoenicia and even a bronze stand for a temple basin, with a sphinx creature from Cyprus or possible Phoenicia.

These creatures, like the ones seen in Ezekiel, were attempts to depict abstract concepts – power, majesty, leadership – in physical

---

[11] The four creatures were later interpreted by Christian commentators as pictures of the four gospel writers – and linked to the four creatures around the throne in Revelation 4.6–8. The first written evidence of this link is in Irenaus of Lyons, who took the link from the opening scenes of each gospel. Luke begins with Zacharias offering sacrifice, so he's the ox; Matthew begins with Jesus' human genealogy, so he's the human; Mark introduces the Holy Spirit quite early on, so he gets the eagle; and John, because of his emphasis on the power and leadership of Christ, gets the lion (Irenaeus, *Against Heresies* 3. 11. 8). Later writers such as Jerome and Augustine changed the order. However Luke is always the ox. Apart from finding the numerous pictures of an ox with a pen rather ludicrous, I can't help wondering if he'd be pleased. See Jensen, R.M. "Of Cherubim and Gospel Symbols." *Biblical Archaeology Review* 21(Jul/Aug 1995).

[12] Isaiah also describes winged beings, but these he calls seraphim (Isa. 6.1–3). Elsewhere the same Hebrew word is translated as snake or serpents (See "Mythical Animals" in Ryken, *et al.*, *Dictionary of Biblical Imagery*). This suggests that the seraphim may be more like dragons than anything else. Anyway, I don't propose to discuss the difference here for the following reasons: (a) I don't think there is any difference and (b) it's Tuesday morning, I haven't had a coffee yet and the whole thing is doing my head in.

[13] Toorn, Becking and Horst, *Dictionary of Deities and Demons in the Bible*, 189

terms. So they could only do so by taking the best elements from the creation around them. Cherubim are like this. They are winged creatures. Since Ezekiel's have hooves, it's reasonable to think they were winged bulls with human faces. In depicting the cherubim, the Bible writers were trying to find physical images to describe metaphysical concepts. Ezekiel saw the ultimate creatures,

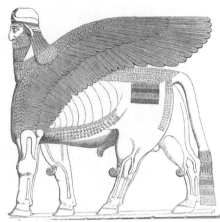

An Assyrian winged bull. These huge statues were placed at the entrance to temples and palaces as "gatekeepers."

creatures who were the pinnacle of creation; and the only language he had to describe them was the language of the creation around him; a creation which was home to majestic lions, the raw power of oxen, the soaring flight of eagles and the mystery and majesty of men.

Whatever the case, they were not human figures and the many depictions of the cherubim on top of the Ark as winged human-figures are probably wrong.[14] Cherubim are not small babies with wings.

So, if your baby is described as "cherubic" I would seek the help of a qualified paediatrician. And possibly someone from the local safari park.

---

[14] I've done this myself in at least two books. Ah well, you live and learn.

The Church of the Nativity in Bethlehem. Built in 325 AD on the traditional site of Jesus' birth, it is one of the oldest churches in the world.

WHERE WAS JESUS BORN?

Every Christmas, in every pre-school, playgroup, nursery and junior school, Mary and Joseph, riding on a donkey, arrive in Bethlehem. There they knock on the door of an inn and are met by an innkeeper – or several innkeepers, depending on how many children have to be found speaking parts. They ask whether there is a room available, but the innkeeper shakes their head (or heads). There is no room at the inn; eventually, however, they are offered a stable round the back and there, in the cosy straw, surrounded by children wearing animal masks they have made themselves out of cereal packets, Jesus is born.

Innkeepers everywhere have been recovering from this PR disaster ever since. And you've got to feel sorry for them; because in all likelihood it never happened like that at all.

Here's what Luke says

> Joseph also went from the town of Nazareth in Galilee to Judea, to the city of David called Bethlehem, because he was descended from the house and family of David. He went to be registered with Mary, to whom he was engaged and who was expecting a child. While they were there, the time came for her to deliver her child. And she gave birth to her firstborn son and wrapped him in bands of cloth, and laid him in a manger, because there was no place for them in the inn (Luke 2.4–7).

Now there are a number of intriguing facts here. The first, which has divided historians for centuries, is the nature of the census. Some deny that such a census ever took place; others say that, even if it did, Roman law registered people in their place of residence which, for Joseph would have been Nazareth. But Luke is clear: Joseph returned to "his own town."

There are several reasons why Joseph might have had to return to Bethlehem. He might have had some land there; he might simply have wanted to get Mary out of Nazareth. A town alive with rumor and scandal is not the best place for a young girl to give birth. Joseph is also described in the Bible as a "righteous" man; maybe he realized that the Messiah had to be born in Bethlehem, to fulfil the prophecy in Micah (Mic. 5.2).

Either way, they made the long journey; some seventy miles from Galilee to just south of Jerusalem. And while they are in Bethlehem, in a taut, sparse passage, Luke records the "time came for her to deliver the child."

No miraculous intervention here – unless you count the everyday miracle that is childbirth. Just a woman bearing the pain brought in by her great-great-great, etc. grandmother, Eve.

So they're in Bethlehem. But where did this take place? Where were they staying? Who were they with? That depends on two tiny details: the manger and the "inn."

YOU SAY KATALUMA, I SAY PANDOCHEION

They give it a bit of the fairytale, those two words; they give the event the whiff of romance. From those small seeds a thousand school nativity plays have blossomed; from the "inn" and the "manger" we have conjured up stables and innkeepers and cattle gently lowing and an entire sub-genre of Renaissance painting.

The truth is Luke may not mean "inn" at all. The Greek word he uses is *kataluma,* which can mean "inn", but just as easily can mean guest room or spare room or anywhere you might put visitors. And, if we look elsewhere in his gospel, there are indications that he is, indeed, using the word this way.

Luke uses the word *kataluma* twice in his gospel: once in this passage and once to describe the room in which the Last Supper took place; the "upper room." The relevant verse is Luke 22.11, where two disciples are told to go and ask "Where is the *guest room*, where I may eat the Passover with my disciples?" (my italics). Now no-one, as far as I know, has yet suggested that the Last Supper took place in an inn. In fact, the whole tone of Jesus' preparations for the Last Supper indicate a concern to find a private space, a space away from threats and interruptions, and away from the vast crowds in Jerusalem for the Passover.

Furthermore, when Luke does come to talk about an inn, he uses an entirely different word. In the story of the Good Samaritan, the eponymous hero takes the unfortunate victim to an inn (Luke 10.34) and there the word Luke uses is *pandocheion*. So, if Luke had meant a traveling inn, with an innkeeper, he would surely have chosen this word. Either Luke is being inconsistent in his choice of words, or he didn't mean an inn at all. Luke is actually precise in his technical terms; he likes to get the details right, does Luke. So Luke says, not that the inn was full, but that there was no room in the guest room, or spare room. Mary and Joseph weren't at the travel lodge; they were staying with relatives.

Which, when you think about the broader context, makes more sense. We have seen that for Joseph to return to Bethlehem for the census meant that he had to have strong links there: either land or close family. If he'd been a second generation resident in Nazareth, for example, then surely he'd have stayed where he was. To make any sense of his journey for the census, he had to have been a recent resident of Nazareth. Which means that he would have had relatives in Bethlehem; which in turn means that there would have been no need for rented accommodation at all.

And just because Joseph traveled for the census doesn't mean that a lot of other people did. As we have seen, there may have been compelling reasons for him to escape Nazareth for a while, reasons which have little to do with Roman tax administration. Luke gives no indication that Bethlehem was full of crowds waiting to fill in their forms.

Sadly for playgroups everywhere, the story of the hardhearted innkeeper who grudgingly opens the stable round the back may well be a complete misreading. The inn and the innkeeper, it seems, have been invented.

UNSTABLE RELATIONSHIP

As if that wasn't bad enough, there probably never was a stable either.

Well, not as such. There was an animals' feeding place, clearly, for Luke records that the baby was put in a manger. This time there is no conflict about what the word means: it means an animal's feeding trough. The misunderstanding lies in where that feeding trough was located.

To understand this we need to remember that both Mary and Joseph were poor. Luke attributes a song to Mary, a song full of delight that the poor and hungry have been blessed by God. "He [God] has brought down the powerful from their thrones," she sings, "and lifted up the lowly; he has filled the hungry with good things, and sent the rich away empty" (Luke 1.52–53).

This song makes no sense at all unless Mary – and the man she was to marry – were "lowly", poor and, even hungry. The language is full of the idea that God has chosen to bless the oppressed, rather than the oppressors. And quite clearly Mary was "lowly" in a number of ways. She was the subject of scandal and she was a virgin. This probably means that she was quite young; although older marriages did occur, the usual age for a Jewish girl to be married was between thirteen and sixteen. Parents usually arranged marriages through intermediaries. Betrothal was legally binding and could thus be dissolved only through death or divorce – hence Joseph's reluctance to do something as drastic as breaking off the engagement.[1]

The fact that Mary and Joseph were poor is backed up by the sacrifice they later give at the Temple. Luke records that they sacrificed "a pair of turtledoves or two young pigeons" – which was the sacrifice you gave if you were too poor to sacrifice a sheep.[2]

Given that data, we can assume that Joseph came from a simple, peasant background.[3] And simple homes did not have stables. The homes of ordinary poor families of the time were frequently built on two levels: there was the lower level where the everyday living took

---

[1] Jewish weddings usually lasted a week, with a lot of feasting among one's friends. The well-off were known to invite large numbers of guests – sometimes the entire village – to the wedding. They were joyous occasions; the fact that Mary didn't appear to get her wedding is just one more sacrifice she had to make.

[2] The regulations are in Leviticus 12.8.

[3] There has been a great deal of debate about this word "peasant"; scholars such as Crossan believe that's exactly what Jesus was. Crossan, J.D., *The Historical Jesus: The Life of a Mediterranean Jewish Peasant*, (Edinburgh: Clark, 1993), 124ff. Others argue that his family were working class, but not peasants. Shanks, H., and Witherington III, B., *The Brother of Jesus: The Dramatic Story & Meaning of the First Archaeological Link to Jesus & His Family*, (London: Continuum, 2003), 101; others that they were quite well off. Thiede, *The Cosmopolitan World of Jesus: New Findings From Archaeology*, 19–20. By using the word, I'm not indicating any perjorative meaning. I'm using it as a description of a simple, rural working-class lifestyle.

place, and an upper, mezzanine level where the family slept. Or, if they were caves (and many people did live in caves at the time) the family would have slept in the central parts and to the back, with the animals kept at the entrance.[4] Israel can get very cold at night, so the animals would have been a heating source for the house; a kind of primitive central heating. What Luke is saying is that there was no spare room in the residential part of the house. The place was packed out. So they had to go to the lower level, where the animals were kept. This would explain why a stable is never mentioned. There wasn't one; the animals were kept downstairs in the home; what happened was that Jesus was put downstairs with the animals, because the rest of the house was full.

A REAL STORY

What difference does this make, apart from ruining many a nativity play? Well, for one thing it shows the truth of the incarnation, of Jesus becoming man. He wasn't just born as a general "man", but in a specific place at a specific time. And the place was a cramped peasant's home in the tiny town of Bethlehem.

We can see that Jesus was born into a lower class family. It blows apart the cosy Christmas card picture of a nice, warm, clean stable, with golden straw illuminated by the glowing halo round Jesus' head. In many ways it's a much more "ordinary" scene. In some ways Jesus' birth was highly unusual: very few births are announced by angelic choirs. But in other ways it was almost painfully normal. The home was an ordinary peasant dwelling; the first cot an animal's feeding trough. In some ways, as well, the birth is more shocking. The Son of God is laid, not in some kind of rustic cot, not in the latest model in Mothercare's Mediterranean Peasant Range, but in the place where usually the animals ate. He slept in hay full of ticks and fleas, in a home that was small and cramped. His parents were poor; his mother was incredibly young.

Most of us accept the idea that Jesus was born into a poor family, but we don't stop and picture what that meant. The Renaissance

---

4   Thiede, *The Cosmopolitan World of Jesus: New Findings From Archaeology*, 16.

paintings which inform our view of the event were painted for rich, wealthy patrons. They did not want to see conditions of slum-like poverty, even had the artist managed to interpret the text correctly. So we have become conditioned to seeing a roomy stable full of colorful characters. We have sanitized the unsanitary stable. We have swept it clean from the dirty straw, given the animals a wash and brush up, sprayed a bit of myrrh around to cover up the unsavory smell of sweat and animal dung.

To do so is to miss the point. The point behind Luke's depiction of the birth of Jesus is that it was dirty and smelly and poor and cramped and hard and utterly, utterly, wonderful.

And that, in my opinion, is a much more wonderful, deeper truth.

WHY DOES RACHEL
WANT MANDRAKES?

Most days, my email is full of curious messages inquiring as to the state of my love life and offering me a range of drugs which are guaranteed to help. The latest one, rather strangely, contains a bullet point list of the advantages of this particular brand, including "It keeps you ready" and "No need to plan around meals." The mind, frankly, boggles.

Spam email may be a relatively recent invention, but human beings have been seeking medicinal help with sex for thousands of years; either through supposed aphrodisiacs or herbs to aid fertility. They crop up in the Bible as well, notably in the story of Jacob's tangled relationship with his wives. Here the desired plant is a root called a mandrake

> In the days of wheat harvest Reuben went and found mandrakes in the field, and brought them to his mother Leah. Then Rachel said to Leah, "Please give me some of your son's mandrakes." But she said to her, "Is it a small matter that you have taken away my husband? Would you take away my son's mandrakes also?" Rachel said, "Then he may lie with you tonight for your son's mandrakes." When Jacob came from the field in the evening, Leah went out to meet him, and said, "You must come in to me; for I have hired you with my son's mandrakes." So he lay with her that night. And God heeded Leah, and she conceived and bore Jacob a fifth son. Leah said, "God has given me my hire because I gave my maid to my husband"; so she named him Issachar (Gen. 30.14–18).

It seems a lot of fuss over a plant that is related to the potato. But then, this story is about a lot more than mandrakes. It's about prestige and position, about status and, above all, about desperation.

OH, YOU WANTED TO MARRY THAT ONE...

This is a story of two desperate women; sisters at war. The background to this story lies in Jacob's marriage. After falling in love with Rachel, the daughter of his Uncle Laban, Jacob worked for seven years to earn her hand. On the wedding day Jacob was tricked into marrying a substitute: Rachel's elder sister, Leah. Since brides were entirely veiled, all he could see were the eyes, so it wasn't till afterwards that he discovered his Uncle Laban's ruse. Jacob was then allowed to marry Rachel as well, but only in return for a further seven years' labor. This, he was willing to do, since he "loved Rachel more than Leah" (Gen. 29.30).[1]

So, we have two wives; Leah, unloved and unwanted; and beautiful, beloved Rachel. It's not looking good for Leah, but she has a trump card over her sister: she can bear children. "When the LORD saw that Leah was unloved, he opened her womb; but Rachel was barren." (Gen. 29.31)

Leah might not be preferred, but she can get pregnant. She gives birth to Reuben, Simeon, Levi and Judah. Rachel is reduced to sending her handmaid in as a kind of surrogate mother. Bilhah, the maid, bears Rachel two surrogate sons: Dan and Naphthali.[2]

The competition is on. Leah responds by sending *her* handmaid into action. Zilpah is the lucky maid, and she bears Jacob two more sons: Gad and Asher. So the score so far is Leah's team 6; Rachel's team 2. And Rachel, the team captain, hasn't yet scored a single goal.

That's the background to this story, which takes place in May, at the time of the wheat harvest. The writer has compressed time, probably, so Reuben may be in his teens. Years have passed, and Reuben, the eldest boy, is out in the fields when he finds some mandrakes.

FANCY A DUDA?

The Hebrew word is *duda'im* which sounds similar to the words for love and lover. Whether the plants referred to are mandrakes is open to question, and probably depends on where this episode

---

[1] See Genesis 29 for the full story.

[2] This was usual practice of the time and was a way for the wife to secure her status in the clan. The maid becomes a kind of "secondary" wife to the husband; she was not on the same level as the wife, and if she sought to abuse her status, she could be punished but not expelled. Research has shown similar laws in other cultures of the time. See Van Seters, J. "The problem of childlessness in near Eastern law and the Patriarchs of Israel." *Journal of Biblical Literature* 87 (1968), 403ff.

takes place. Zohary, in his book *Plants of the Bible,* argues that it cannot mean mandrakes as the mandragora plant has never grown in Mesopotamia.[3] However, mandrakes do grow all over Israel and also in Syria, so it's not out of the question that it could have been found at the time. Perhaps Rachel's desire for the mandrakes is also linked to the rarity of the plant in their part of the world.[4] If they weren't mandrakes, it is clear from the passage that they were assumed to have similar properties.

Mandrakes are generally found in stony places. Their association with fertility probably comes from the fact that they have an odd-shaped root, which sometimes resemble a human figure. Strangely, mandrake roots contain both sedatives and stimulating hormones which may act as aphrodisiacs; experiments have shown that the greater quantity of sedatives may cancel out any effect of the stimulating hormones. In other words, they'll provoke the desire, but make you too sleepy to do anything about it. This hasn't stopped them gaining a reputation across the centuries. The Greeks considered the mandrake a love potion, when it was soaked in wine; they also, as in this story, believed that it helped a woman to conceive.[5] Aphrodite, the Greek goddess of love was sometimes called "the Lady of the Mandrake."[6]

What's really interesting about this story is the discovery of the mandrakes reveals the true dynamics between Leah and her sister Rachel. As the elder sister, one would expect Leah to have the authority, but it is Rachel who appears to have gained a privileged position within the family. She is the favorite wife and she, therefore, gets the privilege of deciding who Jacob gets to sleep with and when. Crucially, however, she has not yet born Jacob a son.

The importance in the Old Testament of child-bearing cannot be over-emphasized. Wives were expected to continue the line;

---

[3]   Zohary, M., *Plants of the Bible: A Complete Handbook to All the Plants With 200 Full-Color Plates Taken in the Natural Habitat,* (Cambridge: Cambridge University Press, 1982), 188–89.

[4]   Moldenke, H.N., and Moldenke, A.L., *Plants of the Bible,* (Waltham: Chronica Botanica, 1952), 137–9. Wenham, G.J., *Genesis 16–50,* (Waco: Word Books, 1994), 246–247.

[5]   Zohary, *Plants of the Bible,* 188–89.

[6]   I suppose it's slightly less pungent than being called The Lady of Shallott

to bear their husband a son (or several). Not to do so was seen as a great curse on the woman, and left her in a kind of limbo, without status. That is why Tamar goes to such lengths to seduce her father-in-law Judah; if she does not do so, she will be left without a child (Gen. 38). In these more emancipated times, it's hard to comprehend the status of women in ancient cultures, but, broadly speaking, a woman was defined by her ability to produce children. She had no real identity and status of her own; these were defined by the "men in her life": her father, her husband, her sons. If her husband died, as a woman she could not inherit any property (hence the plight of widows mentioned throughout the Bible); so her only real means of security was to have children to care for her.[7] No wonder Rachel is so desperate. She's the favored wife now, but what happens in the future? She wants those mandrakes, she *needs* those mandrakes.

Leah, for her part, also has problems. True, she can bear children, but she is unloved and unwanted. The sharpness of her response indicates that it is rare for her to get even one night in the marital bed.[8] Her husband had to be tricked into marrying her; her sister bosses her around. She doesn't actually need the mandrakes, but they do, at least, give her a bargaining position.

Leah lacks love, Rachel lacks children. There is a bargain to be struck.

MAN FOR HIRE

So Leah buys Jacob for a night with a load of vegetable roots. The scale of her desperation shows that she's willing to bargain the whole lot for just one night with Jacob. Two sisters competing over the love of one man, with an exploitative father-in-law hovering in the background; it's a scenario straight out of the soaps. It illustrates how often in the Bible the grace of God operates despite human brokenness. The situation for this family is not like those in the

---

[7]   Kirsch, J., *The Harlot By the Side of the Road: Forbidden Tales of the Bible*, (London: Rider, 1997), 136. See also Deuteronomy 21.16–17 and Numbers 27.8–11.

[8]   Wenham, *Genesis 16–50*, 246.

present day[9] but the conflict and tension, the unfulfiled lives and shattered hopes, those are found in every community throughout the world. The great thing is God does work in this environment; he works among these warring, hurting people. But *he* does it, not the mandrakes.

And the great irony is that the mandrakes are shown to be useless, because Leah conceives that very night. The result is Issachar, another son. Then Leah has a sixth son, called Zebulun, and finally a daughter called Dinah (Gen. 30.17–21).

This is what's technically known as "rubbing Rachel's face in it." Still, in the end, God comes to Rachel's aid: "Then God remembered Rachel, and God heeded her and opened her womb" (Gen. 30.22).

The text is making a point here. Leah gives away the mandrakes and conceives three more children. Rachel, who kept and presumably used the mandrakes, gets no result from them whatsoever. In the end, the text makes clear that it is God who answers her prayers, not some folk superstition based on a kind of potato.

So this story tells us about the relationships between the sisters, about one woman's desperation for love and her sister's desperation for a child; about the status of women in ancient Mesopotamia, and about how incredibly useless mandrakes are.

I wonder how Jacob felt about it all? Maybe this incident, with sisters trading objects for rights, reminds him uncomfortably of his own shady deals with his brother Esau – the reason he fled to Haran in the first place. He has been tricked into working for hire for his Uncle Laban, now even his wives are hiring him. Jacob seems helpless in this exchange, it's all being organized by the women.

But then in the end it's about sex. And men are generally reduced to a state of helplessness where sex is on offer.

---

[9]   At least I hope not. Otherwise Social Services will be calling.

A reconstruction of the first-century synagogue at Nazareth, the place where Jesus' teaching was rejected by the people of his hometown.

WERE JESUS' FAMILY
ASHAMED OF HIM?

Every Christmas, Channel 4 like to annoy Christians.[1] They do this normally by producing documentaries showing that the Bible is made up, or that the church has suppressed the truth, or that Paul was really a woman called Betty who lived up a pole in the Syrian desert. In 2006, they did a documentary called *The Secret Family of Jesus* and the blurb did all it could to paint the programme as iconoclastic and revolutionary: "Did Jesus have a real human family? If so, why were they airbrushed from history and excised from the Bible? Robert Beckford tells the story of the people who shared his bloodline."

Jesus had brothers and sisters shock! And cousins! And... er... uncles! And they were excised from the Bible! It's a stunning shock to everyone – or it would be, apart from one tiny detail: they're not excised from the Bible. We know the names of four of his brothers and, with a little digging, we can even find the names of other relatives; his cousins, aunts and an uncle. There's nothing shocking about the existence of his family. The really shocking thing is that they may not have approved of what he was doing at all.

THE RELATIVES OF JESUS

Let's start with what we know. His parents' names were Joseph and Mary.[2] We also know that John the Baptist was a relative of his mother. When Gabriel gives the news to Mary he also tells her about Elizabeth: "And now, your relative Elizabeth in her old age has also conceived a son; and this is the sixth month for her who was said to be barren' (Luke 1.36).

The nature of this relationship isn't stated and the Greek word used for relative is quite vague.[3] Possibly she was a cousin of Mary's. Certainly the relationship is not close enough to be defined more precisely and may have been quite distant, since in John's gospel, John the Baptist claims not to have known Jesus: "I myself did not

---

[1]   Actually they do it all year round, but it's more obvious then.

[2]   For more on Joseph see p.159. On Mary see p.80.

[3]   *The Anchor Bible Dictionary*, II, 475.

know him, but the one who sent me to baptize with water said to me, 'He on whom you see the Spirit descend and remain is the one who baptizes with the Holy Spirit'" (John 1.33).

So the best we're talking about here is a very distant cousin.

HIS BROTHERS

We also know the names of his brothers

> He left that place and came to his hometown, and his disciples followed him. On the sabbath he began to teach in the synagogue, and many who heard him were astounded. They said, "Where did this man get all this? What is this wisdom that has been given to him? What deeds of power are being done by his hands! Is not this the carpenter, the son of Mary and brother of James and Joses and Judas and Simon, and are not his sisters here with us?" And they took offense at him. Then Jesus said to them, "Prophets are not without honour, except in their hometown, and among their own kin, and in their own house."(Mk 6.1–4).[4]

These then are the names of his brothers: James, Joses, Judas and Simon. The sisters are never named.

James was to become a major figure in the Early Church. Judas (or Jude) is credited with the letter that bears his name. Indeed, it's worth noting that, far from being airbrushed out of existence by the Early Church, the letters of James and Jude owe their place in the New Testament precisely *because* they were believed to be written by relatives of Jesus.

Now, admittedly, there are arguments about the exact status of these brothers. The Catholic church, to support the doctrine of Mary's perpetual virginity, argues they were cousins, while the Eastern Orthodox church teaches that they were step-brothers; children of Joseph from a previous marriage. However, the Greek

---

[4] I always like the next line: "And he could do no deed of power there, except that he laid his hands on a few sick people and cured them" (Mark 6.5). He was so off form that all he could do was a couple of miraculous healings.

word for cousins, *anepsios*, is never used of James and the others, either by the gospel writers or early Christians such as Hegesippus, one of the earliest historians of the Early Church, who wrote some time in the second century AD. Since Matthew states that Mary did not have sex with Joseph "until she had given birth to a son" I think it's reasonable to assume that, after the very unusual events of Jesus' birth, they took up life as man and wife. Indeed, the culture of the time assumed that a married couple would have children; it was an obligation, not an option.[5]

What's notable here, along with the information about Jesus' family, is their attitude towards him and his ministry. Not even his own family, it seems, "honor" him as a prophet. Everywhere else people marvel, but not in the small town of Nazareth where he grew up.[6] And not, apparently, even among his own family, among his own "kin" or even in the family home.

This is curious. Surely his brothers, of all people, should have spotted his mission? Surely they should have respected and supported him? But far from being supportive, it seems as though his brothers might even have set out to stop him: "Then he went home; and the crowd came together again, so that they could not even eat. When his family heard it, they went out to restrain him, for people were saying, 'He has gone out of his mind'" (Mark 3.19b-21).

When your family set out to restrain you, because they think you're mad, I think that qualifies for "being without honor." John, too, records negative attitudes from Jesus' brothers. According to his gospel, after the miracle at Cana, Jesus goes down to Capernaum with his "mother, his brothers, and his disciples; and they remained there a few days" (John 2.11–12). Later, some of his brothers try to persuade Jesus to go up to Jerusalem and demonstrate his power

---

[5] For the different views of Jesus' brothers see Shanks and Witherington, *The Brother of Jesus*, 94–95. Brown, R.E., *The Birth of the Messiah*, (London: Cassell, 1993), 132. Bernheim, P., *James, Brother of Jesus*, (London: SCM, 1997), 1–29. Witherington, *The Gospel of Mark: Socio-Rhetorical Commentary*, 192–195.

[6] On the population of Nazareth see p. 62.

So his brothers said to him, "Leave here and go to Judea so that your disciples also may see the works you are doing; for no one who wants to be widely known acts in secret. If you do these things, show yourself to the world." (For not even his brothers believed in him.)... "Go to the festival yourselves. I am not going to this festival, for my time has not yet fully come." After saying this, he remained in Galilee. But after his brothers had gone to the festival, then he also went, not publicly but as it were in secret (John 7.3–5, 8–10).

"Not even his brothers believed him." Which brothers these were is not made clear, but they act in a way which is recognizable among all families – especially those with a lot of boys: "If you're so great, go up to Jerusalem and prove yourself," they say. "Go on. Dare you."

Significantly, when Jesus finally does go to Jerusalem, when he dies on the cross, his brothers don't appear to be there. His mother and (as we shall see) other relatives have followed him but not, apparently, his brothers. For at the cross, Jesus entrusts care of his mother to the beloved disciple, when naturally one would expect his own family to look after her. Crucifixion was the most shameful death in the Græco-Roman world. He had brought the whole family into disrepute; his actions had shamed a family which traced its lineage back to the royalty of ancient Israel. Perhaps the absence of his brothers is because they were ashamed to be associated with him.[7] What is more, after his death, he was not buried by his family, as would normally be the custom; that role went to another follower – Joseph of Arimathea (Mark 15.43–46).

Fortunately for them and for all of us, it didn't end there. For at least two of these brothers became key leaders in the Early Church. And although they weren't in Jerusalem for the crucifixion, they were in Jerusalem a few weeks later. Luke describes how the disciples returned from the Mount of Olives, having seen the ascension of Jesus

---

7   Shanks and Witherington, *The Brother of Jesus*, 105.

> When they had entered the city, they went to the room upstairs
> where they were staying, Peter, and John, and James, and
> Andrew, Philip and Thomas, Bartholomew and Matthew,
> James son of Alphaeus, and Simon the Zealot, and Judas son of
> James. All these were constantly devoting themselves to prayer,
> together with certain women, including Mary the mother of
> Jesus, as well as his brothers (Acts 1.13–14).

So now the brothers are there, along with their mother. What has
changed things? The answer is simple: they saw Jesus. Here's what
Paul tells us: "For I handed on to you as of first importance what
I in turn had received: that Christ died for our sins in accordance
with the Scriptures, and that he was buried, and that he was raised
on the third day in accordance with the Scriptures, and that he
appeared to Cephas, then to the twelve. Then he appeared to more
than five hundred brothers and sisters at one time, most of whom
are still alive, though some have died. Then he appeared to James,
then to all the apostles" (1 Cor. 15.3–7).

James and Jude, at least, had seen the resurrected Christ. And
from initially believing him mad, from thinking him deluded,
from even, perhaps, being too ashamed to be with him in his final
moments, they are transformed. It seems that Peter's was not the
only experience of denial and forgiveness in the Early Church.[8]

From this point on, James becomes a "pillar" of the church, to use
the words of Paul. In particular, he is associated with a Jewish kind
of Christianity; one that sometimes came into conflict with Paul's
outreach to the Gentiles. Hegesippus paints a portrait of James as
a man of strict Jewish observance, whose holy life led to him being
called "James the Just." James, of course, is the traditional author of
the letter which bears his name, which is generally agreed to be the
most "Jewish" of the New Testament letters in tone and message.
The death of James has also been recorded, this time by the Jewish

---

[8]　The apocryphal gospel called the *Gospel of the Hebrews* (which is largely a different form of
Matthew's gospel) relates how James took a vow not to eat until he saw the risen Jesus. Jesus
appeared to him with some bread, broke it, gave thanks and said "My brother, eat thy bread, for
the Son of Man is risen from among them that sleep." This is a late second century invention, but
it may preserve some historical content, particularly James' reputation as an ascetic. James, *The
Apocryphal New Testament*, 4.

historian Josephus, who writes that, during a power vacuum created by the death of the Roman governor Festus, the Jewish leaders seized James and some others and had them stoned to death.[9]

There is another New Testament letter – the letter of Jude – which is attributed to another of Jesus' brothers.[10] So the brothers of Christ, far from being expunged from church history, are there at the very beginning of it. They may have been unconvinced by his ministry, they may even have been ashamed of him at times, but they became "pillars" of the church and links to its Jewish roots.

We also know that Jesus had at least one sister-in-law. In 1 Corinthians 9.5 Paul talks about those apostles who take their wives around with them on their travels. He includes the brothers of the Lord in the list.

So far, we've identified four brothers, some sisters, a mother, a (step)father, a distant relative (John) and some sisters-in-law.

What's that? You want more? OK. How does a pair of cousins and an aunt and uncle grab you?

THE COUSINS OF THUNDER

The different gospels list different women around the cross

- Mark has Mary Magdalene, and Mary the mother of James the younger and of Joses, and Salome (Mark 15.40).
- Matthew has Mary Magdalene, and Mary the mother of James and Joseph, and the mother of the sons of Zebedee (Matt. 27.56).
- John has Jesus' mother, and his mother's sister, Mary the wife of Clopas, and Mary Magdalene (John 19.25).

---

[9]   In Shanks and Witherington, *The Brother of Jesus*, 168. In later Christian accounts this tale was embellished with James being thrown down from the pinnacle of Temple Mount, surviving the fall and finally being beaten to death with a fuller's club. See Eusebius, *The Ecclesiastical History and the Martyrs of Palestine*, 58–59. For more on James, see Bernheim, *James, brother of Jesus*, and Shanks and Witherington, *The Brother of Jesus*, 91ff.

[10] Some experts argue that the authorship of this letter is not genuine, but even if that were true, it would still prove that Jude was *believed* to be a follower of Jesus; else why attribute authorship to him?

Some of these may be the same person, but named according to different relationships. In particular, Matthew puts in "the mother of the sons of Zebedee", whereas Mark has "Salome."[11] It may be that these were the same people, but Matthew, aware that his readers didn't know who Salome was, prefers to explain her significance. The intriguing possibility is that she is the same as the person John calls "his mother's sister." If this is so, it would make the apostles John and James Jesus' cousins on his mother's side. Admittedly the women referred to may be different women; all three gospel writers say that these women were "among" the women who were there; but this identification does make sense of the mother's request that her sons be given special precedence in heaven (Matt. 20.20–23). After all, they were *relatives* and everyone knew that, in earthly kingdoms, the relatives of the king got the best seats. That would also inform Jesus' response which specifically points out that the disciples should not behave like "the rulers of the Gentiles" (Matt. 20.25).[12]

UNCLE CLOPAS AND AUNTIE MARY

And it doesn't stop there. Another story from the Early Church tells how the successor to James as leader of the Jerusalem church was a man called Symeon, the son of Clopas. Here's what Eusebius writes: "He [Symeon] was a cousin – at any rate so it is said – of the

---

[11] Bauckham has Salome as Jesus' sister, rather than his aunt, see Bauckham, R., *Gospel Women: studies of the named women in the gospels*, (Edinburgh: T & T Clark, 2002), 225f.

[12] Bauckham says, rightly, "We must resist the rather prevalent temptation to deduce from these lists [i. e. the lists of the women at the crucifixion] that a woman named in one Gospel's list is the same person as a woman designated differently in another Gospel." Bauckham, *Gospel Women*, 298. Fair enough, but let's compare Matthew 27. 55–56 with Mark 15. 40–41: "There were also women looking on from a distance; among them were Mary Magdalene, and Mary the mother of James the younger and of Joses, and Salome. These used to follow him and provided for him when he was in Galilee; and there were many other women who had come up with him to Jerusalem." (Mark 15.40–41) "There were also many women there, looking on from a distance, who had followed Jesus from Galilee, ministering to him, among whom were Mary Magdalene and Mary the mother of James and Joseph and the mother of the sons of Zebedee." (Matt. 27.55–56) The closeness of the accounts is obvious. Matthew has edited the information slightly (we've lost the "to Jerusalem", reordered it, and otherwise changed only one detail: "Salome" becomes "the mother of the sons of Zebedee." So it seems not unreasonable to assume that this is not a different person, but an editorial explanation by Matthew of who Salome was.

Saviour; for indeed Hegesippus relates that Clopas was Joseph's brother."[13]

Having had one relative of Jesus in charge, it is natural, perhaps, that they would choose another one. So they selected Symeon, Jesus' cousin on his father's side. Go back to the women around the cross and we find "Mary of Clopas", i.e. Mary, wife of Clopas (John 19.25). Put all that together and you get Joseph's brother Clopas, his wife Mary, and their son Symeon who succeeds his cousin James to the leadership of the Jerusalem church.

Indeed, Clopas appears elsewhere in the gospels, on the road to Emmaus

> Now on that same day two of them were going to a village called Emmaus, about seven miles from Jerusalem, and talking with each other about all these things that had happened. While they were talking and discussing, Jesus himself came near and went with them, but their eyes were kept from recognizing him. And he said to them, "What are you discussing with each other while you walk along?" They stood still, looking sad. Then one of them, whose name was Cleopas, answered him, "Are you the only stranger in Jerusalem who does not know the things that have taken place there in these days?" (Luke 24.13–18).

Cleopas is the name Luke gives, but the probability that Cleopas is the same as Clopas is extremely high.[14] That would mean that the person whom Jesus encounters on the Emmaus road is his own uncle. Origen took this one step further and identified the unnamed disciple walking along the road as Clopas's son, Symeon.[15]

After all this, we can draw a family tree like this:

---

[13] Eusebius, *The Ecclesiastical History and the Martyrs of Palestine*, 78.

[14] For a full discussion of Mary of Clopas and the Cleopas/Clopas identification, see Bauckham, *Gospel Women*, 203–23.

[15] Origen *Contra Celsus* 2. 62. See Bauckham, *Jesus and the Eyewitnesses*, 43.

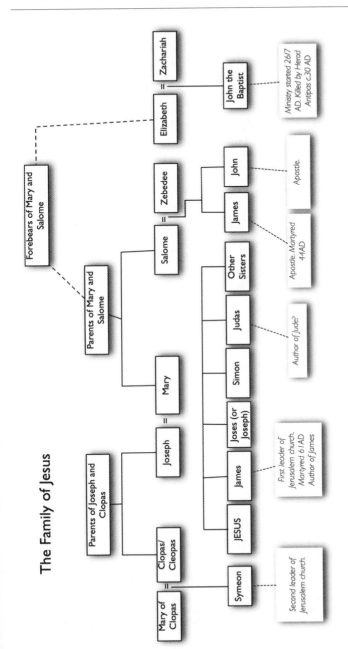

Family of Jesus. As suggested by the gospels and the tradition of the Early Church.

So to sum up, far from being edited out of the Early Church, Jesus' family are all over the place.[16] One relative preached of his coming. Two more cousins may have been part of the twelve disciples. We have the names of four brothers, two of which became major figures in the Early Church. Finally, we know of an aunt, an uncle and another cousin. His aunts were standing near the cross when he died. He appeared to his brother and his uncle after his death. They became leaders of the Early Church and letter writers.

If this is airbrushing out of history, I think the church needs a better airbrush.

---

[16] There is one final intriguing snippet from Hegesippus, reported in Eusebius' History. The emperor Domitian summoned the final three remaining relatives of Jesus, known as the "grandsons" of his brother Jude. When he found out how poor they were, how hard and calloused their hands were from work and how the kingdom they were talking about was not of this world, he "despised them as men of no account, let them go free and by an injunction caused the persecution against the church to cease." While this doesn't seem a credible story, it does reflect a tradition that there were descendants of Jesus' family, who remained influential in Palestine and Syria for many years. Eusebius, *The Ecclesiastical history and the martyrs of Palestine*, I, 80–81.

WHAT HAPPENED TO
THE ARK OF THE COVENANT?

In *Raiders of the Lost Ark*, Indiana Jones faces a race to secure one of the most precious objects ever made: the Ark of the Covenant. In one scene, he explains to two American Secret Service men what the Ark was and what happened to it. Indiana and his academic boss Dr. Brody relate how the Israelites put the ark in the Temple of Solomon, and then how it suddenly and mysteriously disappeared.

So where did it go? Indy has a theory: the Ark was taken by an Egyptian Pharaoh named Shishak, who invaded Jerusalem and took the Ark back to the city of Tanis. God's wrath at Shishak for stealing the Ark resulted in the sudden, mysterious disappearance of Tanis in a huge sandstorm just a year later.

The success of the film is not just testimony to the directing skills of Steven Spielberg, it's also testimony to the enduring power of this object; to the fascination that it still exerts on scholars, explorers and myth-makers today. In the film the Ark is depicted as a kind of relic of mass destruction, a box from which angels of death pour forth, killing everyone who gazes on them.[1] Like the Holy Grail (another object of Indy's searching) people still believe that it can be found. But there is one significant difference between the Ark of the Covenant and the Holy Grail: the Ark of the Covenant was real.[2]

A BRIEF HISTORY

The Ark of the Covenant was basically a box. A very posh box, admittedly, but still, fundamentally, a box.[3] Originally the Ark

---

[1] Indy and his heroine, Marion, are spared, because they refuse to look, although quite how this saves them is never made clear. In the film, the Ark ends up in a government storage facility, crate #9906753.

[2] There was a cup used at the Last Supper of course, but the idea of the special cup, the Holy Grail, does not appear until the 12th century. Before then it isn't mentioned at all.

[3] The cover of this book shows an ark which was found in the treasury room in Tutenkhamun's tomb. The photo has been doctored to remove the head of a jackal, not so much for religious purposes (although it has to be admitted that books featuring the jackal-headed god Anubis don't go down that well in many Christian bookshops) more to give an idea of what the Ark might well have looked like.

contained the two stone tablets on which God had written the ten commandments.[4] It was 1.5 cubits high, 1.5 cubits wide and 2.5 cubits long (about 114 x 68 x 68 cm or 3.75 x 2.25 x 2.25 feet). The box itself was made of acacia wood, a hard, dense wood, resistant to woodworm and ideal for carving. It was covered with gold leaf and had a rim of gold around the top lid. Each side of the box had two gold rings, to allow it to be carried by long wooden poles. On the lid of the Ark were two statues of cherubim, their wings outstretched (Exod. 25.10–22; 37.1–9).[5]

This is where the Ark appears to transcend its box-like status. It became a way for Moses to communicate with God. For God would "appear" to Moses from between these two cherubim (2 Kgs. 19.15; 1 Chr. 13.6).

When carried, the Ark was always wrapped in three layers: the curtain from the Tabernacle and then some kind of leather,[6] and finally a blue cloth, so that it was carefully concealed, even from the eyes of the Levites who carried it (Num 4.5–6).

The key thing is that the Ark indicated God's presence: it was a sign that he was with Israel. That is why it was carried ahead of them when they marched through the wilderness, or even when they went into battle (Num. 4.5–6; 10.33–36). It is also associated with his power. When they crossed the Jordan, the river grew dry as soon as the feet of the priests carrying the Ark touched the water (Josh. 3.7–13). It was present at the siege of Jericho (Josh. 6.1–5) and after the final victory at Ai it is present at a ceremony between Mount Ebal and Mount Gerazim (Josh. 8.33). After the conquest of the land it was stored at Shiloh (Josh. 18.1; 1 Sam.

---

[4] Some verses state that, later, some manna was stored in the Ark and, possibly, the staff of Aaron that budded into a tree (Exod. 16.32–34; Heb. 9. 4) However, 1 Kings 8. 9 states that there was nothing in there except the two tablets of stone.

[5] Meiggs, *Trees and Timber in the Ancient Mediterranean World*, 59. Durham, J.I., *Exodus*, (Waco: Word Books, 1986). For the appearance of cherubim, see p.69.

[6] The Hebrew word is *tachash* and scholars are uncertain what animal that means. NRSV and CEV settle for "fine leather"; the NIV has "sea cow" the ESV "goatskin"; the NEB "porpoise-hide" and the AV, rather bizarrely, "badger skin." It must be some kind of leather, since in Ezekiel the material is used for sandals (Ezek. 16.10). It may be related to the Arabic word for "dolphin," which is why many translators think it must be some kind of sea mammal such as dolphin, porpoise or seal. Frankly, how you come across such a material in the middle of the desert is a mystery. Budd, P.J., *Numbers*, (Waco: Word Books, 1984), 48.

3.2–3) although it also seems to have spent some time at Bethel (Judg. 20.26–27).[7]

The Ark is powerful, but also dangerously unpredictable. To put it bluntly, sometimes it worked, sometimes it didn't. Having the Ark carried before you into battle was no guarantee of success. In the most disastrous example of this, the Israelites blithely march into battle carrying it before them, only to suffer disastrous defeat and have the Ark captured by the Philistines.[8] The Philistines found it no more easy to handle; wherever they put it, it caused destruction. First it destroyed the statue of their god, Dagon (1 Sam. 5.1–5); then, wherever it went, it caused a plague to break out (1 Sam. 5.6–12). Eventually, after seven months of suffering, they placed it on a wagon and allowed it to make its own way home (1 Sam. 6).

Even back in Israel the Ark is characteristically dangerous: when it returns, some seventy people died simply because they do not seem to have shown enough enthusiasm.[9] Not unnaturally, they were only too glad to get rid of the thing: "Who is able to stand before the LORD, this holy God? To whom shall he go so that we may be rid of him?" (1 Sam. 6.20). It was hurriedly sent on to Kiriath-jearim, where it stayed in the house of Abinadab for "a long time" (1 Sam. 7.2).[10] Interestingly, this location may testify to the way the Ark was viewed by both sides. The area seems to have been a kind of neutral buffer-zone between Philistia and Israel; both sides may have seen this as a bit like placing a nuclear weapon in

---

[7] It seems to have been stored in the tent, although they may have created a permanent structure to house it Bright, J., *A History of Israel*, (London: SCM, 1960), 146–147.

[8] Some scholars argue that the defeat is a comment on the inadequacy of the Shiloh priesthood (1 Sam. 2. 22–25). But the loss of the Ark and the death of 34,000 men seems something of an overreaction to the wrongdoings of two priests. See Campbell, A.F. "Yahweh and the Ark: A Case Study in Narrative," *Journal of Biblical Literature* 98 (1979), 35. However, archeological evidence seems to show that Shiloh fell to the Philistines who destroyed the shrine. Samuel moved to Ramah. See Bright, *A History of Israel*, 165.

[9] 1 Samuel 6.19 NRSV. Other versions follow a different reading where the people "look into" or "look upon" the Ark.)

[10] Although the text says "twenty years", it's difficult to reconcile this with the chronology. It must have been longer, because it is not until after the reign of Saul and the establishment of David on the throne that the Ark is moved from Kiriath-jearim. At least fifty years is more likely: Blenkinsopp, J. "Kiriath-Jearim and the Ark." *Journal of Biblical Literature* 88 (1969), 145.

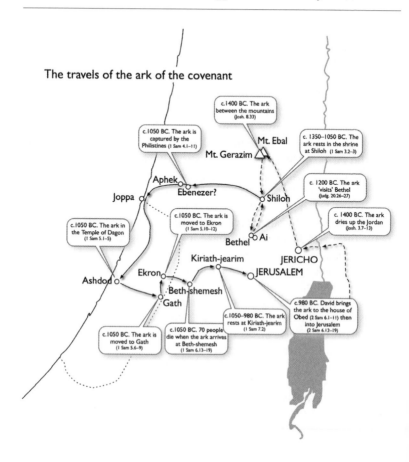

The travels of the ark of the covenant

c.1400 BC. The ark between the mountains (Josh. 8.33)

c.1050 BC. The ark is captured by the Philistines (1 Sam 4.1–11)

c. 1350–1050 BC. The ark rests in the shrine at Shiloh (1 Sam 3.2–3)

Mt. Ebal
Mt. Gerazim

c. 1200 BC. The ark 'visits' Bethel (Judg. 20.26–27)

Aphek
Joppa
Ebenezer?
Shiloh

c. 1400 BC. The ark dries up the Jordan (Josh. 3.7–13)

c.1050 BC. The ark is moved to Ekron (1 Sam 5.10–12)

c.1050 BC. The ark in the Temple of Dagon (1 Sam 5.1–5)

Bethel · Ai

Kiriath-jearim

JERICHO
JERUSALEM

Ekron
Ashdod

Beth-shemesh
Gath

c.1050–980 BC. The ark rests at Kiriath-jearim (1 Sam 7.2)

c.980 BC. David brings the ark to the house of Obed (2 Sam 6.1–11) then into Jerusalem (2 Sam 6.12–19)

c.1050 BC. The ark is moved to Gath (1 Sam 5.6–9)

c.1050 BC. 70 people die when the ark arrives at Beth-shemesh (1 Sam 6.13–19)

a neutral country.[11] This danger, this unpredictability, may explain why Saul did not use the Ark much (1 Chr. 13.3). Saul was pretty unstable himself; perhaps he knew when he was outclassed. David, however, decided that such a prized object should be in Jerusalem. But while moving it, a man called Uzzah put out a hand to steady it and was immediately killed. David was so shocked he postponed its transfer to Jerusalem, while he pondered the advisability of bringing such a dangerous object into the city (2 Sam. 6.6–11).

---

[11] Klein, *1 Samuel*, 60.

In the end, David overcame his fears and, after a three month stay at the house of Obed-edom the Gittite, the Ark was brought into Jerusalem, where it was placed in the Tabernacle. David planned to build a temple to house it, but that was left to his son, Solomon, who built a special chamber, a holy of holies, to house the Ark (1 Kgs. 6.19).

So, at the end of Solomon's reign, the Ark is in the Temple, in pride of place. After which it gets harder to track.

WE'D RATHER NOT TALK ABOUT IT

In *The Mystery of Silver Blaze*, Sherlock Holmes is, as usual, trying to give broad hints to a rather plodding detective.

> "Is there any other point to which you would wish to draw my attention?"
> "To the curious incident of the dog in the night-time."
> "The dog did nothing in the night-time."
> "That was the curious incident," remarked Sherlock Holmes.[12]

The Ark, as we've seen, was a hugely significant object during the time of the Exodus, the conquest of Canaan and into the reign of David – a period of about four hundred years. But after that it disappears. And the "curious incident" is not only its physical disappearance – its apparent removal from the Temple – but the fact that it disappears from the text itself. The silence is deafening. There is, to extend the Holmesian metaphor, scarcely a woof.

The chart on page 104 illustrates the point; there are more than two hundred separate references to the Ark of the Covenant up until the time of Solomon (c. 970–931 BC); but after his reign, it is almost never mentioned again.

---

[12] Conan Doyle, A., *Memoirs of Sherlock Holmes* (London: George Newnes, 1899), 16

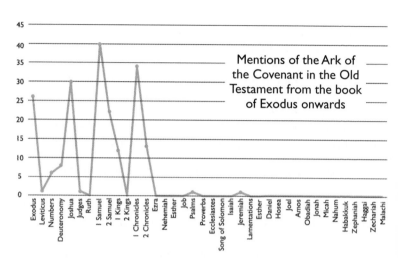

Mentions of the Ark of the Covenant in the Old Testament from the book of Exodus onwards

The only mention in any historical account, subsequent to Solomon's reign is in 2 Chronicles

> Josiah kept a passover to the LORD in Jerusalem; they slaughtered the passover lamb on the fourteenth day of the first month. He appointed the priests to their offices and encouraged them in the service of the house of the LORD. He said to the Levites who taught all Israel and who were holy to the LORD, "Put the holy Ark in the house that Solomon son of David, king of Israel, built; you need no longer carry it on your shoulders. Now serve the LORD your God and his people Israel" (2 Chr. 35.1–3).

Josiah was a reforming king, who came to power following two evil kings, Manasseh and Amon. Here, it appears that he is putting back the Ark into the Temple, but the text is difficult to interpret: had the Ark been brought out for a special occasion? Or had it been removed from the Temple and is it now being returned?

Either way, this is the only "physical" mention of the Ark in all the reigns of the kings after Solomon. It is mentioned twice more in the rest of the Old Testament: once in Psalms (Ps. 132.8, which is a poem recounting the recovery of the Ark by David) and once in Jeremiah (Jer 3.16).

It's almost as if they don't want to talk about it.

WHERE IS IT NOW?

Type in "Ark of the Covenant" into Google and you'll find well over 700,000 citations. And many of these will have their own theories about what happened to it. Here are some of the more popular claims, in order of plausibility.

1. It was lost during the reign of Manasseh

Let's look first at that final appearance in 2 Chronicles. As we've seen, Josiah is cleaning up the mess made by Manasseh and Amon. Manasseh was one of the worst kings of Judah.

Other kings had taken up the worship of foreign gods, but none of them had dared to change the Temple itself. Solomon built high places outside Jerusalem, and during the reign of kings like Jehoram, Athaliah and Ahaziah, a special "house" was built in Jerusalem for the worship of Baal. But no-one tampered with the Temple until Manasseh arrived. Manasseh changed the nature of the Temple itself; he built altars in the outer courts (2 Kgs. 21.4–5) and constructed houses for male temple prostitutes (2 Kgs. 23.7); and he made a carved image of Asherah, which he put in the Temple itself (2 Kgs. 21.7–9). Typically in near-eastern temples, the statue of the god(s) always stood in the last room, the equivalent of the Holy of Holies. The clear inference, therefore, is that Manasseh removed the Ark and the cherubim and placed Asherah's statue in there instead.[13]

Fifty years later, Josiah came to the throne, removed the Asherah and beat it to dust, and even desecrated the dust by throwing it on graves (2 Kgs. 23.6). Then, as we've seen in the passage above, he held the first Passover "since the days of the Judges" (2 Kgs. 23.21–23). Curiously, in the account of this event in Kings, there is

---

[13] Haran, M., "The Disappearance of the Ark." *Israel Exploration Journal* 13 (1963), 50–51.

no mention of the Ark of the Covenant, but the verse in Chronicles implies that the Levites had somehow been "carrying" it.

Some scholars would argue that the verse is an addition by the writer of Chronicles, who tends to emphasize the priestly side of things and who was a big fan of the Ark and the Temple. The absence of any reference to the Ark in 2 Kings is certainly suspicious. Yet we don't have to reject this verse completely to spot two possibly significant clues.

First, although the instruction is given, there is no indication that it actually happened. It's certainly implied, but it may be that the Levites didn't actually have the Ark to put back. Second, if they did have the Ark, they had to have kept it safe for at least fifty years. That implies some kind of sanctuary or hiding place in which it could be put.

The possibility exists, though, that it wasn't found. Jeremiah says: "And when you have multiplied and increased in the land, in those days, says the LORD, they shall no longer say, "The Ark of the Covenant of the LORD." It shall not come to mind, or be remembered, or missed; nor shall another one be made' (Jer. 3.16).

And this prophecy is attributed to "the time of Josiah" (Jer. 3.6). Josiah reigned from 640–609BC. The statement is part of a general call to repentance, beginning in 3.1. Obviously it refers to a future age when people no longer worry about the Ark; but he does seem to be referring to a question that the Israelites are asking in the present, a question that "they will no longer say." One has to ask, if the Ark has been returned to the Temple, why is he lamenting its loss? If Josiah has overseen the return of the Ark, why is Jeremiah telling people to forget about it?

2. It was taken by Egyptians

The Egyptian Pharaoh Shishak[14] invaded Israel and Judah around 918BC. 1 Kings records the story: "In the fifth year of King Rehoboam, King Shishak of Egypt came up against Jerusalem; he took away the treasures of the house of the LORD and the treasures

---

[14] The Hebrew rendering of the Egyptian name Shoshenq. He was actually Libyan, not Egyptian. Bright, *A History of Israel*, 213.

A stone relief carving from Capernaum, dating from the 1st century AD. It shows the Ark of the Covenant. The sculptor has depicted it as a kind of miniature temple on wheels.

of the king's house; he took everything. He also took away all the shields of gold that Solomon had made..." (1 Kgs. 14.25–26).

Although an inscription in the Amon temple in Karnak lists more than one hundred and fifty cities in Judah and Israel that this pharaoh claims to have captured, he didn't actually conquer and enter Jerusalem, but laid siege to it. Rehoboam paid him off by giving him the contents of the treasuries.[15] So, despite Indiana Jones's statement, it's by no means certain that the Ark was part of this payment.

3. It was taken by the Babylonians
Just over three hundred years later, the Babylonian army certainly did invade Jerusalem. Nebuchadnezzar's forces sacked the city; the Temple was burnt, the pillars, basin and other bronze furniture were broken up and taken to Babylon (2 Kgs. 25.9–17). Some scholars believe that the Ark was among the treasures, but it is not listed, nor is it listed among the treasures that were later brought back from Babylon. However it is possible that Jeremiah's statement refers to the loss of the Ark at this time.[16] There is also a reference in the *Tosefta* (a secondary compilation of the Jewish oral

---

[15] De Vries, S.J., (1985), *1 Kings*, (Waco: Word Books), 185. Bright, *A History of Israel*, 214.

[16] Ackroyd, P.R., *Exile and Restoration: A Study of Hebrew Thought of the Sixth Century B.C*, (London: SCM, 1968), 24–25.

law from a similar period to the *Mishnah* (around 70–200AD) that says it was taken to Babylon.[17]

4. It's hidden on Temple Mount

Others claim that it remains hidden on Temple Mount in Jerusalem. The Temple platform stands atop of a warren of cisterns, caves and tunnels, all guarded by its Moslem authorities. One tradition in the *Mishnah* records that the Ark was buried under the "Wood Chamber of the Second Temple" which was on the northeastern side of the Court of Women.[18] In the *Tosefta*, it is claimed that the Ark was "concealed in its place" (i.e. below the Holy of Holies).[19] If this is the case, however, one would expect it to have been recovered after the exile, or discovered during the building works of Herod the Great, when he created the great mount on which the Temple stood. But nothing was ever found.[20]

5. It's on Mount Nebo

This theory comes from 2 Maccabees, a book written in what's called the intertestamental period (i.e. the period between the end of the Old Testament and the beginning of the New). There it's recorded that Jeremiah took the Ark (and the Tabernacle) and hid them in a cave on Mount Nebo

> ...the prophet, having received an oracle, ordered that the tent and the Ark should follow with him, and that he went out to the mountain where Moses had gone up and had seen the inheritance of God. Jeremiah came and found a cave-dwelling, and he brought there the tent and the Ark and the altar of incense; then he sealed up the entrance. Some of those who followed him came up intending to mark the way, but could not find it. When Jeremiah learned of it, he rebuked them and

[17] *Tosefta*, Sotah 13, 1; Grierson, R., and Munro-Hay, S.C., *The Ark of the Covenant*, (London: Phoenix, 2000), 109–112.

[18] *Mishnah*, Sheqalim 6, 1, in Danby, *The Mishnah, Translated From the Hebrew*, 158.

[19] *Tosefta*, Sotah 13, 1

[20] See Grierson, and Munro-Hay, *The Ark of the Covenant*, 114–115.

declared: "The place shall remain unknown until God gathers his people together again and shows his mercy (2 Mac. 2.4–7).

You'd expect such an important event to be recorded in Jeremiah or even in one of the post-exilic works such as Chronicles or Ezra. The book dates from the first or second century BC, at least four hundred years after the events it describes, and the passage reads more like wish fulfilment than anything else.[21]

6. It's in Ethiopia

The belief that the Ark is in Ethiopia, taken there by the son of Solomon and the Queen of Sheba, comes from the claims of the Ethiopian church and the legends in a book called the *Kebra Negast* or *The Glory of the Kings*. According to this legend, Solomon and the Queen of Sheba had a son, Menelik, born after the Queen returned home. He later went to see his father in Jerusalem and then left, taking the Ark with him. The one tiny problem with this claim is that there's not a shred of evidence that Solomon and the Queen of Sheba had a son. Or even tried for one. Admittedly, Solomon did have a tendency to marry anything that was (a) female and (b) breathing, but the Bible doesn't record such a union. Nor is it likely that the most powerful king in Israel's history would let a ten-year old escape with a large, gold-covered box. The earliest linking of the Ark with Ethiopia seems to date from around 1200, at least 1700 years after the Ark's disappearance; *The Glory of the Kings* was written later.[22]

7. It's in the "Cave of Two Columns"

There have been claims that a scroll discovered in one of the Qumran caves contains a reference to the Ark of the Covenant. The

---

[21] Grierson, and Munro-Hay, *The Ark of the Covenant*, 115–116.

[22] Grierson, and Munro-Hay, *The Ark of the Covenant*, 247. Some scholars argue that it was a replica of the Ark which Menelik took home with him. Grierson and Munro-Hay argue that there was not one Ark, but many, each containing copies of the stone tablets. It is some of these which, according to the authors, have made their way to Ethiopia. Graham Hancock argues that the Ark arrived in Ethiopia via Egypt. During Manasseh's reign it was taken to Elephantine in Egypt where it was housed in a Jewish temple. See Porten, B., "Did the Ark Stop at Elephantine?" *Biblical Archaeology Review* 21 (May/June 1995).

Copper Scroll (known as 3Q15 or 3QTreasure) is unique among the Dead Sea Scrolls, not only because it is made of copper (the clue was in the name) but because it is a list of hidden treasure. The scroll lists some sixty-four hiding places, which, in total, contain between 58 and 174 tons of precious metal – although where all this stuff came from is not clear. Some scholars think it was from the Temple, others that the scroll lists treasure hidden during the second Jewish revolt.[23] Sadly for this theory, the fact is that the scroll doesn't mention the Ark at all. Various expeditions have set out to find the treasure, so far with no result.[24]

8. An angel put it in the earth

All right, I accept we're getting silly now. But in a work known as the Second Apocalypse of Baruch, the writer records that just before the destruction of Jerusalem by the Babylonians, an angel came down and took the contents of the Holy of Holies, and "the earth opened up its mouth and swallowed them up" (2 Bar. 6.7–10).[25] Since this text was written after the destruction of the Temple in 70AD, (i.e. over six hundred years after the events it purports to describe) it's probably not that reliable.

9. It's been found by various Americans

Various people have published books/videos/promotional T-shirts claiming to have found the Ark. Perhaps the best known of these was the late Ron Wyatt, an ex-dental nurse. In 1989, he claimed to have broken into a chamber beneath "Golgotha", the site of Jesus' crucifixion. This was not the traditional site, but the so-called place of the skull in Jerusalem, identified by General Gordon. There, Wyatt claimed to have seen the Ark and taken photographs. Strangely, only Ron was present at the time and all

[23] For a good overview see Shanks, H., *Understanding the Dead Sea Scrolls: A Reader From the Biblical Archaeology Review*, (London: SPCK, 1993), 228–241. Wolters, A.M., *The Copper Scroll: Overview, Text and Translation*, (Sheffield: Sheffield Academic Press, 1996). Vanderkam, J. C., *The Dead Sea Scrolls Today*, (Grand Rapids: Eerdmans SPCK, 1994), 68–69.

[24] García, M., Florentino, T., and Eibert J.C., *The Dead Sea Scrolls Study Edition*, (Leiden: Brill, 1997). Campbell, J.G., *Deciphering the Dead Sea Scrolls*, (London: Fontana Press, 1996), 87.

[25] Charlesworth, J.H., *The Old Testament Pseudepigrapha*, (London: Darton, Longman & Todd, 1983), 623.

the photos came out blurry. He also claimed that his excavations revealed that the blood of Jesus had dropped down from the cross, through a crack in the ground and onto the Ark of the Covenant itself.[26] He also claims to have found, in the same cave, "the seven branch candlestick, a giant sword (with no inscriptions, but possibly Goliath's), an ephod, the wilderness Tabernacle, the altar of incense among other things."[27]

ALL RIGHT THEN, WHERE IS IT?

No-one knows. If I had to hazard a guess, I'd guess that it was hidden and lost about the time of Manasseh. The absence of references to it in the Babylon ransacking of Jerusalem indicates to me that it was long gone.

The really noticeable thing is that, apart from that brief reference in Jeremiah, no-one really missed it. You'd have thought, given its power and its significance, that the Bible would be stuffed with laments about its loss; that there would be wailing and gnashing of teeth; that it would be a loss comparable to the destruction of Jerusalem.

But there is nothing. Nada. Zilch. As the graph shows, in the latter books of the Bible it's not even mentioned. And this, surely, is the real historical enigma: not that an immensely valuable golden chest should go missing, but that its loss should be followed by such a deafening, improbable silence.

Perhaps the reasons we hear no more about it is that people realized that it was no longer necessary. The prophets came along calling for personal commitment; Jeremiah's verse about not missing the Ark has also to be seen in the context of a new

---

[26] Since it is now almost universally agreed that Gordon's Golgotha was not the site of Jesus' crucifixion, whatever traces of blood Wyatt found could not have belonged to Jesus.

[27] Taken from http://www.wyattarchaeology.com/ark.htm. On other trips, Wyatt claims to have discovered remnants of Noah's ark, Sodom and Gomorrah and a golden chariot wheel from the Egyptian army drowned in the Red Sea. Another American, Tom Crotser, also claims to have found the Ark. Not to mention "the Tower of Babel, Noah's ark, the City of Adam, and the great stone of Abel, where the son of Adam was killed." Some guys have all the luck. Shanks, H. "Tom Crotser Has Found the Ark of the Covenant—Or Has He?" *Biblical Archaeology Review* 9 (May/June 1983).

understanding about the nature of the covenant between God and his people, an agreement not written on stones kept in a box, but engraved on the human heart.

> The days are surely coming, says the LORD, when I will make a new covenant with the house of Israel and the house of Judah... I will put my law within them, and I will write it on their hearts; and I will be their God, and they shall be my people. No longer shall they teach one another, or say to each other, "Know the LORD," for they shall all know me, from the least of them to the greatest, says the LORD; for I will forgive their iniquity, and remember their sin no more (Jer. 31.31–34).

It's perfectly possible that the Ark was hidden in a cave to avoid the attentions of an idol-worshipping king or a marauding, invading army. It's equally possible that it was taken, among other booty, by invaders such as the Egyptians or the Babylonians.

But that's not the point. The point is that, for some of them at least, the disasters that befell the Israelites taught them something new about God. It taught them that God could be with them wherever they were. It taught them that he was not confined to temples or tents. They stopped talking about it because, for all its power and mystery, they realized that God could not be – and had never been – contained in a box.

Were the Ark to be found it would, undoubtedly, be the greatest archeological find ever. But maybe there's a warning there: for in the Bible, whenever anyone tries to use the Ark for their own ends, things turn out badly.

Perhaps we should listen to the silence of the later generations and just let it go.

WHY DID JUDAS KISS JESUS?

In one of my favorite films, *The Princess Bride*, the little boy is being told a story by his grandfather. He stops the grandfather just before a climactic romantic moment. "Stop!" he says. "This is not going to be a *kissing* story, is it?"

The fact that Judas kisses Jesus is one of the most shocking moments of that shocking night. Suddenly, a story of deceit and betrayal becomes a bizarre, dark, baffling "kissing" story.

But why did Judas do it? Even Jesus seems baffled by it. "While he was still speaking, suddenly a crowd came, and the one called Judas, one of the twelve, was leading them. He approached Jesus to kiss him; but Jesus said to him, 'Judas, is it with a kiss that you are betraying the Son of Man?'" (Luke 22.47–48).

"Are you going to betray me like that?" Why, when Judas could easily have pointed Jesus out, did he need to resort to this subterfuge?

IT'S IN HIS KISS

The New Testament contains a fair bit of kissing. Jesus rebukes Simon the Pharisee for not welcoming him with a kiss, comparing him unfavorably with the woman who kisses his feet (Luke 7.45). Paul and Peter urge other believers to greet each other with a "holy kiss." When Paul parts from the elders at Ephesus, they have to be beaten off with a stick, such is the display of emotion (Acts 20.37).

Which is odd, because the culture of the time rather frowned on such displays of public affection. By Jesus' time, the public kiss was probably not practised among Jews. One ancient commentary on Genesis says that "In general kissing leads to immorality: there are however three exceptions, namely kissing someone to honor that person, or kissing upon seeing someone after a long absence, and the farewell kiss."[1]

Other writers also allow the kissing of relatives, but apart from these instances, mostly Jews were not eager to pucker up in public. The same was true of the wider Græco-Roman world. We are used,

---

[1] Gen. Rab. 70 [45b] quoted in *The Anchor Bible Dictionary*, IV, 90–91. Examples of these three types of kisses are given as Samuel kissing Saul (1 Sam. 10.1) Aaron kissing Moses (Exod. 4.27) and Orpah kissing Naomi (Ruth 1.14).

due to numerous Hollywood excesses, to think of the Romans as engaging in one long mass orgy, but actually public displays of affection were frowned upon. Cato the Elder threw a man called Manilus out of the Senate because he kissed his wife while his daughters were present: the Romans did not use what we would call the "social" kiss – at least, only among the aristocracy.[2]

Today, many cultures feel the same. In much of Western society kissing is a feminine activity; so it's OK for women to kiss each other, and it's OK for men to kiss their women friends. But man to man? Well, we shake hands or occasionally hug, in a manly back-slapping kind of way. I have never kissed any of my close male friends.[3]

Yet, despite all this, kissing was big in the Early Church. So much so that Paul has to lay down the rules of the holy kiss. Paul talks about kissing in several places, most notably in the closing to his letters, where he usually uses the formula "Greet one another with a holy kiss."[4] Although the holy kiss became a part of the liturgy of the Early Church, Paul is writing before a time of formal liturgy. So the likelihood is that kissing was already a distinctive of the Early Church and that it was *because* the first Christians were so accustomed to kissing one another, that it was later formalized into part of the service. What we have is a "distinctively Christian act" which would be shared between Christians, not just in their meetings but at other times as well.[5] The fact that this injunction occurs in 1 Thessalonians – one of the earliest Christian writings – shows that the practice was established early on (1 Thess. 5.26).[6]

For the first Christians, therefore, the kiss was an identifier, a distinctive practice which showed that they were a family. It showed

---

[2]   Harvey, K., *The Kiss in History*, (Manchester: Manchester University Press, 2005), 197. Brown, R.E., *The Death of the Messiah: From Gethsemane to the Grave: A Commentary on the Passion Narratives in the Four Gospels*, (London: Geoffrey Chapman, 1994), 255.

[3]   Well only occasionally. And only after several large glasses of wine.

[4]   See Romans 16.16; 1 Corinthians 16.20; 2 Corinthians 13.12; 1 Thessalonians 5.26. It's also mentioned by Peter in 1 Peter 5.14

[5]   Phillips, L.E., *The Ritual Kiss in Early Christian Worship*, (Cambridge: Grove Books, 1996), 7–8.

[6]   Later it had to be controlled. In 176AD Athenagoras instructed people not to kiss a second time just because it was enjoyable! While Clement of Alexandria complained that there were those who "do nothing but make the churches resound with a kiss." Klassen, W. "The Sacred Kiss in the New Testament: An Example of Social Boundary Lines" *New Testament Studies* 39. 1993, 134.

that there were deep relationships there. It was a true expression of the fact that "In Christ there is neither male nor female, Jew nor Greek, slave nor free" (Gal. 3:28). This is an astonishingly radical proposition from Paul, for it allows a woman to kiss a man in public – a man, moreover, who is not related to her. The kiss broke boundaries and blended people together. It mixed people of different social and ethnic backgrounds into one family. As one writer has put it, it was more than a liturgical gesture, it was "an expression of revolutionary social bonding and of radical equality."[7] The holy kiss, therefore, was a sign of acceptance, a sign that you were part of the family.

But where did this come from? It could not have originated in the Gentile church, because, as we've seen, the Græco-Roman world frowned on public displays of affection. Nor could it have originated in the practices of Judaism. Perhaps they did it because that was what Jesus did. We have seen that Jesus rebuked Simon the Pharisee for not kissing him, unlike the woman who "was a sinner." Why would he say that, given that kissing was not the norm in Judaism? Perhaps it's because kissing *was* the norm among Jesus' followers. Jesus, unlike other Jewish leaders, was accustomed to kissing his disciples, and the Early Church followed his example. The Early Church, therefore, adopted the kiss because they associated it with Jesus, because it was encouraged or even initiated by their founder. It was a sign of discipleship. It was one of the things that the followers of Jesus did. [8]

BACK TO THE GARDEN

Back to Judas, then. Why the kiss?

It is usually argued that it was an identifier, a signal to the outsiders which would arouse no suspicion to those inside the group. Which would be OK if the arrest were a covert act. But

---

[7] Kreider, A., *Worship and Evangelism in Pre-Christendom*, (Cambridge: Grove Books, 1995), 28. Some suggest that Paul sees it as a sign of sharing the Holy Spirit among each other. Hence the fact that it is a holy kiss. See Klassen, "The Sacred Kiss in the New Testament: An Example of Social Boundary Lines", 10–13.

[8] Brown, *The Death of the Messiah*, 255.

what happens is that Judas marches up, accompanied by soldiers, kisses Jesus and then the soldiers arrest him. This is not a covert operation; he's not lulling anyone into a false sense of security. So there would be no need to keep the others in the dark or to reassure them by faking intimacy. They can't help but know that the game is up, the moment the soldiers enter the garden. The disciples' suspicions have not so much been "aroused", as got up, had a shower, dressed and gone to work.

But what if kissing was the normal sign of greeting among Jesus' followers? What if the adoption of the practice by the Early Church really did reflect Jesus' practice? Maybe, if that's the case, Judas kissed Jesus because that was the normal sign of greeting: that was the special thing that Jesus' disciples did.

That's one of the reasons why this kiss stings so badly, why this act of betrayal cuts so hard and deep. It's not just that Judas is identifying Jesus, he's identifying him using a kiss; their own greeting. He's not just betraying Jesus, he's betraying their rituals, their unique behaviors. He's taking something they consider special and using it as a weapon. He's breaking the fellowship apart, using the one act which was supposed to bind them together.

It seems such a callous act, looked at like that. It seems so wantonly cruel. But perhaps it was more instinctive. The practices of three years spent following this man had left their mark, woven themselves into the fabric of his being. Maybe it was so ingrained, such a habit, that when the moment came to greet Jesus, that was what Judas did. He didn't think about it, he just did it.

Maybe he just could not help himself. He'd spent three years greeting this man with a kiss. Now, whatever else he was betraying, the one thing he could not betray was the force of habit.

WHO KILLED GOLIATH?

There are two major theories of history: the conspiracy theory and the cock-up theory. Personally, I believe which theory you subscribe to depends on whether you get out much. If you have no real social life and spend most of your time surfing the Internet, you will naturally gravitate to the belief that everything in life is a huge conspiracy. As soon as you step outside, though, you realize that most of life is governed by the mistakes, blunders and general idiocies that fill our lives. Human beings just get things wrong. It looks like a conspiracy, but it's a cock-up.

Example? Ladies and gentlemen, I give you 2 Samuel 21.19.

The death of Goliath is one of the most famous stories in the world. The courage of the young David; the cowardice of the older king and his troops; the satisfyingly romantic triumph of the small boy against the hairy giant; the delicious irony of a giant being felled with a tiny pebble[1] – it's become part of the world culture, so that, even in today's non-biblical culture, people still talk of a "David and Goliath" story, even though many of the details about the story are slightly hazy.[2] Here are the concluding verses

> When the Philistine drew nearer to meet David, David ran quickly toward the battle line to meet the Philistine. David put his hand in his bag, took out a stone, slung it, and struck the Philistine on his forehead; the stone sank into his forehead, and he fell face down on the ground. So David prevailed over the Philistine with a sling and a stone, striking down the Philistine and killing him; there was no sword in David's hand. Then David ran and stood over the Philistine; he grasped his sword, drew it out of its sheath, and killed him; then he cut off his head with it. When the Philistines saw that their champion was dead, they fled (1 Sam. 17.48–51).

---

[1] Actually it wasn't a tiny stone, ancient slings would chuck quite big rocks, about the size of a cricket or baseball. See Yadin, Y., *The Art of Warfare in Biblical Lands in the Light of Archaeological Discovery*, (London: Weidenfeld and Nicolson, 1963), 10, 364. The idea that a nine foot man can be killed by a small pebble is ridiculous. It was a large rock that hit him in the forehead.

[2] The reason I think children like the story so much is that it taps into two fundamental truths about children: (a) they are all smaller than everyone else and (b) they all love throwing stones.

All very clear, then. David has killed Goliath the Philistine and there's his head to prove it. So it's a bit of a shock to come across a verse, at the other end of the book of Samuel, that seems to cast doubt on this theory: "Then there was another battle with the Philistines at Gob; and Elhanan son of Jaare-oregim, the Bethlehemite, killed Goliath the Gittite, the shaft of whose spear was like a weaver's beam" (2 Sam. 21.19).

Hold on! How can two warriors kill one man? Has there been some massive conspiracy to credit David with the victory?

For many scholars, that's exactly what has happened. This little verse in 2 Samuel is proof of a gigantic conspiracy theory. It's the verse on the grassy knoll. It's the smoking gun (or sling). It's proof that David did nothing at all.

HOW DO YOU READ IT?

There are, as you might expect, a number of theories to explain this, and which theory you believe will depend on your view of the Bible.

Those who believe that the Bible is inerrant, infallible and that every word is exactly what was intended are faced with a problem. The usual explanation here is that this was a different Goliath, who just happened to be a giant with the same weapon as the other one. This explanation scores high on convenience, but low on probability. We know that there were quite a few very large Philistines around; indeed there seems to have been a veritable rash of over sized warriors. 2 Samuel 21 describes four of the "descendants of the giants": Ishbi-benob, Saph, Goliath the Gittite, and an unnamed giant who had "six fingers on each hand, and six toes on each foot, twenty-four in number."[3] But it's not likely that there would have been two giants called Goliath.

Another theory is that Elhanan, son of Jaare-oregim, and David, son of Jesse are one and the same. This theory is based on the idea that David had a family name and a throne name. "Elhanan" was

---

[3] 2 Samuel 21. 16–22. I'm betting his parents were cousins.

David's real name, while "David" was his official, King's name.[4] This theory rather struggles against the relative absence of throne-names elsewhere and the problem of why David's father should require an alternative throne-name when he wasn't a king.

The other extreme of biblical views embraces the conspiracy theory. This proves, according to them, that David never slew Goliath, and that a later propagandist took over the feat and ascribed it to David. Here's a typical passage: "It is certain that this account [David's defeat of Goliath] is a fabrication. Elhanan son of Dodo is credited with killing Goliath (2 Sam. 21.19)... the Goliath story displaces to David... the accomplishments of his warriors in other contexts."[5]

It's all a conspiracy, you see. David never killed any big blokes; it was all the work of other people. Now, there are some interesting things about this view. The first is, like all conspiracies, it only works one way – in the direction of the powerful, the winners. Why has it got to be that way? Surely it's just as logical to argue that Elhanan is trying to claim credit for David's victory. But that wouldn't be much of a conspiracy, would it? Nothing very newsworthy there. No, better to go in the other direction. Discrediting King David is much more fun than discrediting Elhanan; and more likely to get your book published as well.[6]

And you've got to admire the writer's confidence. It's "certain" that David didn't kill Goliath. So there you have it. Case solved. The whole thing is a giant conspiracy designed to make David look good.

There's a serious flaw in the argument, though.

Apparently we're supposed to believe that the creator of the book of Samuel is sophisticated enough to spin the story of King David, but stupid enough to leave the incriminating verses in.

---

[4] Honeyman, A.M. "The Evidence for Regnal Names among the Hebrews." *Journal of Biblical Literature* 67 (1948), 23–25.

[5] Halpern, B., *David's Secret Demons: Messiah, Murderer, Traitor, King*, (Grand Rapids: Eerdmans, 2001), 276–276. He equates this Elhanan with the one in 2 Samuel 23.24.

[6] It's a strange occasion where both the liberals and the ultra-conservatives are in agreement. Both would argue that the text is accurate, the liberals because they believe it shows the real giant-killer and discredits the David myth, the ultra-conservatives because you can't have any errors in the text of the Bible.

He's clever enough to create a detailed, false account of the battle, but too stupid to leave the real account out. He's shrewd enough to conspire against David, but not clever enough to remove the incriminating evidence.

It's not how writers write. If I was creating propaganda, I'd make sure that the opposing view didn't get a toe-hold. If I was crediting David with greatness, I'd take great pains to make sure that there were no cracks in the facade. I'd make certain that the enemies were at the very least discredited, and at best wiped out of the picture altogether. In other words, you've got to answer the serious question of why this verse got left in. Why wasn't the giant's name changed, at least?

I don't think what we have on our hands is a conspiracy. I believe what we have is a cock-up.

THE SAME, ONLY DIFFERENT

There's another version of 2 Samuel 21.19. In Chronicles we read: "Again there was war with the Philistines; and Elhanan son of Jair killed Lahmi the brother of Goliath the Gittite, the shaft of whose spear was like a weaver's beam" (1 Chr. 20.5).

At first glance it looks as though the writer of Chronicles has simply tidied up the account. He's clever enough to realize that you can't have two Goliath slayers, so he adds in a brother. A closer look, though reveals that maybe he was working off the same source as the writer of 2 Samuel. And you'll notice that he hasn't got "Jair-oregim", but just "Jair."

Oregim means "beam" or "shuttle" so its appearance in a proper name is a bit suspect. What appears to have happened is that the copyist of 1 Samuel has got confused. He's missed a line, so that the term "-oregim" gets inserted twice. R.K. Harrison suggests the verse should read "And Elhanan, the son of Jairi the Bethlehemite, slew the brother of Goliath."[7]

One final point about this passage: it may be that the phrase "the descendants of the giants" (2 Sam. 21.16,18, 20, 22) doesn't

---

[7]   For the full argument (including all the Hebrew!) see Harrison, R.K., *Introduction to the Old Testament*, (London: Tyndale Press, 1970), 704.

mean the "children" of the giants, but refers to a group of fighting men, a warrior-association. These may be big men (as in Goliath's case); they are described as "one of the descendants of Haraphah or Raphah" which may be an allusion to the Rephaim, the mysterious giants who lived in Canaan before the Israelites (Gen. 15.20; Deut 2.10–11; Num. 13.33; 3.11). Or they may be members of an elite force of warriors, based in Gath and devoted to a god named Rapha.[8]

One thing that might back this up is the repetition of the weaver's beam; both Goliath and his brother have spears "like weaver's beams." This might not be anything to do with the size; rather the spears had a loop in the middle, at the balance point, so that the warriors could put their fingers through. This was common in Greek javelins; it allowed the thrower to put a spin on the javelin, which would keep it going in straight, like the rifling of a gun on a bullet.[9] Not only were these crack warriors, they had some unique weaponry as well. When the Israelites saw them, the only thing they could liken it to was the weaver's beam with its loops of thread attached.

COPYIST'S ERROR

There you have it. Elhanan, son of Jair, killed Goliath's brother Lahmi, who was a member of the Philistine version of the SAS.

There is no conspiracy; there is just a copyist's mistake. Of course, for many people that doesn't solve things very much. A mistake in the Bible? How could that be? While I was researching this I came across a discussion of this verse on an Internet site. It's a verse which pops up fairly frequently. Amidst the explanations, there came this plaintive voice: "I wish there weren't all these copiest [sic] 'problems' in the Bible."

That would be nice, I guess. But the fact is that there *are* difficulties in the Bible. There are different accounts edited together, collections of stories, misquoted verses, small scribal errors. We're

---

[8]   See Anderson, *2 Samuel*, 244–45.

[9]   Yadin, Y. "Goliath's Javelin and the ארגים מנור." *Palestine Exploration Quarterly* 86 (1955), 58–69.

dealing with material collected over thousands of years by many, many people. There are bound to be some contradictions in that, even if, as here, they're only apparent contradictions.

The important thing is to remember that the Bible is not God; it points us to God. Sometimes I get the feeling that people worship the Bible as much (or maybe more) than they worship God. It becomes unquestionable, inviolable. What this little incident shows us is that the Bible has its fissures and its flaws; it has phrases we don't understand, language so ancient that people don't really know what it means; and it reflects a culture about which, for all our research, we don't know much.

But behind it, beyond it, surrounding it and flowing through it, is a God who longs to know us; who longs to resource us, and who is thrilled when we defeat the descendants of giants.

WHERE DID JESUS LIVE?

"Foxes have holes, and birds of the air have nests, but the Son of Man has nowhere to lay his head." said Jesus (Luke 9.58). And from that, we conjure up an image of Jesus as permanent traveler, always on the move, always sleeping rough. Except that he *wasn't* always on the move. For a substantial time of his ministry, he was based in once place. So where did he live?

We know he was born and brought up in Nazareth. But after his baptism by John and his encounter in the wilderness he relocated, according to the gospels. He moved about twenty miles north-east, to Capernaum, on the north shore of Lake Galilee.

> He left Nazareth and made his home in Capernaum by the sea, in the territory of Zebulun and Naphtali, so that what had been spoken through the prophet Isaiah might be fulfilled: "Land of Zebulun, land of Naphtali, on the road by the sea, across the Jordan, Galilee of the Gentiles – the people who sat in darkness have seen a great light, and for those who sat in the region and shadow of death light has dawned." From that time Jesus began to proclaim, "Repent, for the kingdom of heaven has come near" (Matt. 4.13–17).

A village of around a thousand people in New Testament times, Capernaum lay on a frontier between the territory of Herod Antipas and Philip.[1] Which is why there were tax-collectors there, who collected the customs duties as goods crossed the border, and also why there was a detachment of soldiers led by a centurion (Luke 7.1–2). Indeed, archeologists have discovered and restored the synagogue in Capernaum and although the remains we can see today are of the fourth-century synagogue, it probably stands on the site of the original, first-century one, which was funded by the Roman centurion (Luke 7.5). In other ways, Capernaum was an insignificant place. The Jewish historian, Josephus, only mentions it twice; and one of those is just because he fell off his horse and broke some bones.[2]

---

[1] Horsley, R.A., *Galilee: History, Politics, People*, (Pennsylvania: Trinity Press, 1995), 194–95.

[2] Theissen, G., and Merz, A., *The Historical Jesus: A Comprehensive Guide*, (London: SCM Press, 1998), 166–167.

So, we know Jesus lived in Capernaum. But where? Sleeping rough on the ground? In the first-century equivalent of the YMCA? The obvious answer is that he stayed with friends.

AT HOME WITH THE MESSIAH

Jesus relied on supporters to fund his work, by which I don't mean that he had a large number of staff, a communications department and Matthew the Tax-collector asking people to gift aid. He needed food, clothing and housing, and those were provided by supporters. Luke tells us that many women were involved in providing food for him (Luke 8.1–3). There would also, presumably, have been a number of men and women who could offer him somewhere to stay.

So one answer to this question is simply that he stayed in the house of disciples and friends; and since he traveled around a fair bit that was usually the case. In Capernaum, however, we know of four disciples who had houses there: Simon and Andrew (Mark 1.29); and also James and John, the sons of Zebedee. Zebedee was a fisherman, wealthy enough to have hired men, so James and John probably had a house nearby (Mark 1.20). There is a hint elsewhere in the gospels that John and James were cousins of Jesus (see p.95); this would explain where Jesus might have stayed.

However, Mark implies that he seems to stay with Peter. Following the calling of the four men, Jesus goes to the synagogue, where he teaches and heals a possessed man. Mark then says: "As soon as they left the synagogue, they entered the house of Simon and Andrew, with James and John. Now Simon's mother-in-law was in bed with a fever, and they told him about her at once. He came and took her by the hand and lifted her up. Then the fever left her, and she began to serve them" (Mark 1.29–31).

That evening many people come for healing (Mark 1.32). The next morning Simon and Andrew find Jesus is missing (Mark 1.35–36). So the implication, at the beginning at least, is that Jesus stayed at the house of Simon and Andrew. Following this initial stay, Jesus goes out into the towns around, then stays in the countryside (Mark 1.38–39,45).

After a little while he returns to Capernaum, and here we have some evidence that he has a place of his own, or at least a space that he could call home. Mark says: "When he returned to Capernaum after some days, it was reported that he was at home" (Mark 2.1).

At whose home? It doesn't say, but we know what it looked like, or at least that it had a flat roof, because as soon as the crowd find out he's back, they gather round and start ripping open the roof to let someone down (Mark 2.1–4). After this, he goes out by the lake and teaches the crowd. Then he meets Levi son of Alphaeus at a toll-collecting booth and calls Levi to "Follow me." Then the verse tells us that "Levi got up and followed him." Now, here's the thing; the next verse (Mark 2.15) is usually translated like this: "And as he sat at dinner in Levi's house…" (Mark 2.15).

Except that the text doesn't mention Levi. The Greek just says "his" house, which translators usually take to mean Levi's. The ESV, however, follows the actual text: "And as he reclined at table in his house, many tax collectors and sinners were reclining with Jesus and his disciples, for there were many who followed him" (Mark 2.15 ESV).

So the house could just as easily be Jesus' place. In fact, given the context – the fact that the section begins with Jesus being "at home", then Levi getting up and following Jesus, it's quite reasonable to envisage a scenario where instead of eating at Levi's house, Jesus invites Levi back to his place.

Was he still at Simon's? Or had his friends arranged a place in Capernaum for him to live? It's not an earth-shattering point, I know. It's not going to shake the foundations of Christian doctrine. All it shows is that Jesus could have had a house in Capernaum – a house that was his home. And which, apparently, needed roof repairs.

In fact, it doesn't have to have been a case of either/or. He could have had a place of his own, and still been living with Simon and Andrew and their family.

The reason is that archeologists have identified, within ancient Capernaum, what they call "clan-dwellings."[3] These consist of a

---

[3] *The Anchor Bible Dictionary*, I, 866–69.

central courtyard, around which are lots of small rooms or houses with doors facing inward. The houses were made of blocks of dark basalt stone. Inside, they would have been decorated with pebbles. The floors would have been of blocks of stone, with pebbles packed in between, sometimes covered with a layer of yellow-colored earth. A gate from the street led into the first of the courtyards and from there one could gain access into the other rooms or houses. Windows from these rooms opened onto the courtyard, not onto the street, and the main family life would have taken place in the courtyards, where there would have been fires for cooking, millstones for grinding corn and hand presses for olives. Stairs within the courtyards allowed access to the roofs of the houses. The roofs were made of beams, covered with layers of packed mud – ideal for dropping paralysed people through.

PETER'S PLACE

In 1968, archeologists in Capernaum were working in the remains of a splendid, octagonal church dating from Byzantine times (c. 5th century AD). Octagonal churches were generally built to commemorate significant events in Christian history, linked with the site. The Church of the Nativity in Bethlehem was originally octagonal, as is the Church of the Ascension on the top of the Mount of Olives. So this was a significant church, but what did it commemorate?

Further excavations showed that the octagonal church was built over an earlier church with Christian symbols and graffiti, inscriptions to Jesus and Peter; and beneath *that* there lay the remains of an ordinary house. The house dated back to the first century AD (and possibly before that). Originally built of large blocks of the dense black basalt rock of the area, at some time this house had been converted into a church: the largest room in the house had been strengthened with an arch, so that its roof could be raised to form a kind of central hall.

The house was part of a clan-dwelling, with two courtyards. In the first courtyard the cooking would have been done and the food prepared. This courtyard was surrounded by rooms on the

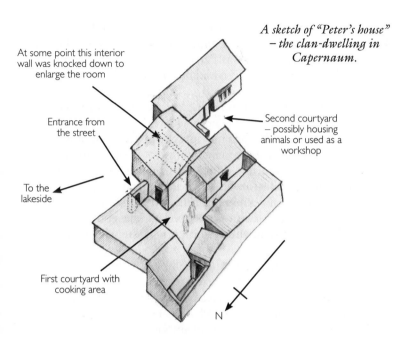

A sketch of "Peter's house" – the clan-dwelling in Capernaum.

At some point this interior wall was knocked down to enlarge the room

Entrance from the street

Second courtyard – possibly housing animals or used as a workshop

To the lakeside

First courtyard with cooking area

N

north and west. The second courtyard might have housed animals or been used as a workshop area. Also, at some time in the first century AD, the floor, walls and ceiling of the main room were plastered. It's the only house in Capernaum with plastered walls; in Roman times the only rooms which were plastered were rooms used as gathering or meeting places.

So, we have a building that had once been a house. The house was significant and people began to meet there. Soon more people gathered there, so that a wall was knocked down to create more space. And then, much later, a splendid church was built on the original site.[4]

---

[4] For a full account of the discovery see Strange, J.F., and Shanks, H. "Has the house where Jesus stayed in Capernaum been found?" *Biblical Archaeology Review* 8 (Nov/Dec 1982). Theissen, and Merz, *The Historical Jesus: A Comprehensive Guide*, 167. Thiede, C.P., *Simon Peter, From Galilee to Rome*, (Exeter: Paternoster Press, 1986), 25.

What we have here, therefore, is a good candidate for Simon Peter's house in Capernaum and, indeed, for one of the earliest churches in the world. If it is Peter's house, then it's probably the place which Jesus, during his residence in the village, called home.

CAPERNAUM, CRADLE OF CHRISTIANITY

We transform Jesus. We turn him into a white-robed, other-worldly figure who floated around Galilee staring at people and saying Very Wise Things. But he spent a lot of his time in peoples' homes: in the homes of tax-collectors and friends, in the homes of supporters, and in the homes of people like Simon Peter. And maybe within that dwelling, in one of those rooms off the courtyard, was his place. When he was in there, the crowds knew that he was "at home."

Interestingly, Jesus didn't find it all plain sailing in Capernaum. Despite the crowds, he had a mixed reception. The town received a withering condemnation from Jesus, who described its stubbornness as worse than Sodom's (Matt. 11.23–24).

When we think about the most important places in the history of Christianity, our minds drift, naturally, to the big cities: to Jerusalem, Rome, Ephesus or Antioch. But Capernaum, this tiny community on the north bank of Galilee, has a good claim to be the most important place in the history of Christianity. For it was here that Jesus worked out who he was and what his purpose was. It was here that he called his first disciples (Mk 1.16–20); that he taught with authority (Mark 1.21–22) and that he demonstrated that he had the power to forgive sins (Mark 2.1–12). It was in Capernaum that his habit of eating meals with entirely the wrong sort of people began.

He was known as, and we still talk about, Jesus of Nazareth. But Jesus from Capernaum was the man who really made an impact.

WHY DID THE ISRAELITES
HATE THE PHILISTINES?

"I'm Sick to Death of Meddling Philistines" ran the headline in *The Times*. The story went on to issue a savage denunciation from the head of a major London arts venue, who claimed that the "Government arts policy is forged by ignorant bureaucrats and posturing barbarians."

Naturally, this is not the sort of thing that someone like myself[1] could let pass, so I wrote at once to the editor.

Philistine values

Sir, There are often unwarranted slurs on the reputation of the Philistines, illustrated by the headline "I'm sick to death of meddling Philistines" (*Times2*, April 17), referring to government interference in the arts.

This is being Philistineist. The Philistines were a highly sophisticated society with a written culture and a strong tradition of beautiful ceramics. They were skilled at working in ivory and gold, pioneered iron and bronze technology and excelled in urban planning, developing large, fortified cities with industrial zones and elite housing.

The problem with this Government is not that it is Philistine, but that it isn't Philistine enough.

NICK PAGE, Eynsham, Oxon[2]

You see, the truth is that the Philistines have had a bad press. If someone shows ignorance of art or culture, if someone prefers basketball to Bach or *Coronation Street* to *Coriolanus*, we call them an "ignorant Philistine."

It's a misconception. The trouble is, when we think of the Philistines, we think of one Philistine in particular: Goliath, the giant warrior, a man of prodigious height, breadth, strength and, probably, hair. Goliath is the biblical yob par excellence; he's a kind

---

[1] i. e. bizarre, slightly obsessed and probably needing to get out more.

[2] *The Times*, Letters Page, April 23 2007

of James Bond villain; nine foot of muscle with the IQ of a house brick.

And we think all Philistines were like him: big, hairy and brutal. This story, with its powerful image of the enormous Philistine warrior, completely colors our view of the Philistines themselves. So when faced with the question of why the Israelites were at war with the Philistines, we conclude that that was what the Philistines were like; that was all they were capable of doing. The problem with the Philistines was that, well, that they were Philistines. They were the bad guys, the enemy, the thugs, the brutes.

Which is not quite true. They were clever, cultivated people. They had a sophisticated written culture and produced beautiful pottery and ceramics. They were not ignorant at all. Indeed, the conflict between Israel and the Philistines was not because the Philistines were more brutal than the Israelites. It was because they were more refined.

At least, their metal was...

A BIT ABOUT THE PHILISTINES

The Philistines probably arrived in Canaan from two routes: overland via Anatolia, and overseas from Crete. Indeed a verse in Numbers (24.24) probably refers to the first wave of invading forces. They clashed with the Egyptians in about 1190BC and were defeated by Rameses III, who seems to have used them as mercenaries and settled them in the coastal towns of Gaza, Ashkelon and Ashdod.[3] However, about forty years later they drove out the Egyptians and took over the two extra cities of Ekron and Gath. This confederation of five city-states became the core of Philistia.

Soon, they spread north and then east, into Israelite territory, occupying the hill country.[4] Such was the pressure, however, that at one point one of the tribes of Israel, Dan, was forced to relocate in order to find refuge. They inflicted a crushing defeat of Israel at Ebenezer (the Philistines had already reached Aphek), where the

---

[3]   In Deuteronomy 2:23, where "Caphtorim" refers to the Philistines.

[4]   cf. 1 Samuel 10:5; 13:23–14:16, and also 2 Samuel 23:13–17.

Israelites lost the Ark of the Covenant (1 Samuel 4 – see p.101). It was pressure from the Philistines that led Israel to call for a king (1 Sam. 8), which led, in turn, to the appointment of Saul. So one reason why the Israelites were in conflict with the Philistines was simply over land. If that were the only issue, then there wouldn't be much reason for re-evaluating our image of the Philistines; militarily, they were stronger than the Israelites. But why were they stronger? How come they managed to win the battles, even when the Israelites tried to deploy the Ark of the Covenant?

The answer is that they weren't only stronger than the Israelites, they were *cleverer*.

They were more technologically advanced. They knew how to work gold and carve delicate ivory and their pottery and ceramics show artistry and craft. As one writer has put it, "Philistine material culture stands out against the bleak background of the world in which they lived."[5] They transformed their city-states into large, well-planned, fortified cities with industrial zones and elite housing. They had their own language (although only a few examples of it have been found) so were obviously a written culture. There is unquestionable evidence for writing on papyrus in Philistia during this period.[6]

But it's all very well making nice pottery. What was it that enabled this relatively small nation to thrive? What made them so powerful?

The answer to that is metal.

ANY OLD IRON?

A couple of verses show us a glimpse of the back story concerning the conflict:

> Now there was no smith to be found throughout all the land of Israel; for the Philistines said, "The Hebrews must not make

[5] Dothan, T. "What We Know About the Philistines." *Biblical Archaeology Review* 8 (July/August 1982).

[6] Kelm, G.L. and Mazar, A., "Excavating in Samson Country—Philistines and Israelites at Tel Batash." *Biblical Archaeology Review* 15 (Jan/Feb 1989).

swords or spears for themselves"; so all the Israelites went down to the Philistines to sharpen their plowshare, mattocks, axes, or sickles; the charge was two-thirds of a shekel for the plowshares and for the mattocks, and one-third of a shekel for sharpening the axes and for setting the goads. So on the day of the battle neither sword nor spear was to be found in the possession of any of the people with Saul and Jonathan; but Saul and his son Jonathan had them (1 Sam. 13.19–22).

The Philistines had mastered the art of making iron and bronze. It was this that led to Philistine superiority, rather than the size of their warriors. Their technology was better, and they were keeping it to themselves.

The Iron Age became the age of the blacksmith. From this point on, until relatively recently, no community was complete without its blacksmith, working at the forge, creating the tools and weapons that the community needed. Iron became an everyday, utilitarian substance. As this passage shows, the Philistines knew how to work iron, and they would not allow the Israelites to do the same. This had drastic effects because iron was used for objects requiring strength and hardness; useful objects such as axes and chisels, hoes and plowshares and, above all, weapons.

Relative to working with bronze, iron technology is difficult and complicated. One simple reason was that it required more heat. Bronze was made using copper and tin and copper melts at about 1100°C. Iron, however, melts at 1530°C. Those extra 400° required a lot of technological know-how. Similarly, pure wrought iron is quite soft; but if you add a bit of carbon into the mix, by exposing the iron to the coal in the furnace for a bit longer, you effectively turn iron into steel.

Also, when you plunge red-hot carburized iron into water, it forms on its surface a substance called martensite. Martensite is extremely hard – only a diamond is harder – but it's also unstable. In order to stabilize it, you have to temper the object: that is, reheat it at temperatures above 150°C. This decomposes some of the martensite and makes it less brittle. I've probably lost you by now (I've certainly lost myself) but all this shows is that, compared to pouring melted copper and tin into a mold, making objects of iron required a lot more skill.[7] It had to be learned by trial and error. It wasn't that the Iron Age smiths knew about carbon (the element wasn't even discovered until the end of the 18th century AD), it was that they found out what worked. And they passed that knowledge on to others.

So the Philistines had mastered iron technology. And the text implies that any Israelites who mastered it were deported – a sort of Iron-Age brain-drain. This monopoly on the best technology – whether military or agricultural – gave the Philistines enormous power.[8] Israel became dependent on them for the simplest repair job to their agricultural tools, for which they were charged exorbitant prices: just sharpening the ax cost half as much as the entire cost of the object (1 Sam. 13.21).[9]

This is probably why only Saul and Jonathan had iron weapons. They were so scarce that only the leaders were allowed them. One can imagine them being smuggled across the border, an illegal and highly expensive set of iron weapons. An early form of gun-smuggling.

Bronze still had its uses. Goliath's armor, for example, is made out of bronze, but his spear is made of iron

> And he had a helmet of brass upon his head, and he was armed with a coat of mail. … And he had greaves of brass upon his legs, and a target of brass between his shoulders. And the staff of his spear was like a weaver's beam, and his spear's head weighed six hundred shekels of iron; and one bearing a shield went before him (1 Sam. 17:5–7).

---

[7] The full process is outlined in Muhly, J.D. "How Iron Technology changed the Ancient World and gave the Philistines a military edge." *Biblical Archaeology Review* 8 (November/December) 1982.

[8] This explains why most of the iron tools and weapons found in Israel before about 1000BC come from sites that show signs of Philistine occupation or influence. Iron weapons are found at Philistine sites only. At the Israelite sites there are iron agricultural implements, but not weapons. In fact, iron did not become common in Israel until after the Philistine culture went into decline in the tenth and ninth centuries BC.

[9] Klein, *1 Samuel*, 128.

So the Philistines were suppressing the Israelites not through sheer physical size, not through brutishness and physical strength, but through technology. This places the context of the battle in a different light. We tend to think that all battles in the Old Testament had a kind of theological basis, that they were wars against foreign gods. But this war has a much more mundane and even modern basis. It was a fight for technological superiority.

That's why the Israelites hated the Philistines. It was not only that they were grabbing their land, they were withholding technology.

Which brings us back to that letter in *The Times*. Who are the Philistines today, I wonder? Today, withholding technology is still an established way of controlling other nations. As technology advances, the developed world remains in control. We don't want other nations to have access to the tools we have. We'll allow them some access, of course, but we'll keep the best bits for ourselves. And by retaining the expertise we can charge high prices for repairs. The Internet, the latest medicines, nuclear technology; even down to some simple tools like the right papers or permits; the country which controls those has the power. We've got it all and we'll let you have some of it. For a price. And if you can't pay, well, tough.

One postscript to the Philistine story. The Greek historian Herodotus, along with Persian sailors and travelers, called them *palastinoi* and their country *palastium*. The Romans followed this usage and applied the name to the entire area. Emperor Hadrian officially called the province of Judaea *Provincia Palaestine*, and by the 4th century AD, Palestine had become the accepted name for the entire area.

The Philistines may be gone, but their name lives on. Ironically the Palestinians, who have inherited the name of the Philistines, along with the places where they live, are now subject to Israeli control. The boot is on the other foot.

WHY DID BARNABAS GO
AND FETCH PAUL?

Think about your favorite film for a moment. Now, can you tell me the name of the director? What about the name of the stars? Fine. But what about the name of the producers?

The job of a film producer is a vital yet strangely anonymous one. The producer brings together the right elements to make the film work: notably the director and the stars. They raise the money and oversee the entire project, yet most people don't know who produced their favorite film. The directors and stars get all the plaudits, but the producers? Who remembers their names?

If we think about the stars of the Early Church, a few names spring to mind. Paul, certainly; Peter, of course; maybe some others like Stephen and Philip. But one of the most important people in the Early Church, certainly in terms of the impact his actions were to have, is often overlooked. His name was Joseph Barnabas.

Acts 11 contains some of the most important developments in the history of the church, all packed into a handful of verses

> Now those who were scattered because of the persecution that took place over Stephen travelled as far as Phoenicia, Cyprus, and Antioch, and they spoke the word to no one except Jews. But among them were some men of Cyprus and Cyrene who, on coming to Antioch, spoke to the Hellenists also, proclaiming the Lord Jesus. The hand of the Lord was with them, and a great number became believers and turned to the Lord. News of this came to the ears of the church in Jerusalem, and they sent Barnabas to Antioch. When he came and saw the grace of God, he rejoiced, and he exhorted them all to remain faithful to the Lord with steadfast devotion; for he was a good man, full of the Holy Spirit and of faith. And a great many people were brought to the Lord. Then Barnabas went to Tarsus to look for Saul, and when he had found him, he brought him to Antioch. So it was that for an entire year they met with the church and taught a great many people, and it was in Antioch that the disciples were first called "Christians" (Acts 11.19–26).

Luke describes how persecution in Jerusalem pushed the faith into new areas. Like pouring water on a chip pan fire, instead of quenching the flames, it just spread it further afield. Originally in Phoenicia, Cyprus and north to Antioch, conversion was centered on the Jews, but as the message spread, Gentiles too came to embrace this new set of beliefs. For the first time, the Christian faith spreads outside the boundaries of Judaism.

It's not difficult to see how Christianity came to Antioch; Nicolaus, one of the seven Greek Jews called to serve as deacons in Jerusalem, was a "proselyte from Antioch" (Acts 6.5). Antioch was an incredibly diverse city, with different races and nationalities crammed together in a tiny space; restricting such a life-changing belief as Christianity to one ethnic group would be an impossible task. Soon, outsiders from Cyprus and Cyrene start talking to the "Hellenists" – the Greek Gentiles.

Back in Jerusalem, James and the other leaders hear what is going on. Nervous about this new development, they sent a trusted troubleshooter to check up on things. The man they sent was Barnabas.

THE NAME'S BARNABAS, JOSEPH BARNABAS

Barnabas was the ideal man for the job. A man of impeccable credentials, he was a Levite from Cyprus (so probably knew some of those who had done the evangelizing in Antioch). His Jewish name was Joseph, but the apostles called him Barnabas, which, Luke explains, means either son of exhortation or son of encouragement (Acts 4.36).[1] He may have been one of the seventy-two disciples mentioned in Luke 10.1. As a respected figure in the Jerusalem church, his name would carry a lot of clout. It was he who had introduced Paul of Tarsus to the Jerusalem church, some three years after Paul had been leading the persecution. Like Paul[2] he had a trade, although we don't know if it was the same as Paul's (1

---

[1] Witherington III, B., *The Acts of the Apostles: A Socio-Rhetorical Commentary*, (Grand Rapids: Eerdmans, 1998), 209.

[2] I know he's called "Saul" in this part of his life, but I'm going to use Paul for the sake of clarity and consistency.

Cor. 9.6). This was a man with a track record; a "good man, full of the Holy Spirit and of faith." Indeed, he's the only man in Acts called "good."[3] Hengel describes him as a "link man" between different groups.[4] And that indeed was what he excelled at: making links, joined-up thinking.

Barnabas went to Antioch, took a look at the new church and immediately recognized its potential. Loads of people were coming to Christ; it was expanding rapidly. Then, "Barnabas went to Tarsus to look for Paul..."

Now why on earth did he do that?

A BIT OF BACKGROUND

Let's get the timing sorted first. There's a lot of argument about when Paul was converted. Personally I think those first few chapters of Acts take place in a compressed period of time and that Paul was probably converted shortly after the resurrection, around 34AD. After that, according to his own autobiography, he spent three years in Damascus and Arabia (Gal. 1.15–17), presumably trying to come to terms with what had happened, but also talking to other Jews about Jesus. This came to a head in Damascus, when he had to be smuggled out of the city in a basket (Acts 9.23–25). That takes us to around 37AD.

He then went down to Jerusalem for his first meeting with the apostles – the meeting at which Barnabas vouched for him (Acts 9.26–27). After the apostles accepted that he had truly joined them, Paul, typically, went straight to the Hellenistic synagogues – the synagogues for Greek-speaking Jews – where his arguments led to threats against his life (Acts 9.28–29). The apostles, wondering, no doubt, if this was going to be the normal state of things with this man, sent him home to Tarsus (Acts 9.30), some 500km away. There was then, what Luke describes as a period of peace. Whether this was because Paul left the district, he doesn't say.

---

[3] Luke also calls Joseph of Arimathea "good" in his gospel – there must be something about the name Joseph (Luke 23.50)

[4] Hengel, M., and Schwemer, A.M., *Paul Between Damascus and Antioch: The Unknown Years*, (London: SCM, 1997), 216–17.

Some nine or ten years passed, then Barnabas went to Antioch and suddenly Paul was back in the frame. So why did Barnabas suddenly think of Paul? What was it that brought Paul to Barnabas's mind?

Antioch was an incredibly important city; the third biggest city in the empire after Rome and Alexandria, it was a cosmopolitan melting pot. The Romans used it as the base for their control of all Syria and Palestine, so there was a huge Imperial presence. It was also a major commercial center, describing itself on its coins as "Antioch, metropolis, sacred, and inviolable, and autonomous, and sovereign, and capital of the East."[5] There was a large Jewish population in the city, and many non-Jews had become followers of Judaism there.[6] These non-Jewish converts took two forms, later described as Proselytes of the Sanctuary and Proselytes of the Gate. The former were people who were circumcised and took on the full "law" of Judaism; the latter were what the book of Acts calls "God-fearers" who followed the teaching of Judaism and some of the ceremonial purity rituals, but didn't follow all the rules.[7]

But this new church contained Gentiles; people who were not Jews, proselytes or even God-fearers. With the benefit of hindsight, we can see that Paul was absolutely the right man for the job. A Roman citizen, raised as an ultra-orthodox Jew in a Gentile city: he was the ideal applicant. Barnabas obviously brought in Paul because of his background, and because he had the expertise to help. But Barnabas didn't *know* that Paul was good at dealing with Gentiles. Antioch, according to Acts was the first Gentile church. Unless...

WANTED: SMALL, BALD GUY WITH BANDY-LEGS

Some commentators believe that Barnabas was merely recalling the work Paul had done at Damascus.[8] Paul knew, right from the

---

[5] Witherington, *The Acts of the Apostles: A Socio-Rhetorical Commentary*, 366. Now that's what I call a city mission statement.

[6] Josephus, *The Jewish War*, 377–78

[7] Ramsay, W.M., *St. Paul the Traveler and the Roman Citizen*, (London: Hodder and Stoughton, 1908), 43.

[8] Witherington, *The Acts of the Apostles: A Socio-Rhetorical Commentary*, 370. Ramsay, *St. Paul the Traveler and the Roman Citizen*, 45.

beginning, that God had called him to preach to the Gentiles, but even so, for him to suddenly pop into Barnabas's mind is scarcely credible. It's unbelievable that Barnabas should wave goodbye to Paul in Jerusalem, then, ten years later, when he's struggling with the growth of this new Gentile church, suddenly say to his friends, "What was the name of that bloke... you know, did all the persecuting? He'd be ideal."

No. The fact that Barnabas travels to find Paul must mean two things:

1. He knew where Paul was living.

2. He knew what Paul had been up to.

Barnabas must have kept in contact with Paul. This would not have been difficult. The Roman empire had made communication easier than in previous times, and travel safer. It would have been quite possible for Barnabas to meet up with Paul in the intervening years: Barnabas' home was in Cyprus and Cyprus is a short boat journey to Tarsus. Similarly, from Antioch it is not far to Tarsus.

Tarsus was a rich, cosmopolitan city, in a wealthy region. Cilicia Pedias – Cilicia of the Plain as the Greeks called the region – was rich agricultural country, growing wheat, sesame and rice. Its vineyards produced a muscatel-type wine, and it had a flourishing textile industry.[9] Tarsus and the other cities in the area derived their wealth not only from the agriculture but also from the trade routes which passed through the region, then through the Cilician gates to the north. It made a perfect missionary base. Paul could already have made some forays north in Cappadocia.[10]

However, Luke's phrase "and when he [Barnabas] had found him [Paul]" is intriguing. It hints that perhaps finding Paul wasn't as easy as all that. Some scholars wonder if Paul has been disinherited for his faith and thrown out of the family home.[11] Intriguingly, there

---

[9] Jones, A.H.M, and Avi-Yonah, M., *The Cities of the Eastern Roman Provinces*, (Oxford: Clarendon Press, 1971), 191.

[10] Jones, and Avi-Yonah, *The Cities of the Eastern Roman Provinces*, 206. Riesner, R., *Paul's Early Period: Chronology, Mission Strategy, Theology*, (Grand Rapids: Eerdmans, 1998), 266–267.

[11] Bruce, F.F., *Commentary on the Book of the Acts: The English Text*, (London: Marshall, Morgan & Scott, 1954), 240.

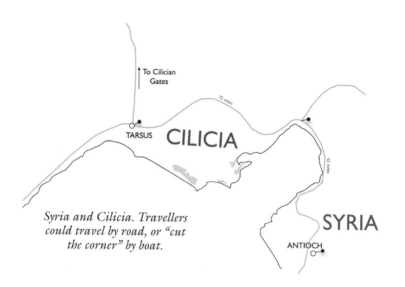

Syria and Cilicia. Travellers could travel by road, or "cut the corner" by boat.

is another account of someone looking for Paul, which was written much later. The apocryphal gospel *The Acts of Paul and Thecla* was written by an unnamed church leader in Asia.[12] It's a curious story about a young woman Thecla, who becomes devoted to Paul and who undergoes many trials and is miraculously delivered. But it describes a time when a man is searching for Paul and there is a description: "And he saw Paul coming, a man small in size, bald-headed, bandy-legged, well-built, with eyebrows meeting, rather long-nosed, full of grace. For sometimes he seemed like a man, and sometimes he had the countenance of an angel."[13]

Whilst *The Acts of Paul and Thecla* is a work of fiction (for which its author was deposed from his office) this description is so unflattering that it very well may contain a kernel of truth. Anyway, Barnabas knew roughly where Paul was; but he also had to have known what he'd been doing. You don't travel all the way to Tarsus just on the whim that Paul might be good at this sort of thing; you go to get him because you *know* he's good at this sort

---

[12] Eusebius, *The Ecclesiastical History and the Martyrs of Palestine*, II, 79–80.

[13] "Acts of Paul and Thecla" in *Church Fathers – The Ante-Nicene Fathers*. Edited by Roberts, A. and Donaldson, J., Oak Tree Software.

of thing. What that implies is that Paul had not been quiet all those years in Tarsus; let's face it, the idea of Paul being quiet about Jesus for more than about ten minutes is hard to imagine; let alone ten years. Those ten years would have been spent talking to people: arguing, explaining, refining his own theories: above all, engaging with the people of that region: Jews as well as Gentiles. Paul must have been doing this, and Barnabas must have known he was doing this. Indeed, Paul's letter to the Galatians indicates that reports of his activities might have spread south: "Then I went into the regions of Syria and Cilicia, and I was still unknown by sight to the churches of Judea that are in Christ; they only heard it said, 'The one who formerly was persecuting us is now proclaiming the faith he once tried to destroy.' And they glorified God because of me" (Gal. 1.21–24).

This might mean that they were "glorifying God" following news of the meeting in Jerusalem; or it could mean that the church in Judea had heard of his activities in Cilicia and Syria. But whether they'd heard or not, Paul has to be active in Tarsus and the area around, and Barnabas must have been aware of this.

There's a possible hint of this in a variant version of Acts, the so-called Western text.[14] This runs: "When [Barnabas] found him he exhorted him to come to Antioch. When they came, for a whole year a considerable crowd was stirred up…" Given that Luke normally smooths things over, this image of Paul as someone who needed to be persuaded, and who, when he was persuaded, immediately started stirring things up, may well be authentic.[15] The idea that Paul needed persuading indicates that there was something else he was doing. He surely must have been engaged in mission work among the Gentiles and it must have been working. As Hengel puts it: "An unsuccessful missionary would not have been much help to Barnabas in building up the church in Antioch."[16]

---

[14] This is a group of mss. of Acts originating mostly in the West, which contain a number of alternative and expanded readings. See Neil, W., *Acts: Based on the Revised Standard Version*, (Grand Rapids: Eerdmans, 1981), 70–71. Witherington, *The Acts of the Apostles: A Socio-Rhetorical Commentary*, 65–68.

[15] Witherington, *The Acts of the Apostles: A Socio-Rhetorical Commentary*, 370.

[16] Hengel and Schwemer, *Paul Between Damascus and Antioch: The Unknown Years*, 179.

There's another clue later in Acts when, after the Apostolic Council in Acts 15, Paul suggested to Barnabas that they "return and visit the believers in every city where we proclaimed the word of the Lord and see how they are doing" (Acts 15.36). As things turn out, they didn't go together – following a disagreement over John Mark, Paul traveled with Silas instead. And where did he go? He did not follow the route of his first missionary journey, straight to Iconium, Derbe, and Lystra; instead "He went through Syria and Cilicia, strengthening the churches" (Acts 15.41). In other words, he visited churches that he had *already* planted.[17]

This theory also helps to reconcile the different account Paul gives of his trials and hardships in 2 Corinthians, with Luke's account in Acts. The number of shipwrecks, beatings and general Paul-associated disasters don't add up (2 Cor. 11.24–26), but if we assume that in these "hidden" years he was active in Syria and Cilicia, then suddenly all that makes sense. In particular the "synagogue punishments" mentioned – "Five times I have received from the Jews the forty lashes minus one" may well have been meted out during the first years of activity, because there was a strong, powerful Jewish presence in Tarsus and around.[18]

Why doesn't Luke make this clear? Well, part of the reasons might be that it *wasn't* that clear. History is never quite as clear cut as we'd like; it's always a bit messy. It would be nice to think that Antioch was the first Gentile church, but you can't bottle up the message of salvation that neatly; once you pop the cork, it has a habit of fizzing all over the place. We know, for example, Christianity spread rapidly to Damascus; hence Paul's journey there. We know it went to Cyprus and Cyrene. Luke has tidied things up slightly, and Antioch was probably the first major Gentile congregation, but there must have been others. Maybe he's also being diplomatic; creating the impression of an ordered expansion overseen by the Jerusalem church, but he put hints in there. As one

---

[17] Hengel and Schwemer, *Paul Between Damascus and Antioch: The Unknown Years*, 156. Bruce, *Commentary on the Book of the Acts: The English Text*, 240–241.

[18] Osborne, R. E. "St. Paul's Silent Years." *Journal of Biblical Literature* 84 (1965), 60–61.

writer puts it: "He wanted to have readers who sometimes could also read between the lines."[19]

All of which means that the church at Antioch may well not have been the first Gentile church; just the first one big enough to register on the radar. And the famous first missionary journey of Paul was probably the first "official" missionary journey of Paul. Above all, it shows that the expansion of the church was a more gloriously messy affair than we sometimes imagine, that it probably happened more quickly and in a far less organized way. For it can't have just been Paul who talked to their Gentile neighbours about Jesus. In the tight, compressed, multi-ethnic world of the Græco-Roman cities, the good news would have leapt across boundaries.

What's more, it means that the church owes an incalculable debt to Barnabas, who not only recognized the validity of what was happening in Antioch, but also knew just the right man for the job. We don't know a great deal about him, and following a disagreement with Paul in Acts 15.36–39, he drops out of history. But he was the man who knew what would work. He was the man who kept his finger on the pulse through the hidden years. He was the man who saw in Paul the man who could take the church forward. He was the one who lit the blue touch paper, stood back and watched the rocket soar.

So let's hear it for the producer of the Gentile church: Joseph Barnabas.

---

[19] Hengel and Schwemer, *Paul Between Damascus and Antioch: The Unknown Years*, 156. As I. Howard Marshall puts it, "One is tempted to say that Luke cannot win either way: if the narrative is lacking in concrete details, he is said to have no sources at his disposal, and if he paints a detailed picture of an episode, it is dismissed as legendary embellishment." Marshall, I.H., *The Acts of the Apostles: An Introduction and Commentary*, (Leicester: Inter-Varsity Press, 1980), 200.

A cross stands by a doorway outside the Church of the Holy Sepulchre, Jerusalem – the church which is built over the traditional sites of Jesus' death and burial. The original building was begun in 326, and dedicated in 335 AD.

HOW DID JESUS DIE?

There are many books on Jesus' death. Almost all focus on the theological aspects: the atoning nature, the theological significance. There is one question that I always wondered about it: how did he die? He was crucified, of course, but actually, nobody dies of "crucifixion." Horrible as it sounds (and much of this chapter is horrible, I'm afraid) having nails driven through your hands and feet does not kill you.

Medical opinion is divided as to how, exactly, crucifixion causes death. But as we start to explore some of the truth of what crucifixion means, we will see just how far Jesus was prepared to go for all of us.

THE SLAVES' DEATH

Despite the many thousands of sermons, books and articles describing the crucifixion, we actually know very little about how it was done. The Græco-Roman world didn't like to talk about it. "The very name 'cross' should not only be far from the body of a Roman citizen, but also from his thoughts, his eyes and his ears" said Cicero.[1] The passion narratives are, in fact, the most detailed ancient accounts of crucifixion, but even they skip over the details: "And they crucified him…" says Mark (Mark 15.24). He, and all his readers, knew what it was like, but nobody wanted to dwell on the detail. They knew it was done; they knew how it was done, but so shameful was the deed that one simply didn't talk about it.[2]

But that was the point. It was designed to be humiliating; its entire purpose was to terrify both victim and onlookers. One of the reasons was that it was a way of imposing Imperial control. There were two main groups of people for whom crucifixion was the punishment: slaves and rebels. Indeed, crucifixion was known as "the slave's death", because so many slaves were killed in this way.

Rome's economy, its very existence, was built upon the concept of slavery. There were millions of slaves in the Roman empire; the authorities simply could not let a group that large get out of

---

[1] Cicero, *Pro Rabirio perduellionis* 5. 16

[2] Carroll, J.T., and Green, J.B., *The Death of Jesus in Early Christianity*, (Peabody, Mass: Hendrickson Publishers, 1995), 167–70.

control. So they used terror to control them, and chief among its terror weapons was crucifixion. The great slave rebellions of the second century BC ended, not only in defeat for the slaves, but in mass crucifixions; the victorious Crassus had six thousand slaves crucified, lining the main road into Rome. For everyday use, as it were, the Roman historian Tacitus records that there was a special place in Rome for the punishment of slaves; the Campus Esquilinus.[3] No doubt the numerous crosses that were set up there served as a constant reminder to slaves of the fate that awaited them, should they step out of line. It may well be that the Romans set up similar "reminders" in all the major cities of their empire, one of which may have been Golgotha. However, a slave could expect this terrible punishment for a number of offenses. For instance, the Emperor Nero revived the practice of executing (often by crucifixion) all the slaves in the household if the master was murdered. In one extreme example, Horace reports a man who had his slave crucified because he tasted some fish soup while bringing it to the table.[4]

The same was true of the other countries which Rome conquered. There were always more people in these countries than troops occupying them. So at the slightest hint of rebellion, Rome stamped hard. It punished severely and obviously; and crucifixion was about as severe and obvious as it could get. It was designed to maximize the opportunity for public ridicule and shame. Crucially, the victims were often denied burial. It was, in the words of Borg and Crossan, an act of "imperial terror."[5]

From our perspective, we can see that Jesus' death fits into both these categories. Historically and politically, he was condemned as a revolutionary, as one who had disturbed the *pax romana*. He was accused of having led a rebellion and claimed to be king of

---

[3] Hengel, M., *Crucifixion in the Ancient World and the Folly of the Message of the Cross*, (London: SCM, 1977), 54. Horace called the vulture "the Esquiline bird" Horace, *Satires* 1. 8. 14ff.

[4] Hengel, M., *Crucifixion in the Ancient World*, 59–60. Horace called the master "quite mad by any reasonable standard."

[5] Borg, M.J., and Crossan, J.D., *The Last Week: What the Gospels Really Teach About Jesus's Final Days in Jerusalem*, (San Francisco: HarperSanFrancisco, 2007) 146. Burial of crucifixion victims was rare, but not unknown. See Lyons, W.J. "On the Life and Death of Joseph of Arimathea." *Journal for the Study of the Historical Jesus* 2 (2004), 47–48.

the Jews. When he appeared before the Sanhedrin, the charge was a theological one: blasphemy (Matt. 26.65). When he appeared before Pilate, the high priest changed the charge to a political one – telling people not to pay their taxes and claiming to be a king (Luke 23.2).[6]

From a theological perspective, we can see in Jesus' death his willingness to become a slave. It is this understanding that is reflected in one of the hymns of the Early Church, quoted by Paul in Philippians

> Let the same mind be in you that was in Christ Jesus, who, though he was in the form of God, did not regard equality with God as something to be exploited, but emptied himself, taking the form of a slave, being born in human likeness. And being found in human form, he humbled himself and became obedient to the point of death – even death on a cross (Phil. 2.5–8).

He was a slave and a revolutionary. Just not in the way that anyone imagined.

A STANDARD PATTERN

Given the shameful connotations, and its association with rebels or slaves, it is hardly surprising that Græco-Roman literature doesn't preserve the details. We do know, however, the general process. Crucifixion by Romans seems to have followed a standard pattern: the victim was flogged beforehand, then their arms were strapped or tied to the crossbeam of the cross and they were forced to march to the crucifixion site, where they were crucified. There, for many victims, death came slowly, sometimes over several days. Jesus' death was unusually rapid, brought on, no doubt, by a beating of such severity that someone else had to carry his crossbeam (Matt. 27.32).

The crucifixion itself could take a variety of forms. As Hengel has put it, "Crucifixion was a punishment in which the caprice

---

[6] Jensen, E.E. "The First Century Controversy over Jesus as a Revolutionary Figure." *Journal of Biblical Literature* 60 (1941), 262–263.

and sadism of the executioners were given full rein."[7]Josephus recounts how the Roman soldiers besieging Jerusalem "amused" themselves by crucifying their victims in different poses and positions: "Scourged and subjected before death to every torture, they [captured prisoners] were finally crucified in view of the wall... The soldiers themselves through rage and bitterness nailed up their victims in various attitudes as a grim joke, till owing to the vast numbers there was no room for the crosses, and no crosses for the bodies."[8]

Seneca reported on a mass crucifixion that he saw: "I see crosses there, not just of one kind but made in many different ways: some have their victims with their head down to the ground, some impale their private parts, others stretch out their arms" [9]Mostly, however, the Romans would have used a quick, brutal, straightforward method. The evidence from the only crucifixion victim, discovered by archeologists, indicates that the crossbar was set in place and the victim's hands or wrists nailed, then his legs were lifted up and he was sat on a small peg. A single nail was then driven laterally through his ankles.[10]

The whole thing was designed for economy of effort and speed by the Romans. Jesus did not have a long march to his place of execution: it is just a few hundred yards from Herod's Palace, where Pilate was, to the traditional site of the crucifixion. Once there, the job was done with a brutal efficiency. Since wood was so scarce in Jerusalem, Jesus was probably allocated a crossbeam that had been used before.[11]

---

[7] Hengel, *Crucifixion in the Ancient World*, 25.

[8] Josephus, *Jewish War* (London: Penguin Books, 1981), 326

[9] Seneca L.A., in Michaelis H.C., ed. *De Consolatione ad Marciam*, quoted in Maslen, M.W. and Mitchell, P.D. "Medical theories on the cause of death in crucifixion." *Journal of the Royal Society of Medicine* 99 (2006), 185. This strengthens the traditional story that Peter was crucified upside down, if he was crucified as part of the mass crucifixions of Christians ordered by Nero.

[10] See Haas, "Anthropological Observations on the Skeletal Remains from Gi'vat ha-Mivtar", *Israel Exploration Journal* 20 (1970), 49ff. This reconstruction has been challenged by others, who claim that his arms were actually hung over the crossbeam and his feet nailed into each side of the main upright. See Zias J. and Sekeles, E. "The Crucified Man from Giv'at ha-Mivtar: A Reappraisal", *Israel Exploration Journal* 35 (1985), 22–27.

[11] Zias J and Sekeles, "The Crucified Man from Giv'at ha-Mivtar: a reappraisal", 22

CAUSE OF DEATH

Pathologists have theorized at length as to how crucifixion actually killed its victims. At least ten different theories have been proposed, with many writers suggesting a combination of these different theories.[12] For many victims, as we have seen, the cause of death was blood loss, from the beating they took beforehand. Many actually died during the beating.[13]

The main suggestion for the cause of death in crucifixion is usually asphyxiation. Eyewitness accounts of the "crucifixion" of prisoners in Dachau and during the First World War show that when victims were left hanging by the arms with their feet off the ground their muscles went into spasms. Unable to keep lifting themselves to exhale, they died quickly. This has long been the standard explanation, but more recent research has claimed that people only die of asphyxiation when their arms are directly over their heads.[14] Nor does this explanation square with the historical facts, which indicate that the victims survived, on the cross, for a long time. Jesus lasted three hours; others, as we've seen, lasted a lot longer. In those cases, the victims were not purely suspended by their arms, but sitting on a small peg or block of wood, called a *sedile* ("seat"), and fixed halfway up the main upright. Alternatively they might have had a *suppedaneum* or footrest.

Towards the end, the victim might have their legs or other bones broken. Many scholars have argued that this would speed up the process of death, since it would make the victim unable to support himself, but as we've seen above, there were other means of support. If it did speed up death, it would have been simply through inflicting even greater pain and trauma on the victim. In this case, the breaking of limbs – what the Romans called *crurifragium* – was just another level of degradation, one final act of suffering imposed on their most despised enemies. [15]

---

[12] For a list, see Maslen, M.W. and Mitchell, P.D. "Medical theories on the cause of death in crucifixion", 185–188.

[13] Hengel, *Crucifixion in the Ancient World*, 29 n. 21

[14] Brown, R.E., *The Death of the Messiah: From Gethsemane to the Grave*, 1088–1092

[15] Brown, R.E., *The Death of the Messiah: From Gethsemane to the Grave*, 1175–1176

In Jesus' case, however, this final barbaric act was not inflicted: when the soldiers came to break his legs, they found that he was already dead. Compared to what the historical accounts tell us of the length of time it took for crucifixion victims to die, Jesus seems to have died unusually quickly; so much so that it is remarked on in the gospels

> When evening had come, and since it was the day of Preparation, that is, the day before the sabbath, Joseph of Arimathea, a respected member of the council, who was also himself waiting expectantly for the kingdom of God, went boldly to Pilate and asked for the body of Jesus. Then Pilate wondered if he were already dead; and summoning the centurion, he asked him whether he had been dead for some time. When he learned from the centurion that he was dead, he granted the body to Joseph (Mark 15.42–45).

What this indicates is that Jesus was already badly injured before he was nailed to the cross. We know that he was too weak to carry the crossbeam to the execution site. The distance from Herod's Palace, where Pilate was based, to the traditional site of Golgotha is not far: around three hundred meters or so. But Jesus had been so badly beaten that he could not make it. Given he was too weak to carry the cross that relatively short distance, he must have already been seriously weakened by loss of blood. In that event, he would have succumbed to what is termed hypovolaemic shock. This is when the victim has lost so much blood that there is not enough left for the circulation to deliver it – and especially the vital oxygen carried by the blood – to the organs.

Normally we have around five liters of blood in our bodies: a loss of more than 10–15% can start to drive the body into shock. After a loss of around 30% someone lying down would be in severe shock; if they were upright and nailed to a cross, a smaller volume might have a proportionately greater effect. Hypovolaemic shock can be caused by both external and internal bleeding. Given the beating that Jesus took beforehand, and the probable loss of blood, it would not take much more to kill him. A friend of mine who is a doctor, explained it like this: "Both internal or external bleeding can cause hypovolaemic shock, and so the spear in Jesus' side and internal bleeding could trigger the whole cycle of organ shutdown, shock and very swift death – if he was not dead already, or close to death."

Jesus died on the cross, that is certainly true. But the beating he took must have been savage. In many ways, the Romans had already executed him before they drove the nails in.

The authors of the gospels and the writers of the Early Church did not dwell on the details of Jesus' crucifixion and, in some ways, one can understand this. Crucifixion was a part of Roman society that all understood, but few wished to dwell upon. What mattered to them was not how Jesus died, but the fact that he chose to do so. And that, perhaps, is what all historians who look into this most brutal of punishments should remember. How Jesus died is one thing; why he died is far more important.

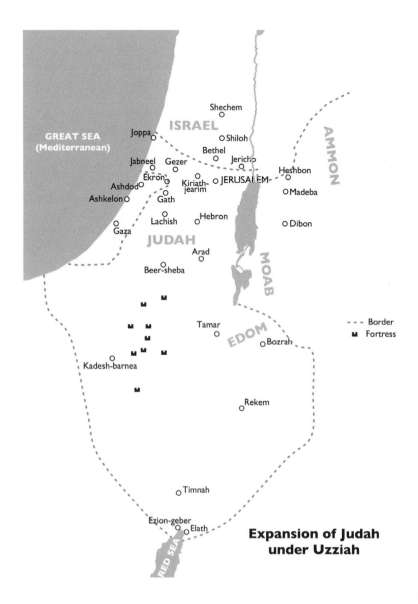

Expansion of Judah under Uzziah

King Uzziah campaigned against the Philistines, building settlements in their territory. He rebuilt the port of Ezion-geber on the Red Sea and established a chain of fortresses in the Sinai wilderness.

WHAT DID UZZIAH'S MACHINES DO?

Let's face it, most of us skip the books of Kings; all those monarchs of Judah and Israel with their unpronounceable names and inability to recognize the claims of God. They're too confusing, too difficult to get your head around. Yet, these books contain some of the most fascinating stories in the Old Testament. You just have to do a bit of digging.

Here's a classic example. It's a king called Azariah, who was also known as Uzziah[1]

> In the twenty-seventh year of King Jeroboam of Israel King Azariah son of Amaziah of Judah began to reign. He was sixteen years old when he began to reign, and he reigned fifty-two years in Jerusalem. His mother's name was Jecoliah of Jerusalem. He did what was right in the sight of the LORD, just as his father Amaziah had done. Nevertheless the high places were not taken away; the people still sacrificed and made offerings on the high places. The LORD struck the king, so that he was leprous to the day of his death, and lived in a separate house. Jotham the king's son was in charge of the palace, governing the people of the land. Now the rest of the acts of Azariah, and all that he did, are they not written in the Book of the Annals of the Kings of Judah? Azariah slept with his ancestors; they buried him with his ancestors in the city of David; his son Jotham succeeded him (2 Kgs. 15.1–7).

Hardly what you'd call high praise. "Could do better" seems to be his "end-of-reign" report. All we know is that he didn't do enough to get rid of false worship, and that he suffered from leprosy. His leprosy made it, at times, impossible for him to fulfil his duties and his son ruled as a kind of deputy-king, overseeing the royal estates and buildings. During the latter part of his father's reign, it is highly likely that Jotham was co-regent.

Yet if we look a little closer, there are some interesting snippets here. For a start, Azariah reigned for a long time – fifty-two years, so it seems rather a short report for such a long reign.

---

[1] 2 Kings 15.13,30,32,34

A quick check in Chronicles reveals more details. And there we find a much richer and more exciting picture. It seems that Azariah/Uzziah was more than just a king with a skin problem who did OK. He was a farmer, town-planner and military strategist. His reign was a golden age for Judah. And apparently he invented the catapult three centuries before the Greeks.

GOOD KING UZZIAH

Uzziah was a young man when he came to the throne. Indeed, he seems to have been propelled into the job as the result of a coup. His father, King Amaziah, had started his reign successfully, with victory over the Edomites. But then he turned away from God, decided to attack King Joash of Israel, was defeated and captured. Joash even marched as far as Jerusalem, destroying a large portion of the walls, looting treasure from the Temple and withdrawing with hostages (2 Chr. 25.20–24). So much for a shared ancestry. Although time passed, the resentment of this defeat doesn't seem to have abated, and a conspiracy grew against Amaziah. He fled to Lachish, but the conspirators pursued him and assassinated him, leaving his sixteen-year-old son, Uzziah, to be placed on the throne of Judah (2 Chr. 25.25–28).

And the thing is, Uzziah was really, really good at being king. He repaired the damage to Jerusalem done by Joash and took control of the southern desert and the Negev. Israel and Judah were at peace with one another and, with the major trade routes passing through their territories, their markets must have been full of goods and their treasuries full of tolls and custom charges. The recapture of Elath was particularly important, since it gave Judah a port on the Red Sea with access to its rich trade routes.[2] The population grew and new settlements were planted.[3] Some of this rebuilding might have been in response to an earthquake which rocked the country, some time in Uzziah's reign (Zech. 14.5). He expanded his territory to the west as well, defeating the Philistines

---

[2]   Ben-Tor, A., and Greenberg, R., *The Archaeology of Ancient Israel*, (New Haven: Yale University Press, 1991), 327.

[3]   Bright, *A History of Israel*, 238–40.

and even building cities in their territory.[4] He also oversaw the formation of a large standing army (2 Chr. 26.11–13).

So this was an astute military strategist, who not only defeated his enemies but successfully occupied their territory. The Chronicles account says "He built towers in the wilderness and hewed out many cisterns." Archeologists have discovered fortress towers dating from this time as well as a seal bearing Uzziah's name, in a cistern. The towers were to protect the trade routes, but may also have served as storehouses for food, or refuges for those tending his large flocks of livestock.[5]

Indeed, Uzziah seems to have been particularly interested in agriculture and farming. Chronicles describes him beautifully as someone who "loved the soil" (2 Chr. 26.10b). The word "love" here does not mean, obviously, a romantic attachment, but has a richer depth. Like "loving" your neighbour, it has an active, practical flavor; it means serving, helping, being of use to. If Uzziah was alive today, he'd be into organic farming in a big way. He was the Prince Charles of his day. He expressed his "love" for agriculture by building irrigation systems in the wilderness. The Bible records that "he had farmers and vine dressers in the hills" (2 Chr. 26.10) which may indicate that he encouraged terraced farming and vineyards. But his innovation extended beyond farming, and here's where the text gets intriguing: "In Jerusalem he set up machines, invented by skilled workers, on the towers and the corners for shooting arrows and large stones. And his fame spread far, for he was marvelously helped until he became strong" (2 Chr. 26.15).

His "skilled workers" invented some kind of machines, which were mounted on towers. But what were they? The Hebrew is obscure; a literal translation would run "devices, the devising of devisers."[6] So a bit of a problem describing them, then.

---

[4] 2 Chronicles 26.6. As the *Word Biblical Commentary* puts it, "The practice of building towns in conquered territories has a striking analog in our own times in the practice of Israel in encouraging Jewish settlements in the Golan and West Bank, territories conquered in the Six-Day War." Dillard, R.B., *2 Chronicles*, (Waco: Word Books, 1987), 208.

[5] Dillard, *2 Chronicles*, 208–209.

[6] Japhet, S., *I & II Chronicles: A Commentary*, (London: SCM, 1993), 883.

Although they are described as "shooting" the stones, it's very unlikely that they were catapults or ballistas. The first primitive catapults were a bit like crossbows, capable of shooting arrows; they don't really make much of an appearance until the third and fourth centuries BC – some four hundred years after the reign of Uzziah.[7] Similarly the ballista (machines capable of hurling great stones) are attributed to Archimedes who used them during the siege of Syracuse (214–212BC).[8] Uzziah inventing these would be like King Charles I inventing the machine gun. If he had, we would expect other nations to have followed suit, but there's no indication of anything like this in Assyrian or Babylonian armies.

So what were they? Well, there are two clues in the verse:

First, they were set up in Jerusalem, so these were defensive devices. Second, they were positioned on "towers and corners", so they were raised up high. This has led the eminent archeologist Yigael Yadin to suggest that what we're talking about are "special structures built on the towers and battlements ... to facilitate the firing of arrows and the casting down of 'great stones'."[9]

The amazing thing is that we might even have a picture of these. In the British Museum are huge relief carvings showing the Assyrian army's assault on Lachish.[10] On a few of the towers you can make out pictures of raised platforms, with rows of shields. Yadin speculates that these are the devices invented by Uzziah's skilled workers. The shields would have allowed the defenders the use of both hands to fire down arrows, while others behind them threw down or dropped heavy stones on the attackers.

Although Lachish eventually fell to the Assyrians, that was not until 701BC, some forty years after Uzziah's death. And, although the Assyrians besieged Jerusalem, it held firm, until a miraculous plague forced the Assyrians to retreat (2 Kgs. 18.13–19.37). An

---

[7] Hacker, B.C. "Greek Catapults and Catapult Technology: Science, Technology, and War in the Ancient World." *Technology and Culture* 9 (1968), 34–50.

[8] Whitehorn, J.N. "The catapult and the ballista." *Greece and Rome* 15 (1946), 49–60. Landels, J.G., *Engineering in the Ancient World*, (London: Constable, 2000), 99ff.

[9] Yadin, *The Art of Warfare in Biblical Lands in the Light of Archaeological Discovery*, 326.

[10] The panels came from the palace of Sennacherib at Nineveh. See also Mitchell, T.C., *The Bible in the British Museum: Interpreting the Evidence*, (London: SCM, 1988), 60–63.

inscription from Sennacherib's palace describes Hezekiah – the king of Judah at that time – as being "shut up in Jerusalem his royal capital like a bird in a cage." But Jerusalem was not captured; the Assyrian records list only one attack on it, so maybe Uzziah's defenses held firm.[11]

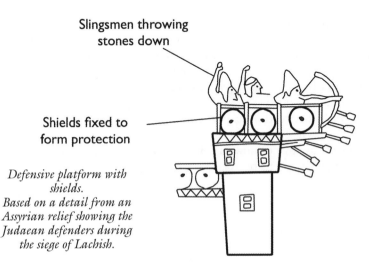

Slingsmen throwing stones down

Shields fixed to form protection

Defensive platform with shields.
Based on a detail from an Assyrian relief showing the Judaean defenders during the siege of Lachish.

LATER YEARS

Uzziah was undoubtedly one of the greatest kings of Judah, yet the irony is that he's not really remembered for his military victories or his agricultural success, or even the "devices, the devising of devisers." What he's remembered for is the leprosy which marred the end of life. The writer of Chronicles links this with a moment of pride, when he took on the role of a priest, offering incense in the Temple.[12] Although the Bible talks about leprosy, the term is

---

[11] Wiseman, D.J., *1 and 2 Kings: An Introduction and Commentary*, (Leicester: Inter-Varsity Press, 1993), 274–276.

[12] Hamilton, V.P., *Handbook on the Historical Books: Joshua, Judges, Ruth, Samuel, Kings, Chronicles, Ezra-Nehemiah, Esther*, (Grand Rapids: Baker Academic, 2001), 452–453.

widely used to cover a range of skin diseases. The effect, though, was that as an unclean man, he could not take part in the worship in the Temple. He was isolated, living apart, while his son, Jotham, took over the administration of the kingdom.[13] His disease meant that, even when he died, he was buried near but not in the royal cemetery.

According to most translations, Uzziah ended his life living in a "separate house" (2 Kgs. 15.5). It paints a picture of isolation, of a successful monarch in a kind of quarantine, kept apart from the rest of his people. It is hard to imagine what that was like for this king, so obviously an active and energetic ruler.

But maybe it wasn't that bad. The literal reading of the Hebrew is "house of freedom"; perhaps, freed from the affairs of state, Uzziah was liberated.[14] Perhaps he had the chance to think, to plan, to dream dreams of new machines and new irrigation systems.

Or maybe just to potter about in his garden.

---

[13] One wonders if it was really as bad as it was made out. Given that both his father and his grandfather had been assassinated, perhaps the leprosy gave the various power cliques of his court a convenient excuse.

[14] Wiseman, *1 and 2 Kings: An Introduction and Commentary*, 251.

HOW OLD WAS JOSEPH?

There's a painting by Guido Reni which shows a baby being held by a very old man, possibly the oldest man in captivity. Looking at this painting, I wondered who it was. The baby's grandfather? His great-grandfather? Father Christmas without his uniform? No, it's Jesus and his adopted father, Joseph.

The painting follows the convention with regard to Joseph: in virtually every nativity scene, he is depicted as an old man. Yet the Bible doesn't give any indication of his age. So how come he's always portrayed as a wrinklie? And what do we actually know about the man who brought up the Son of God?

IN THE BACKGROUND

Joseph isn't mentioned much in the Gospel accounts. Not a single word of his is recorded in any of the gospels and his appearances are mainly confined to the accounts of Jesus' birth:

- He discovers Mary is pregnant (Matt. 1.18–25; Luke 1.26–27)
- He takes Mary to Bethlehem for the birth (Luke 2.1–7)
- He is with Mary when the shepherds visit (Luke 2.8–20)
- He goes with Mary and the baby to Jerusalem (Luke 2.21–24)
- He takes the family into exile in Egypt (Matt. 2.13–15)
- He brings the family back to Israel, then to settle in Nazareth (Matt. 2.19–23)
- When Jesus is twelve, his father and mother are with him in Jerusalem (Luke 2.41–51)
- He is mentioned by people (from Tiberias?) when they find Jesus in Capernaum (John 6.42).

We know that he was a carpenter, or *tekton* (see p.62). We know that he is described as an "upright" or "righteous man" (Matt. 1.19) which indicates that he was a devout Jew, familiar with the teachings of the *Torah*. He was careful, for example, to take Jesus to the Temple after eight days as the law demanded (Luke 2.22–29) and it was his habit to take his family to the Temple each year to observe the Passover (Luke 2.41). We know that he was descended from the royal line of King David; indeed, this pride in both ancient and more recent Jewish heritage can be seen in the names he gives his children: they are named after Bible heroes (Jesus and James are the Greek forms of the names Joshua and Jacob) and also after two heroes of the Maccabean revolt, when Israel gained independence (Judas and Simon).[1]

St. Joseph and the Infant Christ, by Guido Reni. c. 1635

There is nothing in any of this information to indicate that he was an old man. That assumption is an argument from silence – or absence at any rate. It's based on the fact that Joseph was not present at the crucifixion and that he was no longer around to look after his wife. "When Jesus saw his mother and the disciple whom he loved standing beside her, he said to his mother, 'Woman, here is your son.' Then he said to the disciple, 'Here is your mother.' And from that hour the disciple took her into his own home" (John 19.26–27).

So the assumption is that Joseph is dead by that point, which seems reasonable. But remember, we're talking about an event at least thirty years after Jesus' birth. So if he did die, when did he die?

LATER APPEARANCES

One of the reasons that Joseph is regarded as being older is that he is assumed to have been a widower when he married Mary. This

---

[1]   Bernheim, *James, Brother of Jesus*, 33–34.

idea has a long pedigree; a second century apocryphal work called the *Protevangelium of James*, which embellishes the story of the nativity with a series of bizarre episodes, has Joseph refusing to marry Mary with the words "I have sons and am an old man, but she is a girl..."[2]

The *Protevangelium* is clearly a work of fiction, written, probably, to defend Mary's reputation and refute allegations that Jesus was an illegitimate child. It works hard to glorify Mary, portraying her as a kind of female version of the prophet Samuel, dedicated to the Lord and dwelling in the temple. Despite being rejected as apocryphal, the book proved highly popular and played a significant role in establishing the idea of Joseph as an elderly widower with children from a previous marriage.

This depiction, in turn, was used to support the Catholic doctrine of Mary's perpetual virginity. According to this theory, the brothers and sisters of Jesus were actually older step-brothers and step-sisters from Joseph's first marriage. However, the gospels give no reason to believe that Joseph and Mary did not have more children[3] and there is a clear implication that, after the birth of Jesus, Joseph and Mary had a perfectly normal marriage (Matt. 1.25).

Joseph appears again in the story of Jesus being left behind in the Temple: "Now every year his parents went to Jerusalem for the festival of the Passover. And when he was twelve years old, they went up as usual for the festival" (Luke 2.41–43).

If Jesus was born around 4BC, then this means Joseph was still alive in 8AD. A year later, when he was thirteen, Jesus would have come of age and joined his father full-time in the business; although his father would have been teaching him the craft from an early age.[4] We know that Jesus took on his father's trade but whether he worked alongside his father in the family business is uncertain.

By the time Jesus enters his ministry, however, Joseph appears to be more of a memory. The people in Nazareth say: "'Is not this the carpenter, the son of Mary and brother of James and Joses and

---

[2] See James, M.R., *The Apocryphal New Testament*, 42. *Anchor Bible Dictionary*, III, 629–632

[3] See p.90–91

[4] Daniel-Rops, H., and O'Brian, P., *Daily Life in Palestine at the Time of Christ*, (London: Weidenfeld and Nicolson, 1962), 109,113.

Judas and Simon, and are not his sisters here with us?' And they took offense at him" (Mark 6.3).

Joseph is not mentioned, which is significant, since identifying people by the name of their father would be the norm, were that father still alive. The implication, therefore, is that Jesus' father was dead, but his mother was known to the villagers. Certainly to refer to someone as the son of their mother usually indicated that the mother was a widow. Some scholars have argued that to refer to someone as the son of their mother also implied illegitimacy. This can hardly be the case here, unless all of Jesus' brothers and sisters were illegitimate.[5] The likeliest explanation, it seems to me, is that Joseph had died by the time Jesus' ministry started.

HOW OLD?

But none of this, it should be noted, says anything at all about Joseph's age. It doesn't say that there was anything different or unusual about the engagement of Joseph to Mary. The normal age of marrying for a Jewish man in New Testament times would have been about sixteen (and about fourteen for a woman). And so far we've seen nothing in any of the gospel texts that means we should think that Joseph was an old man. In particular it seems to be an argument based on life expectancy from a different age. He must have been old when Jesus was born, because he had died by the time Jesus was thirty.

It would have been perfectly feasible for a man to marry at sixteen years old in 4BC, and to be dead by 30AD. In fact, it would probably have been the norm. Life expectancy in Israel was low. Today, for example, we think of thirty as young, so when we read that Jesus was "about thirty years of age" when he began his ministry (Luke 3.23) we imagine a young man in his prime. However, in Jesus' time he would have been considered at the very least mature, and more likely getting on a bit. Some experts believe that very few people, maybe as low as 3%, survived to the age of sixty and that

---

[5] Brown, *The Birth of the Messiah*, 540–541. Gundry, *Mark: A Commentary on His Apology for the Cross*, 290–291.

90% were dead by their mid-forties.[6] Hence, perhaps some of the surprise of people who knew him: fancy starting the life of a preacher at his age!

Joseph worked in a hard manual profession. He came from a background of poverty, rather than wealth. He lived in what we today would consider unsanitary conditions. If he married Mary at sixteen and lived to a normal life span, he would have been dead around 20AD; ten years before Jesus had what many onlookers considered to be a late-mid-life crisis.

To sum up; there is no reason to suppose that Joseph was old when Jesus was born. On the contrary, he may only have been a couple of years older than Mary, a young lad by our standards. Which means two things: first that most of the nativity scenes in Western art are wrong and second, that his maturity and willingness to adopt the Son of God are all the more remarkable.

---

[6] Vermès, G., *The Changing Faces of Jesus*, (London: Penguin, 2000), 151–152. Crossan, *The Historical Jesus: The Life of a Mediterranean Jewish Peasant*, (Edinburgh: Clark, 1993), 4.

The Appian Way in Rome. In Roman times this was the main southern route into the city. Paul would have been brought along this road from the "Three Taverns" some thirty miles south (Acts 28.15).

WHAT BOOKS DID PAUL WANT BROUGHT TO HIM IN ROME?

Paul is in Rome. Miserable and abandoned, he feels as though the end is near. In a heartfelt letter to Timothy, his "son", he shares his fears and his feelings: he is being poured out like a drink offering (2 Tim. 4.6). He has had some sort of hearing at which everyone has deserted him and now he is convinced he is facing the end.[1] Then, towards the end of the letter, he suddenly springs a request: "When you come, bring the cloak that I left with Carpus at Troas, also the books, and above all the parchments" (2 Tim. 4.13). Which raises a lot of questions. Who is Carpus?[2] What is so important about the parchments? And why does Paul want his cloak?

Let's look at the situation. Paul is under arrest in Rome. He has had some kind of "hearing" which has gone very badly. He has been deserted and abandoned by some people (2 Tim. 4.10a), while others are apparently absent on other business. Only Luke is with him (2 Tim. 4.11) but he urges Timothy to send Mark. It is as if he is gathering the oldest, most trusted team around him.

So he calls for his friends to come and help him at this crucial time. And he asks them to bring some written documents with them: "the books and the parchments."

What might these have been? Some scholars have suggested that the scrolls were copies of the Hebrew Scriptures – what we would call the Old Testament – which Paul needed for reference. But this doesn't make sense. He's in Rome, and in Rome you can get almost anything you want. Even if he couldn't buy them, he could consult the Scriptures in the synagogues if he wanted (or send Luke to do it for him). Every synagogue had a library which would have contained the *Torah* (the five books of Moses), the

---

[1] 2 Timothy has often been relegated to the status of a pseudepigraphal letter – one attributed to Paul, but not actually written by him. This is not the place to argue in detail against this view, but, as a writer, if there is one thing that convinces me of its authenticity, it is this small detail. If you were fabricating a letter by Paul, one of the great heroes of early Christianity, would you present him as a worried, uncertain figure, anxious about stuff he left at Troas? If you were creating a character for propaganda purposes, would you think to include something as mundane as a request for a cloak? This passage is either genuine, or it's the work of one of the greatest novelists of the ancient world. For a fuller, more detailed and generally more brainy defense, see Witherington III, B., *Letters and Homilies for Hellenized Christians* (Nottingham: IVP Academic, 2006), 26–38, 301–305.

[2] All we know of Carpus is that he was a resident of Troas. Presumably he was Christian and it may have been in his house that the church at Troas met.

scrolls of the *Haftara* (the biblical books read during the service to aid exposition of the *Torah*), and at least one scroll of the Psalms. There were probably other texts there as well, such as non-canonical writings like Enoch and Baruch.[3]

Paul may not have been flavor of the month among the Jews but there must have been ways in which he could have found out the information. In fact, if they were any kind of famous, published books, he wouldn't have needed to have them sent from Troas. He could have sourced them in Rome. So what could they have been?

THE BIBLIA AND THE MEMBRANAE

Paul mentions two different types of written media in this verse: *biblia* and *membranae*.

Biblia literally means "books" (and is the root of our modern word Bible). In Paul's day it meant scrolls such as those housed in a library. It is also used of secular, civil documents, such as the certificate of divorce (Matt.19.7; Mark 10.4), as well as of the writings of the Hebrew Scriptures.

Membranae means "parchment" – the skin of sheep or goats which made a more durable writing material than a papyrus scroll. However, although this letter is written in Greek, the word is actually a Latin word and referred to small notebooks of parchment which people would carry with them. They were the kind of thing someone might write everyday notes in, or a poet use to draw up the first drafts.[4] The notebook consisted of several small sheets of parchment, loosely held by leather bands, a bit like a loose-leaf file.

Originally made, as in Paul's letter, of parchment, some time in the first century someone got the idea that you could make membranae out of papyrus. They folded sheets of papyrus and sewed through the spine. These are called codices (or codex in the singular) and they are the same basic format as the book you have

---

[3]   Thiede, *The Cosmopolitan World of Jesus: New Findings From Archaeology*, 111. This is what happened at Beroea – the Jews in the synagogue listened to Paul and then studied the Scriptures to make up their own minds. In other words, they went to their own theological research library.

[4]   Roberts, C.H. "Books in the Graeco-Roman World and the New Testament" in *Cambridge History of the Bible*, (Cambridge: Cambridge University Press, 1970), I, 53.

Scroll (left) and codex (right). Scrolls were long sheets of papyrus, with writing on one side. A codex was made by taking sheets of parchment or papyrus, folding them, and putting a stitch through the middle to bind it. Codices could also have wooden covers affording them more protection.

in your hand. In other words, when someone took some papyrus sheets, folded them and sewed them together, then wrote on both sides of the page, they invented, in fact, the book.

This new invention took a long time to catch on in the Græco-Roman world. For them, *membranae* were not proper books. Only scrolls were "proper" books. And so the notebooks were relegated to the status of informal, unimportant documents.

Except among one group of people.

CHRISTIANS AND THEIR NOTEBOOKS

One of the remarkable things about Christian literature from the second and third centuries is that it is virtually all from codices. In the Græco-Roman and Jewish traditions, the scroll was ubiquitous; everything was written on a scroll, but Christians used books.

We have some fourteen fragments of Christian literature from the first half of the second century (100–150AD). All of these came from codices. When you compare this to Græco-Roman literature of the same period, only 2.5% is in codex form.[5] Of the remains of Greek books that can be dated earlier than 200AD, more than 98 percent are scrolls; in the same period the surviving Christian books are almost all codices. In fact, it wasn't until the fourth century that the codex use equalled that of the scroll in the wider Græco-Roman

---

5   Gregory, C.R., *Canon and Text of the New Testament*, (Edinburgh: T. & T. Clark, 1907), 322–323.

world. What this shows is that the Christians, for some reason, adopted the use of the codex almost exclusively, in direct contrast to the general expectations of the culture around them.[6]

Given the fact that Christians were choosing to use the codex much more than non-Christians, some scholars have argued that it was a Christian who first folded papyrus and "invented" the book: "Where and by whom the idea was first tried out we do not know; but we do now know that the new form [i.e. the papyrus codex] is directly connected with the earliest days of Christianity and that the inventor may actually have been a Christian."[7]

Why did they do this? We have already seen that the Græco-Roman world didn't view the codex as a "proper" book, yet Christians chose this medium to communicate the most important message they had. Scholars have suggested many reasons why they might have used this innovative new communication method. Some have suggested it could be more easily hidden, or that it offered easier access to the contents. The codex could be held in one hand, leaving the other free to make notes or mark a place. Codices were often bound with wooden covers, which gave the contents more protection. All of those are possible advantages, but they don't really explain why the Early Church made the decision to use this form of media to the total exclusion of the scroll.

I think that there were two main reasons why the first Christians chose the codex form to transmit their teaching.

Firstly, *membranae* were common among craftsmen and traders, who used them as everyday notebooks. Many of the people in the Early Church were from this background – free craftspeople, artisans and small traders, who had some wealth and therefore the ability to travel – they would have been used to this form. It was their media; they understood it.[8] More than that, the language in these early codices was *koine* Greek; the type of Greek spoken by ordinary tradesmen and workers. Christianity made a deliberate

---

[6] Gamble, H.Y., *Books and Readers in the Early Church: A History of Early Christian Texts*, (New Haven: Yale University Press, 1995), 49.

[7] Skeat, T.C, and Elliot, J.K., *The Collected Biblical Writings of T. C. Skeat*, (Leiden: Brill, 2004), 46.

[8] Gamble, *Books and Readers in the Early Church: A History of Early Christian Texts*, 5.

choice to use the language and the media of the ordinary working people of the society around them.[9]

But many scholars believe that perhaps the main reason that Christians used the codex is that they were continuing a tradition which had been established by the most important leaders of their church. They used the codex, because that was the form in which their first Scriptures were recorded. These Scriptures could have been the gospels, or Mark's first record of Peter's reminiscences. However, the earliest writings in the New Testament are not the gospels, but letters written by Paul.

Paul's letters were collected and passed around the church at a very early date. The letters themselves date from around 48/9AD with Galatians, with Thessalonians written a little while later. But at some point the letters were collected and copied to become the first Scriptures of the young church (see 2 Peter 3.15–16). Any collection of Paul's letters – even if we reduce it to those whose authorship is undisputed – would be too long for a scroll. But they could be contained in a codex. Whereas the outside of a scroll was left blank, a codex used both sides of the paper, offering greater storage capacity.[10] So the Early Church, perhaps, brought together Paul's letters – their first Scriptures – in a codex; and from then on, almost in tribute, passed on all their teaching in this new, vernacular form.

BACK TO THE NOTEBOOKS

Which brings us back to the notebooks of Paul. We've seen that they must have contained personal information, since that's what membranae were used for. We've seen that the Early Church preserved a tradition of recording their teaching in the codex – the successor to the parchment notebooks mentioned here. We've seen that Paul is drawing things together, bringing his trusted friends around him and preparing for the end.

It seems likely, therefore, that what he's doing is collecting together his life's work. The scrolls may be official documents,

---

[9] Lee, G.M. "The Books and the Parchments: Studies in Texts: 2 Timothy 4:13." *Theology* 74 (1971), 169.

[10] Quoted in Casson, L. *Libraries in the Ancient World*, (New Haven: Yale University Press, 2002), 124.

perhaps to do with his citizenship, or evidence that he would want to present at a trial. And perhaps the *membranae* contained drafts or copies of the letters that he had sent out over the years. He was preparing to have them copied so that they could be passed on. This would explain how, before the end of the century, a collection of his letters was already circulating in the Christian church.[11]

AND DON'T FORGET THE COAT

A final note about the cloak. The type of cloak mentioned here – a *phailonen* in Greek – was a rough, thick cloak, with a hole in the middle to put your head through, like a poncho. Paul left it in Troas, a port which featured in most of his journeys. Given that traveling by ship sometimes meant having to leave in a hurry (because the wind had changed) and traveling light, it is understandable that he wouldn't necessarily take everything with him. It may have been a special cloak, one he made himself, given the fact that, as a tent maker, he would have been able to weave goats hair.[12]

Or it may not have been a cloak at all. Some scholars think that this doesn't mean "cloak" in this context, but a kind of leather book bag or case for documents. This would make sense in light of the later request. "Bring the bag," Paul is saying, "the one with the documents and the notebooks."[13]

Whatever the case, this verse reminds us of the lengths to which Paul – and others – were willing to go to get the message of Jesus out to the world around them. They were willing to travel as far as they could, talk with whoever would listen, to tell them the good news of Christ.

And they would happily break with tradition where it suited them. They talked in ordinary language of the extraordinary events, and they wrote it down in an innovative form of media, one which the sophisticated people looked down on, but ordinary people understood.

---

[11] Witherington, *Letters and Homilies for Hellenized Christians*, 379.

[12] Still, T.D. "Did Paul Loathe Manual Labor? Revisiting the Work of Ronald F. Hock on the Apostle's Tentmaking and Social Class," *Journal of Biblical Literature* 124 (2006), 781.

[13] Thiede, *The Cosmopolitan World of Jesus: New Findings From Archaeology*, 103.

WHAT WAS SO SPECIAL ABOUT JOSEPH'S COAT?

As I write this, there are a number of men on television trying to be Joseph. In the programme *Any Dream Will Do*, unknown, talented singers are in a weekly competition to star in a new production of *Joseph and his Amazing Technicolor Dreamcoat*. There, the winner will don his "amazing coat of many colors", the coat, which according to the song was "red and ocher and crimson and gold and scarlet and bronze and white with a hint of mauve; and magnolia and fuchsia and purply-brown and…" well, you get the idea.

It's one of the most, if not *the* most famous garment in history. It's up there with the ruby slippers and the little red riding hood, but, as we investigate what it may have looked like, we come to one inescapable conclusion. Andrew Lloyd Webber may be a Lord. He may be a multi-millionaire with a string of hits to his name. He may be an expert in Pre-Raphaelite art.

But he knows diddly-squat about Bronze Age Mesopotamian fashion.

I'LL GET MY KETONET PASSIM

The description of "a coat with many colors" comes from the King James Version:

> And Jacob dwelt in the land wherein his father was a stranger, in the land of Canaan. These are the generations of Jacob. Joseph, being seventeen years old, was feeding the flock with his brethren; and the lad was with the sons of Bilhah, and with the sons of Zilpah, his father's wives: and Joseph brought unto his father their evil report. Now Israel [Isaac] loved Joseph more than all his children, because he was the son of his old age: and he made him a coat of many colors. And when his brethren saw that their father loved him more than all his brethren, they hated him, and could not speak peaceably unto him. (Gen. 37.1–4)

The KJV took this from the Septuagint (the Latin translation of
the Old Testament) which translated the word in the sense of
"variegated." This is the sense that has survived, with popular
depictions of the coat showing it as having many different colored
stripes.[1] Later translations, however, show a much wider range of
descriptions:

- "a richly ornamented robe" NIV
- "a robe of many colors" ESV
- "a fancy coat" CEV
- "a long robe with sleeves" NRSV

In the commentaries, scholars take a similarly wide range of
interpretations:

- "a special tunic" [2]
- "an ornamented tunic" [3]
- "a long colorful tunic" [4]
- "a sleeved tunic" [5]

Why so much variety? Well, it's not just that the Hebrew phrase
– *ketonet passim* – is obscure, it's also a reflection of the fact that
we don't know much about ancient Israelite or Canaanite fashion.
Because it's organic matter, clothing decays, so archeological
discoveries are rare.[6] What archeological records we have come
mainly from statues and relief carvings, from nations around
Israel.

Perhaps the best depiction comes from an ivory carving found
in Megiddo. This dates from the 13th century BC and shows naked
prisoners being brought before a king. There is a figure in front of
him which is either a princess or a priest or a prince – depending
on which book you read. The prince/priest/priestess wears a

---

[1]   Von Rad, G. *Genesis: A Commentary*, (London: SCM, 1972), 351.

[2]   Wenham, *Genesis 16–50*, 346.

[3]   Speiser, E.A., *Genesis*, (Garden City: Doubleday, 1964), 287.

[4]   Hamilton, Victor P., *Book of Genesis: Chapters 18–50* (Grand Rapids: Eerdmans, 1995), 403.

[5]   Westermann, C., and Scullion, J., *Genesis 37–50: A Commentary*, (London: SPCK, 1987), 32.

[6]   See Barber, E.J.W., *Prehistoric Textiles: The Development of Cloth in the Neolithic and Bronze Ages with Special Reference to the Aegean*, (Princeton: Princeton University Press, 1990), 165–167.

decorated head covering and a "decorated cloak that covers their arms to the wrists."[7]

Obviously, the ivory is not colored but we can get an idea of what colors were available from the few small scraps of cloth that archeologists have recovered. There are some traces of a red dye used on thread, plus traces of a blue, white and red fabric from a Philistine temple. In Egypt, archeologists have discovered bright yellow mummy cloths, and there are colored Egyptian linens from around 1500BC – red, green, yellow, blue, brown and black.[8] Dyes came mostly from plants such as safflower, saffron, madder and a range of plants which produced indigo. The shells of sea snails were crushed to produce purple; indeed, if I had to hazard a guess as to the color of Joseph's coat, I'd go for purple. Purple was the costliest dye, and it was reserved for the wealthy and the powerful. Twelve thousand murex snails were required to yield 1.4 grams of pure dye.[9] It was a sign of status. The clothes of the high priests were adorned with purple, as were the curtains in the Tabernacle. It would have come from the Phoenician coast; the names "Canaan" and "Phoenicia" probably mean "purple."[10]

To return to the Hebrew phrase; *ketonet* indicates that it was some kind of garment, but the problem is working out what *passim* means.

One argument is that it's a coat with gold ornaments sewn onto it. These were ceremonial robes, which were decorated with gold rosettes, leaves, discs and other designs, and embroidered with gold thread.[11] Others argue that rather than meaning "color", *passim* refers to the length of the coat, from "pas" meaning extremity, such as the sole of the foot or the palm of the hand.[12] What we have

---

[7] Mazar, B., Avi-Yonah, M. and Malamat, A., *Views of the Biblical World*, (Oxford: Oxford University Press, 1958), 126.

[8] Barber, *Prehistoric Textiles: The Development of Cloth in the Neolithic and Bronze Ages with Special Reference to the Aegean*, 224.

[9] Durham, *Exodus*, 354.

[10] Canaan may derive from the Akkadian *kinahhu* meaning red-purple; while Phoenicia probably comes from the Greek for "dark red", *phoinos*. See King and Stager, *Life in Biblical Israel*, 160–161.

[11] Speiser, *Genesis*, 290. Oppenheim, A.L. "The Golden Garments of the Gods." *Journal of Near Eastern Studies* 8 (1949), 172–193.

[12] Brenner, *Samuel and Kings*, 66. Hamilton, *Book of Genesis: Chapters 18–50*, 409.

here, then, may be a coat with long sleeves, as in the translation
in the NRSV. The same type of coat, perhaps, as we see in the ivory
carving from Megiddo.

This also links in with an Egyptian tomb painting showing a
Canaanite delegation bringing tribute, found in Thebes and dating
from c.1800BC. The Canaanites, presumably dressed in their finery,
are shown wearing long-sleeved fitted garments.[13]

Joseph's coat, therefore, may not have been that highly colored
It may, instead, have had very long sleeves. This implies that it was
clearly not a work coat. As Von Rad says, "it was a luxury which
only those who did not have to work could think of having."[14]

Exactly. Because the main thing about Joseph's coat is not so
much what it looked like, but what it implied.

POWER DRESSING

Ketonet appears in the Bible some 29 times. Twenty of these refer
to some kind of priestly garment, a woven linen "tunic" that was
worn by Aaron and his sons (e.g. Ex. 39.27–28; Lev. 8.7, 13).[15]
It was not, however, solely a priestly garment. Here are the other
wearers of the *ketonet*

- Adam and Eve get a *ketonet* of skins to wear when they are
  expelled from Eden (Gen. 3.21).
- Hushai the Archite, a high-ranking member of David's court,
  wears one (2 Sam. 15.32).
- Isaiah talks of the *ketonet* being removed from Shebna, master
  of the household, and given to Eliakim son of Hilkiah (Isa.
  22.15–25).
- Job talks about God binding himself to Job, as close as the
  neck of his *ketonet*.

---

[13] Hamilton, *Book of Genesis: Chapters 18–50*, 409.

[14] Von Rad, *Genesis: A Commentary*, 351.

[15] This also ties in with the depiction from Megiddo – if the wearer is a priest.

What all these have in common is that the *ketonet* implies some kind of high status.[16] The ketonet is associated with high rank, with priestly importance, or with great wealth and status. Jacob, by giving this coat to his favorite son, is raising him above the others.

Most importantly, there is one other use of the phrase *ketonet passim* in the Bible, and it occurs in the grisly tale of the rape of Tamar, a royal princess and daughter of David. Tamar has been lured to her half-brother's bedside, believing that he was ill. There he violently rapes her. After the act is done, he just wants to throw her out

> Then Amnon was seized with a very great loathing for her; indeed, his loathing was even greater than the lust he had felt for her. Amnon said to her, "Get out!" But she said to him, "No, my brother; for this wrong in sending me away is greater than the other that you did to me." But he would not listen to her. He called the young man who served him and said, "Put this woman out of my presence, and bolt the door after her." (Now she was wearing a long robe with sleeves; for this is how the virgin daughters of the king were clothed in earlier times.) So his servant put her out, and bolted the door after her. But Tamar put ashes on her head, and tore the long robe that she was wearing; she put her hand on her head, and went away, crying aloud as she went (2 Sam. 13.15–19).

And what is she wearing? A *ketonet passim*, a "long robe with sleeves" (NRSV), or a "richly ornamented robe" (NIV); the robe of an unmarried princess.

Of course, it's not the same for Joseph (he was unmarried, but as far as I'm aware no-one has yet claimed he was a princess.) But the point that the writer of the Joseph story is making is that Isaac gives his son a royal robe, perhaps even a priestly robe. It's not just an elevation in the fashion stakes, it's an elevation in status.[17]

---

[16] Brenner, *Samuel and Kings*, 75.

[17] Kidner, D., *Genesis: An Introduction and Commentary*, (London: Tyndale Press, 1967), 180.

FASHION DISASTER

One interesting sidelight more. The story of Tamar also shows how wearing the ketonet is often linked with disaster. In the list above, all the mentions are associated with something bad going on: Adam and Eve are expelled from Eden; Hushai is grieving as David is forced to flee Jerusalem; Shebna will be "thrown" into a far country to die in disgrace; Job is sitting on a rubbish heap, having lost everything. Tamar, of course, has been raped and abandoned. And Joseph is thrown into a well, then sold into slavery. In all, out of the eight non-priests who wear the ketonet – Adam, Eve, Hushai, Shebna, Eliakim, Job, Tamar, Joseph – only Eliakim is not associated with disaster. Even if we look on it as a priestly garment, two of Aaron's sons – Nadab and Abihu – are consumed with fire when offering an incorrect offering (Lev 10.1). And Aaron himself is involved in the creation of the golden calf (Exod. 32) and the complaints against Moses (Num. 12). Like Moses, he never made it to the promised land.

The "coat of many colors", as it is commonly portrayed, is seen as a splendid coat, a coat that signifies love, even if that love is partial and misguided. To Jacob and Joseph and their family it signified that the favored son was now top-dog; that he did not need to work like the others, that he was head of the clan.

But to the listeners, perhaps the *ketonet passim* signified something else entirely. Perhaps it signified that doom was coming. Whatever it looked like, it meant disaster for anyone who wore it.

HOW DID PETER GET IN THE COURTYARD?

It's dead of night. The city of Jerusalem is quiet – well quieter than usual, although no city of the time was really quiet at any time. Suddenly, climbing up through the narrow streets comes an arresting party, torches aflame, weapons clanking and jangling. In the midst of them, hidden perhaps by a throng of guards, is Jesus, the teacher whom they have cornered in an olive grove on the other side of the city. The party rush him up to the gates of a large house, which are opened for them. Inside, beyond the gate, the courtyard looks crowded: it is clear no-one is asleep in that house tonight. The arresting party continue through the gates, which are closed behind them.

A few moments later, through the shadows, some other men come forward. One of them walks straight up to the gate and is allowed through. The other looks alarmed and scared. He wants to enter the courtyard, to see what is going to happen. But the gates are closed.

How on earth is he going to get in?

BACKSTAGE PASS

The story of Peter's denial of Jesus is one of the most important episodes in the last week of Jesus' life on earth. The tale of this great servant's denial of Christ and his eventual reinstatement has inspired, comforted and strengthened the church for two thousand years. We have all been there and, like Peter, we can all be forgiven, we can all be reinstated.

We are familiar with the setting: Peter is in the courtyard of the high priest's house, warming himself at the fire, when the denial takes place. But there is one mystery about the event: how did he get into the courtyard in the first place? How was it that a fisherman from Galilee, a supporter of the man who has just been arrested, gets allowed through security? Who provided him with access? Who gave him the backstage pass?

When Jesus was arrested, Peter at first resisted. He struck off the ear of the slave of the high priest (Luke 22.50; John 18.10) before being stopped by Jesus. Then, according to Mark at least,

These steps, by the church of St Peter Gallicantu (left), date from Roman times. They led from the upper city to the lower city of Jerusalem, and the Kidron Valley. Jesus may well have been taken this way on the night of his arrest, since the high priest's house would have been in the upper city.

Although some Christians venerate the site as the place of Peter's denial ("Gallicantu" is Latin for "cock crow") the house of Caiaphas would probably have been at the top of the hill, where luxurious houses from the Herodian period have been found.

"All of them deserted him and fled" (Mark 14.50). It's not hard to see why they flee: they were scared. It's one thing to take on the servant of the high priest; it's another thing to take on a load of soldiers. Understandably, they thought that they, too, would be arrested and killed. So they ran.

But Peter, as so often in the gospels, does a very brave thing: one of the bravest things this big-hearted man ever did: he stops running. He turns around and follows the arrest party, at a distance, right up to the gates of the high priest's residence.

We must imagine that the whole event takes place in an atmosphere of high security. Remember, it's the early hours of the morning; the night before Passover. The arrest has happened at night, because Caiaphas, the high priest, does not want the crowd to interfere. Indeed, things have been timed specifically so that "the crowds" could not protect Jesus. As Mark tells it: "It was two days before the Passover and the festival of Unleavened Bread. The chief priests and the scribes were looking for a way to arrest Jesus by stealth and kill him; for they said, 'Not during the festival, or there may be a riot among the people'" (Mark 14.1–2).

The last thing the high priest would want is for anything to spoil the plans. Jesus must be arrested, tried and executed before the festival and before support can be rallied. Given this urgency, the last thing that the high priest wants is for any of Jesus' supporters to disrupt proceedings. And yet, in the midst of this, Peter, one of the most visible of Jesus' supporters, gets into the courtyard. How?

John gives us the answer – or an answer at least: he was let in by "another disciple"

> Simon Peter and another disciple followed Jesus. Since that disciple was known to the high priest, he went with Jesus into the courtyard of the high priest, but Peter was standing outside at the gate. So the other disciple, who was known to the high priest, went out, spoke to the woman who guarded the gate, and brought Peter in. The woman said to Peter, "You are not also one of this man's disciples, are you?" He said, "I am not" (John 18.15–17).

So Peter, we are told, was accompanied on that journey across Jerusalem. He was with someone who knew the high priest. Someone who was trusted enough to vouch for Peter. Someone who was known to be a follower of Jesus.

But who?

SOME BIBLICAL PROFILING

We know that it was a disciple but that doesn't have to mean one of "the twelve." The twelve disciples were a core group, a subset of a much larger band of disciples who had decided to follow Jesus. As we have seen there were at least 72 of these in the wider group who were with Jesus in Galilee (Luke 10.1). But there were others elsewhere, including friends like Lazarus, "secret admirers" like Nicodemus and Joseph of Arimathea, and even converts such as Zacchaeus. There were women supporters as well, some of whom were present at the crucifixion, having followed Jesus up to Jerusalem from Galilee (Mk 15.40–41). Indeed, some of these women were influential, such as Joanna the wife of Chuza, the manager of Herod Antipas's household (Luke 8.1–3). So it could have been any of these disciples.

I always like that bit in crime thrillers, when the psychologist builds up a "profile" of the suspect they are chasing. Offender profiling is now a standard part of police procedure, but what we need here is a bit of "disciple profiling"; we need to build up a picture of the type of person this disciple was.

1. The disciple was male.
Some writers have suggested that the disciple was female (usually Mary Magdalene – who generally gets suggested for everything). We have seen that Jesus had female supporters and some of these were with him during the toughest times and certainly a woman would not have been likely to have been arrested (see point 5 below). But the problem is that, in the gospels, those referred to as "disciples" do not appear to be female. This is not because women didn't do what disciples do – the gospels show women who are every bit as courageous and committed as men – it's because disciple is a

masculine term.[1] So, if it had been a woman, I don't think John would have – or could have – used the word "disciple."

2. The disciple was known to the high priest.
The account is clear that the high priest knew this disciple. The word "known" (*gnostos*) means more than just personal acquaintance; it denotes personal knowledge and even friendship. Whoever this man was, he knew the high priest well enough to gain immediate and uncontested access to his residence.[2] So, he may have been a high-standing resident of Jerusalem; or he may have had some previous contact with the high priest.

3. The disciple was known to be a follower of Jesus.
The woman who lets Peter in says to him "You are not also one of this man's disciples, are you?" (John 18.17). The verse implies that she knew that the other disciple was a follower of Jesus. So we're looking for someone who, within the household of Caiaphas at least, was known to be an associate of Jesus of Nazareth.

4. The disciple was not a threat.
Even though he is known to be a disciple, he is not perceived as a threat in any way. This disciple moves about freely, whereas it seems that if Peter had answered "Yes" to the question he would either have been refused entrance or possibly arrested.[3] The doorkeeper's job was to screen the people entering the premises. A servant might fill this role, and in large, wealthy establishments there would have been a full-time porter. They were security, asking peoples' identity and observing those going in and out of the premises. The woman

---

[1]   As one writer has put it "During his public ministry Jesus indeed had committed female followers but there was literally no feminine noun that could be used to describe them; there was no noun that said 'female disciples.'" Even Luke, who is generally very favorable towards women, doesn't call any of them disciples in his gospel (although he does in Acts). See Meier, J.P., *A Marginal Jew: Rethinking the Historical Jesus*, (New York: Doubleday, 1991), 40, 73ff.

[2]   Kruse, C.G., *The Gospel According to John: An Introduction and Commentary*, (Leicester: Inter-Varsity Press, 2003), 353. Abbott, E.A., (1913), *Miscellenea Evangelica I*, (Cambridge: Cambridge University Press, 1913), 29–30.

[3]   Brown, R.E., *The Gospel According to John*, (London: Geoffrey Chapman, 1971), II 822–23.

obviously knew and trusted the first disciple, but asked questions of Peter – questions that were not friendly.[4]

5. The disciple was not likely to be arrested.
The main reason why everyone else ran away was because they were likely to be arrested. Yet this disciple, known to be a follower of Jesus, walks straight in to the courtyard without fear of being arrested. So we are looking for someone who is "bulletproof", someone who will not be arrested.

6. The disciple couldn't be named.
John does not name the person. Yet he names many other disciples of Jesus. So either he didn't know the name, or there are reasons why he cannot or will not name him.

So much for the profile. How does that fit the main candidates?

THE SUSPECTS

First, we can rule out most, if not all of "the twelve" as well as prominent "out-of-town" disciples, such as Lazarus. They would have failed on points 4, 5 and 6. Particularly Lazarus, whom we know that the high priest and the other leaders wanted dead (John 12.10).

But we can't rule out all of them, because many people believe that the disciple is the author of the fourth gospel. The author of John's gospel is never explicitly identified; authorship of the fourth gospel is generally ascribed to the person who describes himself throughout as "the beloved disciple." Here, our suspect is called "another disciple", so is it, perhaps, the same person?

From very early on, the "beloved disciple" and author of the gospel was identified as someone called "John" – usually John the apostle. If we go with this identification, however, we have to believe that a fisherman from Galilee was a personal friend of the high priest. This seems highly unlikely. Some have claimed that John might have been from a priestly family like Zechariah, the

---

4   Keener, C.S., *The Gospel of John: A Commentary*, (Peabody: Hendrickson Publishers, 2003), 1091.

father of John the Baptist, and that he therefore served occasional duty in the Temple. But how likely is it that a part-time priest who served for two weeks each year would have known the high priest? Others have suggested that John's fishing business supplied the house of the high priest with dried fish.[5] It doesn't seem very likely to me that the high priest would be on friendly terms with the dried fish merchant. And anyway, John the Apostle fails the test on points 4 and 5. Further, Mark tells us that the disciples ran away. He doesn't mention John returning with Peter, which he surely would have, if he was recording Peter's reminiscences.

But what if the "beloved disciple" wasn't John the apostle? Others have challenged this identification, not least because John appears elsewhere in the gospel – albeit obliquely – as one of the sons of Zebedee (John 21.2). Given that the gospel generally reflects the stories of those outside of the twelve, it is entirely possible that the gospel was the work of a different disciple altogether – not one of the twelve apostles, but one of the many other people who are disciples of Jesus. The prime candidate here is a man called John the Elder, who lived in Asia Minor in the first century and who is described by an early Christian called Papias as one of the disciples of the Lord.[6]

I suppose John the Elder could have known the high priest. But the real question in this case is whether the "other disciple, who was known to the high priest" is the same as the "beloved disciple." I'm not at all sure that he is. For one thing, the writer of the gospel is generally very precise about the use of this name. In the five other episodes where he "appears" (John 13.23–24; 19.26–27; 20.2–4,8; 21.7,20–24).[7] each time he makes it clear that he is the disciple that Jesus loved.

For example, when Mary runs to tell the disciples that the stone has been moved, he is introduced in the following way: "So she ran

---

[5]   Kruse plumps for John, son of Zebedee and argues that his father was prosperous enough to employ hired hands: Kruse, *The Gospel According to John: An Introduction and Commentary*, 353. Brown argues, rather drily, that this is "imaginative, but hardly persuasive." Brown, *The Death of the Messiah*, 597.

[6]   Richard Bauckham, in his book *Jesus and the Eyewitnesses,* has made a compelling and brilliant case for John the Elder to be the author of the gospel.

[7]   Some argue that he is also the unnamed disciple who is called by Jesus in John 1.35ff.

and went to Simon Peter and the other disciple, the one whom Jesus loved, and said to them, 'They have taken the Lord out of the tomb, and we do not know where they have laid him'" (John 20.2).

So each time it's clear. We're not left wondering who this other disciple is. But not in the trial story; in the trial story it is just "another disciple." If it were the beloved disciple, why is he not identified? Why this vagueness?[8]

Not only that, but the action hardly fits with the actions of this "other disciple." Elsewhere he is a more reflective, not to say reserved character. It is Peter who jumps out of the boat when Jesus appears on the shore, the "other disciple" waits in the boat; it is Peter who rushes straight into the tomb, the "other disciple" waits outside. Yet here, we are asked to believe that he marches straight ahead into the dragon's den. So, in that sense at least, it is almost as if the writer of the gospel is sending out a message; this is *not* the beloved disciple, he's not clearly identified as such, nor does he act in the same way.[9]

OTHER CANDIDATES

So if it wasn't the "beloved disciple", who was it? Let's look at some more candidates.

If we are looking for high-ranking, socially significant followers of Jesus, who moved in the same social and political circles as the high priest, people such as Joseph of Arimathea or Nicodemus might be candidates.

Joseph of Arimathea would certainly have been known to the high priest, but John describes him as "a disciple of Jesus, though a secret one because of his fear of the Jews" (John 19.38). The Jews here – and elsewhere in John (e.g. 7.13; 12.42–3) – means the Jewish authorities. So Joseph fails point 3 because the person who let Peter in was *known to be a follower of Jesus*. The serving girl knew; everyone knew. Nicodemus is probably ruled out for the same reason, and also because you have to ask why John doesn't

---

[8] See Keener, *The Gospel of John: A Commentary*, 1091.

[9] Abbott, *Miscellenea Evangelica I*, 20–23.

name them. He is not coy about describing their role in the burial of Jesus, so why not here?[10]

The reason that the disciple is not named may be down to what is called "protective anonymity." Some scholars have argued that, where writers such as Mark and John do not name the individual "sources" of stories, it might be because they are shielding the person, protecting their identities. That is why, for example, Mark does not name the owner of the upper room; at the time Mark was writing and when the stories were first collected, to be publicly identified with Jesus could have been dangerous to that person. This, it seems to me, is clearly one such case of protective identification, although perhaps not quite in the way we imagine...[11]

THE REAL IDENTITY

There is one person who fits the bill. Indeed, there is only one disciple who fulfils all the conditions. Let's recap: he has to be male, known to be a follower of Jesus; he has to be able to move freely within the high priest's courtyard without fear of arrest; and he has to be considered not to be a threat.

That person was the disciple who had been instrumental in the arrest of Jesus in the first place: Judas Iscariot.

Look at it this way: he is (obviously) present at the arrest. What does he do then? The Bible doesn't say, but it implies that he is not part of the actual arresting team. He isn't mentioned in the list of people who lead Jesus away: "So the soldiers, their officer, and the Jewish police arrested Jesus and bound him" (John 18.12).

One can imagine that the party rush off, leaving Judas behind. He has done his job, and no-one, on either side, wants to be associated with a traitor any longer than absolutely necessary. So he decides to follow the arresting crowd and to tag along. He would already be recognized by those on the gate, as he had been there at other times, and, crucially, earlier in the evening to alert the high priest that the moment for the arrest had arrived. He was

---

[10] For Nicodemus as the disciple, see Tindall, E.A., *Expository Times* 28 (1916–17), 283–84.

[11] See Bauckham, *Jesus and the Eyewitnesses*, 183–201.

known to be a follower of Jesus – that was what made him ideal for setting the trap. And he was not a threat – how could he be? He was on their side.

We know that he followed the arrest and trial closely. Matthew's account tells us: "When Judas, his betrayer, saw that Jesus was condemned, he repented and brought back the thirty pieces of silver to the chief priests and the elders. He said, 'I have sinned by betraying innocent blood.' But they said, 'What is that to us? See to it yourself'" (Matt. 27.3–4).

He passes every one of the tests we set above.

1. He is male.

2. He was known to the high priest; he was more than an acquaintance, for they had planned the arrest together.

3. He was known to be a follower of Jesus, for that was what gained him access in the first place. Given the key role he played in securing the arrest of Jesus, others in the household, including the gatekeepers, would have known to admit him at any time.

4. He was not a threat. He is the one person, known to be a follower of Jesus, who would not try a rescue attempt. Because he's part of the plot, he's "on their side."

5. He was not likely to be arrested. Absolutely not. Instead he is rewarded by the authorities for his work.

I know what you're thinking: "What about point 6: 'The disciple couldn't be named'?" It can't be a case of protecting his identity – by the time the gospel was written Judas was long dead, and anyway, he's betrayed Jesus just a few lines earlier. It's not as if he's got a reputation left to protect.

Well I believe John *is* protecting someone. Just not Judas.

It's hard to overstate how much of a pariah Judas became for the Early Church, just how much his name was loathed and hated. The New Testament preserves two accounts of his death, but later writers go a lot further. Papias, an otherwise reliable source from the late first century, preserves a legend in which: "Judas walked about in this world a sad example of impiety; for his body having swollen to such an extent that he could not pass where a chariot could pass easily, he was crushed by the chariot, so that his bowels gushed out."[12] This change of attitude can also be detected in the gospels, where the depiction of Judas gets steadily darker in Matthew, Luke and John. In John's gospel, Jesus is aware that Judas is a traitor almost from the start (John 6.64); John also adds the detail that Judas used to pilfer money from the common purse (John 12.6). While Matthew's gospel shows signs that Judas repented, John's gospel portrays a harsher picture.

So John isn't protecting Judas here; it's not as if his reputation can sink any lower. The person I believe he is protecting is not Judas, but Peter. You see, it is all very well for the disciples to associate with Judas before he betrays Jesus; after all, they had no idea what he was up to. But to have someone associate with him *after* the betrayal, that would be more difficult to explain. Especially if the person who was with him was one of the leaders of the church. I think the reason John leaves out the name of the "disciple" who let Peter in is simply because he does not want to link Peter in any way with the great betrayer.

And yet, looked at logically, it does fit. Judas would have known that there, among the supporters of the high priest, Peter could not take revenge on Judas. Perhaps he, of all the people there, understood how much the disciples had invested in Jesus and therefore how close the attachment was. Perhaps he thought it couldn't do any harm. Or maybe he just wanted to see another disciple fail, as he himself had failed.[13]

That's the least charitable view. Another possibility is that maybe Judas was trying to help. Maybe he was already aware that he had

---

[12] A later account adds even more with Judas's eyes "so swollen that they could not be seen, even by the optical instruments of physicians; and that the rest of his body was covered with runnings and worms." When he dies, the solitary place of his death is left desolate, and "no one could pass the place without stopping up his nose with his hands." See "Fragments of Papias" in *Church Fathers – The Ante-Nicene Fathers.* Edited by Roberts, A. and Donaldson, J. Oak Tree Software.

[13] I discovered, as is normally the case with any kind of Bible theories, that I am not the first person to come up with this. Various others have proposed the theory, the most recent, as I understand is James Charlesworth in *The Beloved Disciple: Whose witness validates the Gospel of John* (Valley Forge: Trinity Press International, 1995) although I haven't seen a copy of this. Edwin Abbott, the author of *Flatland*, also came up with the same theory. See Abbott, *Miscellenea Evangelica I.* He also raises the way in which the "other disciple" tempts Peter to follow him, lures him in, which is linked to Luke's statement that Satan had entered Judas (Luke 22.3).

done something terribly, tragically, disastrously wrong. Matthew tells how, after betraying Jesus, Judas repented of his actions, threw back the money and committed suicide (Matt. 27.3–5). Perhaps the first pangs of regret and shame hit him in the garden when he saw Jesus being taken away. Perhaps he felt by this little gesture, he would show that he wasn't all bad.

All supposition, I know. All complete conjecture. But someone let Peter into the high priest's court that night.

And Judas fits the profile.

WHY DO THE BEARS KILL THE BOYS?

The second book of Kings contains an account of what can only be called Old Testament anti-social behavior. Elisha is passing through Bethel when he is assailed by a group of children

> He went up from there [Jericho] to Bethel; and while he was going up on the way, some small boys came out of the city and jeered at him, saying, "Go away, baldhead! Go away, baldhead!" When he turned around and saw them, he cursed them in the name of the LORD. Then two she-bears came out of the woods and mauled forty-two of the boys. From there he went on to Mount Carmel, and then returned to Samaria (2 Kgs. 2.23–25).

Nevertheless, scholars have long wondered about the morality of this passage, and even the point of recording it in the first place. A Victorian writer called it "one of the stories which naturally repel us more than any other in the Old Testament."[1] Some experts have even called it "a puerile tale" and viewed the idea of God destroying a load of cheeky street urchins as a rather distasteful myth.[2]

I can't see the problem here. You mock someone for baldness, you get eaten by bears. Sounds fine to me. All right, maybe I'm a trifle biased, in that I share at least one of Elisha's personal characteristics. My faith may be OK, but my hair has been backsliding for years. Even so, I think that for anyone who mocks us baldies, being slaughtered by bears is the least they deserve.

However, I'm prepared to admit that having a lot of cheeky kids eaten by bears does smack a little of an over-reaction. So what's going on here?

Some argue that it is another example of the importance of respecting a prophet. The identification of a prophet with the message, the respect which God demands for those he entrusts with his truth, means that even minor misdemeanors are taken extremely seriously. Others see it as a straightforward morality tale, where rudeness and wickedness is punished. Matthew Henry

---

[1] Quoted in Ziolkowski, E.J. "The Bad Boys of Bethel: Origin and Development of a Sacrilegious Type" *History of Religions* 30 (1991), 333.

[2] Gray, J., *I & II Kings: A Commentary*, (London: SCM, 1964), 428.

wrote: "The Lord must be glorified as a righteous God who hates sin, and will reckon for it. Let young persons be afraid of speaking wicked words, for God notices what they say. Let them not mock at any for defects in mind or body; especially it is at their peril, if they scoff at any for well doing."[3]

I can't help thinking that growing up as one of the Henry kids might not have been a barrel of laughs. He might be right about the need for children to exercise judgment, but I'm not sure that's really what this passage is all about.

What we make of this story depends on how we interpret one key word: children. That's the issue that many people find difficult: we picture these little children, being cheeky to this balding prophet, who, in a display of grumpiness, destroys them with some bears of mass destruction.

NOT SO LITTLE

First, even if they were children, our view of children and the Old Testament view is very different. Our world, where criminal responsibility starts at an older age, would baffle the time of the Old Testament. In the ancient world you were expected to take on more responsibilities at an earlier age – and that included responsibility for your own behavior and moral conduct.

Debate centers around the age of these children. Some argue that they were little children and that they had therefore been taught this taunting song by their parents.[4] Others see in them a kind of forerunner to the groups of pestering children that you see "even today in the streets and markets of the Middle East, to the discomfort of the unwary traveler"[5]

Others argue that they weren't children at all. The Hebrew words used to describe the lads are *na`ar* and *yeled*. Both words can indicate a wide age range, from infant to young adult. *Na`ar* means boy or lad, but also can denote a servant or helper. Mephibosheth's

---

[3] Henry, M., *Matthew Henry's Commentary (Condensed)*. Hypertexted and formatted by OakTree Software, Inc.

[4] e. g. Provan, I.W., *1 and 2 Kings*, (Carlisle: Paternoster, 1995), 176–177.

[5] Cogan, M. and Tadmor, H., *II Kings: A New Translation*, (Garden City: Doubleday, 1988), 39.

servant Ziba is called a *na`ar* (2 Sam. 16:1), and he had fifteen sons (2 Sam. 19:17). So, he must have been a bit older than a child (unless he was a very early developer). Similarly, Boaz put a *na`ar* in charge of his harvesting team (Ruth 2:5–6). Also in 1 Kings 20.14, the *na`aray* are "the young bodyguards who serve the district officials."[6]

Whatever the age, the setting is crucial. Elisha is at Bethel – home of the false worship cult which was established in the reign of Jeroboam (1 Kgs. 12.25–33). He is in enemy territory. So these lads – these *na`ar* – far from being innocent, chubby-cheeked little street urchins, may well have been apprentices or helpers associated with the shrine at Bethel. We should get out of our heads the idea of tiny children skipping along the road and being a bit cheeky to a slaphead. These are gangs, from a city associated with false worship and they were threatening Elisha. Don't think "children", think "gangs." Think young adolescents, threatening and ready for a fight. They're the religious equivalents of football hooligans.

Once we understand this, we can look again at their behavior and see it in a different light.

BALD OR INADEQUATE

Elisha was probably naturally bald, since the law did not encourage the shaving of one's head.[7] One commentary talks about his "extreme natural baldness" which sounds like a Hollywood film to me.[8] But the main issue is not actually his lack of hair, but his lack of a master. It should be remembered that Elisha has not long succeeded Elijah as a prophet. He may have been wearing the cloak that Elijah left behind (2 Kgs. 2.13). Telling Elisha to "go on up" is a snide reference to Elijah and the way that he was carried away by God. So the youths are not just saying "Get lost, baldy", they

---

[6] Messner, R.G. "Elisha and the Bears: A Critical Monograph on 2 Kings 2. 23–25." *Grace Journal* 3 (Spring 1962), 16–18.

[7] De Vries, *1 Kings*, 24. Fritz, V. and Hagedorn, A.C., *1 & 2 Kings: A Continental Commentary*, (Minneapolis: Fortress, 2003), 239.

[8] Cogan and Tadmor, *II Kings: A New Translation*, 28.

are mocking Elisha's prophetic role, denying that he is the true successor to Elijah.

Indeed, when we read about the exploits of Elisha, we find that he did everything that his master did and more. And yet Elijah is always referred to as the greatest of the prophets of Israel. Herod Antipas thinks John the Baptist might be Elijah come back to life, not Elisha. The emphasis on Elisha picking up the fallen cloak and his recognition by a group of apparent followers of the old prophet might indicate that there was some question about the validity of Elisha's succession.[9]

So this is not just a story about mocking someone's lack of hair. It's not about a group of cheeky kids. It's about a physical threat to Elisha by young apprentices at a false shrine. It's about people denying that Elisha is the true successor to Elijah. It's about mocking a prophet – and therefore the message they were carrying. They're challenging Elisha to prove himself. Which he does. Rather decisively.

Note that Elisha does not ask for bears; the bears are just an added bonus. No, Elisha curses them in the Lord's name, because he knows that this is part of the ongoing battle between the true worship of Yahweh and the false worship of the Canaanite fertility gods. It's not really Elisha who proves himself, it's God who acts at Elisha's request.

The Old Testament makes it clear that it is a serious crime to mock those doing God's work. Moses was protected by God when he was verbally abused (Num. 12.9–10). Words matter. The old adage about sticks and stones is not true. Words can hurt people enormously; the tongue – as James pointed out – is a powerful weapon.

More than that, you mock the individual and you mock what they stand for. Mock a prophet and you were mocking the message they carried – and that came from God himself. Prophets were God's ambassadors on earth. And he would do all that was necessary to demonstrate that.

No matter how much hair they had.

---

9   De Vries, *1 Kings*, 27.

HOW DID LUKE GET
ON BOARD THE SHIP?

Luke's description of the sea voyage with Paul to Rome is one of the most remarkable travel narratives in ancient literature. There isn't anything else quite like it. The writing is filled with the breathless excitement of someone who just wasn't used to this kind of adventure.[1] You can taste the salt on your lips and feel the spray in your hair. But the excitement of the voyage begs a question: how did Luke get onto the boat in the first place?

Paul, after all, is a prisoner. He's been a prisoner for two years in Caesarea, removed from Jerusalem for his own safety (Acts 23.16–35). Felix, the governor of the time, has left Paul languishing in jail; but when he is replaced by Festus, Paul is given a hearing before the governor, and also Herod Agrippa II (Acts 25–26). After this, because he appealed to Caesar, it is decided to ship Paul to Rome (Acts 26.30–32).

Acts tells us that he is taken on board a ship, which is heading towards the ports on the south coast of Asia Minor

> When it was decided that we were to sail for Italy, they transferred Paul and some other prisoners to a centurion of the Augustan Cohort, named Julius. Embarking on a ship of Adramyttium that was about to set sail to the ports along the coast of Asia, we put to sea, accompanied by Aristarchus, a Macedonian from Thessalonica. The next day we put in at Sidon; and Julius treated Paul kindly, and allowed him to go to his friends to be cared for. Putting out to sea from there, we sailed under the lee of Cyprus, because the winds were against us. After we had sailed across the sea that is off Cilicia and Pamphylia, we came to Myra in Lycia (Acts 27.1–5).

So Paul is in custody. This is not a pleasure cruise or a business trip, he's a prisoner. So how come he's allowed to take his friends along?

---

[1] Smith points out that he describes everything with the eye of a seasoned traveler, but not with the eye of a mariner; it's not a professional account, see Smith, J., and Smith, W.E., *The Voyage and Shipwreck of St. Paul: With Dissertations on the Life and Writings of St. Luke, and the Ships and Navigation of the Ancients*, (London: Longmans, Green, 1880), 21ff.

ALL ABOARD

We know that Paul was accompanied by Luke and Aristarchus. Aristarchus is mentioned by name (Acts 27.2); Luke isn't actually mentioned, but this is one of the "we" passages, written in the first person plural, implying that Luke is actually there. Some scholars find this a problem. They argue that the writer of Luke/Acts was not present on board and simply cobbled the piece together from other accounts of voyages, in order to give a historical verisimilitude to the piece. As a writer, I don't buy this. There is a sense of marvel and excitement, a concern to note down the details accurately. It is, in fact, the single most detailed account of a sea voyage in the whole of ancient literature. So if it is cobbled together from other accounts, it's an amazing job.

Those who claim that Luke was "filling in the gaps", as it were, will always face the problem of why he didn't do it elsewhere. After all, there are plenty of other spaces where he could have filled in the blanks with a bit of well-crafted historical fiction (the two year imprisonment in Caesarea, for example). But he didn't; because he wasn't there.

Not so in this passage. In this passage, he was there. But how did that happen? How did Aristarchus and Luke get on board? Aristarchus is easy: he was probably a prisoner like Paul. He came with Paul to Jerusalem, as a representative of the church in Thessalonica (Acts 20.4). In a letter written after Paul has arrived at Rome, Paul describes him as "my fellow prisoner" (Col. 4.10). Presumably he was caught up in the Jerusalem riot and maybe arrested at the same time. But Luke is not a prisoner.

We know from another account that prisoners seem not to have been allowed to be accompanied. A letter from Pliny tells of a Roman prisoner called Paetus. When he was brought from Illyricum to Rome, his wife Arria was not allowed to accompany him. He was only allowed to take certain slaves with him.[2]

So how did he get on board the ship? The answer may lie in finding a bit more out about Luke. And a bit more about ships.

---

[2] Pliny *Epist* III. 16, quoted in Ramsay, *St. Paul the Traveller and the Roman Citizen*, 316.

A BRIEF WORD ABOUT SHIPS

The Roman Imperial government did not have special prison ships. In fact, there weren't even any passenger ships in those days. If you wanted to travel by boat, you had to go down to the port and find a trade ship which was heading in the right general direction. You would then approach the captain or ship's owner and barter a passage on the boat. This is what happens in this passage: the centurion finds no ships heading for Rome, so hops on one that is going in the same direction.[3]

Just as there were no passenger ships, there were no cabins and no stewards. The only cabin accommodation as such would have been for the use of the captain or owner, and that would have been a large box.[4] Passengers were allotted deck space, and each night a servant would put up a small tent to cover them, taking it down each morning. Similarly, there were no stewards arriving with Bacardi Breezers or an invitation to join the captain for sherry. Instead, servants had to do the cooking, and obtain all the necessary provisions for the journey. There was a galley on ship which the servants could use, presumably after the crew had been fed. So any passenger would have to take along sleeping quarters, cooking equipment and all the food they needed. If the voyage was a long one across open water, they would need a lot of provisions.[5] However, many voyages were a series of short hops from port to port, which allowed passengers to replenish stores and sleep in an inn. We can see this in the first leg of Paul's voyage, where he is allowed off to spend the night with friends in Sidon (Acts 27.3).

Despite this discomfort, ships were technologically very advanced. In particular, Rome's need for grain led to the development of huge grain ships from Alexandria, and it was onto one of these that Paul was transferred. We know what these ships looked like because one

---

[3] Adramyttium was a seaport on the eastern shore of the Aegean sea, opposite the island of Lesbos; see Smith and Smith, *The Voyage and Shipwreck of St. Paul*, 62–63. This is the same course a smaller ship bound for Italy would take.

[4] See Casson, L., *Travel in the Ancient World*, (London: Allen & Unwin, 1974) in particular pp. 149–162.

[5] Casson, *Travel in the Ancient World*, 154.

Two ancient boats from Herculaneum. In the drawing on the left there is a figure sitting on the deck (presumably the owner) giving instructions. The drawing on the right shows the roof of one of the cabins on deck.

was blown off course sometime around 150AD and ended up in Athens. Like the ship in Luke's account, it was traveling late in the season.[6] The Athenians, for all their sophistication, had never seen anything like this "great monster of an Egyptian corn-ship" and it became a noted tourist attraction. The description from Lucian is so wonderful that it's worth giving in full

> I say, though, what a size that ship was! 180 feet long, the man said, and something over a quarter of that in width; and from deck to keel, the maximum depth, through the hold, 44 feet. And then the height of the mast, with its huge yard; and what a forestay it takes to hold it! And the lofty stern with its gradual curve, and its gilded beak, balanced at the other end by the long rising sweep of the prow, and the figures of her name-goddess, Isis, on either side. As to the other ornamental details, the paintings and the scarlet topsail, I was more struck by the anchors, and the capstans and windlasses, and the stern cabins. The crew was like a small army. And they were saying she carried as much corn as would feed every soul in Attica for a year. And all depends for its safety on one little old atomy of a man, who controls that great rudder with a mere broomstick

---

6   Hirschfeld, N. "The Ship of Saint Paul: Historical Background." *The Biblical Archaeologist* 53 (1990), 26.

of a tiller! He was pointed out to me; Heron was his name, I think; a woolly-pated fellow, half-bald. [7]

These ships were enormous: the tankers of their day, capable of holding over a thousand tons of grain, which is three times as much as any vessel before 1820.[8] Rome's need for grain meant that big money was to be made on these voyages, hence the desire of the ship's owner to sail, even though the safe time for sailing was past (Acts 27.9). Ships generally only sailed between May and October, since after that the weather deteriorated, and poor visibility made navigating difficult (ancient mariners relied on the stars to chart their course, or simply on recognizing landmarks on the coastline).[9]

Paul knew only too well the danger and discomforts of traveling by sea. Although accounts of his voyages suggest he traveled more than three thousand miles on the sea over three decades of ministry, he more often chose to go by land. This time, of course, he had no choice. He was put on a series of merchant ships, without anyone to provide for him, and it was presumably this role that Luke agreed to fulfil. It is possible that Luke booked his passage as an independent traveler, but it is also possible that he was allowed on in some other capacity entirely, a role which, despite the fact that Paul was under guard, would, according to Pliny, have allowed Luke to accompany the prisoner. And it is a role that Luke may have known only too well.

A BIT ABOUT LUKE

There are three references to Luke in the New Testament, all from the time of Paul's imprisonment in Rome. In 2 Timothy 4.11 Paul reports that only Luke is with him and he wants Mark sent

---

[7] *The Works of Lucian of Samosata*, Volume IV tr. by H.W. Fowler and F.G. Fowler (Oxford: The Clarendon Press, 1905).

[8] Casson, *Travel in the Ancient World*, 159. For more on the size of these vessels see Hirschfeld, "The Ship of Saint Paul: Historical Background", 27–28; Smith and Smith, *The Voyage and Shipwreck of St. Paul*, 187–190. Landels, *Engineering in the Ancient World*, 160ff.

[9] Landels, *Engineering in the Ancient World*, 156.

to join them. In Philemon 24 Paul sends greetings from himself and his fellow workers – who include Mark and Luke. And finally, in Colossians 4.14, Paul says "Luke the beloved physician greets you…"

We know that Luke came from or at least lived in Philippi, in Greece. We know this because the "we" passages in Acts begin in Troas (just across the sea from Greece) and continue into Philippi, stop when Paul leaves Philippi, then pick up again some time later when Paul returns via the city. So the likelihood is that Luke came across to Troas to meet Paul, traveled back with him to Philippi and stayed behind there, joining Paul when he returned later. Philippi was a Roman colony, populated by many ex-soldiers and freed slaves.

We know from his writing that Luke was familiar with the Septuagint – the Latin translation of the Old Testament – which may indicate that he had become an adherent at the synagogue before converting to Christianity.[10] I doubt that he was Jewish, as Paul includes him in Colossians 4.10–11 in the group of those who are not "of the circumcision." (Aristarchus, on the other hand, is in the "circumcised" group.)

We also know that Luke was a doctor; the "beloved physician" (Col. 4.14). The trouble is that when we see the word "doctor" we think of trained professionals sitting in a surgery or zooming round a hospital ward in their coats. Doctors today are part of a highly skilled, highly respected (and mainly well-paid) profession.

The same was absolutely not true in New Testament times. Being a doctor in the Græco-Roman world was to be part of a low-status profession. Since most people they treated died, the doctors were often seen as "quacks" or charlatans. Doctors were often Greek, and also frequently slaves or ex-slaves. Rich Romans might have their house physician, a slave who had learnt some medicine and who looked after the health of the household. It is highly likely that Luke was one such doctor: a freed slave, who carried on his profession once he had gained his freedom. Like all freed slaves,

---

[10] Witherington, *The Acts of the Apostles: A Socio-Rhetorical Commentary*, 54ff.

he took the name of his master upon gaining his freedom, which means that his master was called Lucian or Lucius.

This would explain the fact that in his dedication to Theophilus, Luke uses the same form of address that subordinates use to Roman superiors. He was simply used to speaking that way. Luke also depicts craftsmen and artisans in a positive light. We're looking at someone who was educated, who was used to dealing with Roman superiors, who was at home among craftsmen and artisans.[11]

In particular, it gives us a clue as to the capacity in which he served Paul. We know that Paul suffered from some kind of medical complaint throughout his life. It may have been that which not only first brought Luke to Paul's aid, but, as Paul grew older, formed a key role for Luke. He was Paul's personal physician as well.

And maybe that's how he was allowed to be on the boat and to continue in close proximity to this person who was a Roman prisoner. In the letter of Pliny, as we have seen, only slaves were allowed to accompany prisoners. Perhaps, therefore, Luke was not only willing to accompany Paul on the sea, he took up his old role, that of a servant or slave, the person who put the tent up and arranged the meals.

A REAL HERO

Of course, it's possible that he was allowed to travel as a companion, but he would have had to book his own passage. He would almost definitely have needed some form of special permission, as the larger the party, the more hassle it would have been for the centurion to book passage.[12] The likelihood is that he still would have assisted Paul in this way. Luke knew what he was doing. He knew how to look after people. He was not afraid of getting his hands dirty (or,

---

[11] For a detailed account of authorship see Witherington, *The Acts of the Apostles: A Socio-Rhetorical Commentary*, 54ff., Ramsay, *St. Paul the Traveller and the Roman Citizen*, 20–23.

[12] Rapske argues that Luke could have traveled as a fare-paying passenger. "But the closeness of his association with Paul during the voyage must have required, at the very least, some form of official consent. Personally I still feel it unlikely that permission would have been granted for Paul to take some friends; but it may have been granted for him to take a servant or slave. And the presence of the slave would add to his status in the eyes of the centurion and Captain of the ship." See Rapske, B., *The Book of Acts and Paul in Roman Custody*, (Grand Rapids: Eerdmans, 1994), 378.

in this case, wet). He went along with Paul, in whatever capacity he could, to do whatever was needed to help.

For the Early Church, the kind of role that Luke played was to become a defining, identifying characteristic. They, too, took on the role of servants. Like their founder, they were willing to wash the feet of others. Because four years after this journey, the kind of open, unfettered preaching that Paul had toured through Asia and Greece became, if not impossible, a lot more risky. Following the Neronian persecution, it became extremely difficult to talk openly about Jesus. And yet the church kept growing. Why? Because, in the words of one early church writer, "We do not talk about great things. We live them."[13]

It's easy to look at Paul and Peter and talk about them as the heroes of early Christianity. They certainly were heroic, but the truth is that there were thousands of heroic Christians; people who risked oppression, exclusion, stigma and even death to follow "the way." They lived lives that were distinctive, lives that were different, lives which sailed in the opposite direction to those of the people around them. They rescued abandoned children, they stayed with plague victims, they looked after widows and orphans.[14]

Luke may have bought passage alongside Paul on the boat. Or he may have taken up an old role as a slave and acted the part. Whatever the case, he went, knowing the danger, because it was the right thing to do.

How did he get on the boat? The hard way.

---

[13] Minucius Felix Octavius 38. 5 trans. in Kreider, *Worship and Evangelism in Pre-Christendom*, 19.

[14] Stark, *The Rise of Christianity*, 147ff.

BIBLIOGRAPHY

Abbott, E.A. *Miscellenea Evangelica I*, (Cambridge: Cambridge University Press, 1913)

Ackroyd, P.R. *Exile and Restoration: A Study of Hebrew Thought of the Sixth Century B.C.*, (London: SCM, 1968)

Alexander, L. "The Origin of Greek and Roman Artillery" *The Classical Journal* 41 (1946), 208–212

Altschuler, E. L., A. Haroun, B. Ho, & A. Weimar. "Did Samson Have Antisocial Personality Disorder?" *Archives of General Psychiatry* 58 (2001), 202–203

The Anchor Bible Dictionary, ed. D.N. Freedman, (New York: Doubleday, 1999)

Anderson, A.A. *2 Samuel*, (Dallas, Texas: Word Books, 1989)

Avi-Yonah, M. *Map of Roman Palestine*, (London: Oxford University Press, 1940)

Balz, H. and G. Schneider. *Exegetical Dictionary of the New Testament*, (Grand Rapids: Eerdmans, 1990)

Barber, E.J.W. *Prehistoric Textiles: The Development of Cloth in the Neolithic and Bronze Ages with Special Reference to the Aegean*, (Princeton: Princeton University Press, 1990)

Batey, R.A. "Is this not the carpenter?" *New Testament Studies* 30 (1984), 249–258

— "Sepphoris – An Urban Portrait of Jesus" *Biblical Archeology Review* 18 (May/June 1992)

Bauckham, R. *Gospel Women: Studies of the Named Women in the Gospels*, (Edinburgh: T & T Clark, 2002)

— *Jesus and the Eyewitnesses: The Gospels as Eyewitness Testimony*, (Grand Rapids, Michigan: Eerdmans, 2006)

Beasley-Murray, G.R. *John*, (Waco, Texas: Word Books, 1987)

Ben-Tor, A. and R. Greenberg. *The Archeology of Ancient Israel*, (Philadelphia: Yale University Press, 1991)

Bernheim, P. *James, Brother of Jesus*, (London: SCM, 1997)

Bettenson, H.S. *Documents of the Christian Church*, (Oxford: Oxford University Press, 1986)

Blaikie, W.G. *The First Book of Samuel*, (Expositor's Bible, London: Hodder & Stoughton, 1888)

Blenkinsopp, J. "Kiriath-Jearim and the Ark" *Journal of Biblical Literature* 88 (1969), 143–156

Blomberg, C.L. *From Pentecost to Patmos: Acts to Revelation: An Introduction and Survey*, (Nottingham: Apollos, 2006)

Borg, M.J. and J.D. Crossan, *The Last Week: What the Gospels Really Teach About Jesus's Final Days in Jerusalem* (San Francisco: HarperSanFrancisco, 2007)

Brenner, A. *Samuel and Kings*, (Feminist Companion to the Bible, 7; Sheffield: Sheffield Academic, 2000)

Bright, J. *A History of Israel*, (London: SCM, 1960)

Brown, R.E. *The Birth of the Messiah*, (London: Cassell, 1993)

— *The Death of the Messiah: From Gethsemane to the Grave: A Commentary on the Passion Narratives in the Four Gospels*, (London: Geoffrey Chapman, 1994)

— *The Gospel According to John*, (London: Geoffrey Chapman, 1971)

Brown, R.E. and J.P. Meier. *Antioch and Rome: New Testament Cradles of Catholic Christianity*, (London: Geoffrey Chapman, 1983)

Bruce, F.F. *Commentary on the Book of the Acts: The English Text*, (London: Marshall, Morgan & Scott, 1954)

Brueggemann, W. *First and Second Samuel*, (Louisville, Ky: John Knox Press, 1990)

Budd, P.J. *Numbers*, (Waco, Texas: Word Books, 1984)

Busch, F. *The Five Herods* (London: Robert Hale, 1958)

Campbell, A.F. "Yahweh and the Ark: A Case Study in Narrative" *Journal of Biblical Literature* 98 (1979), 31–43

Campbell, G. *The Oxford Dictionary of the Renaissance*, (Oxford: Oxford University Press, 2003)

Campbell, J.G. *Deciphering the Dead Sea Scrolls*, (London: Fontana Press, 1996)

Carroll, J.T, and J.B. Green. *The Death of Jesus in Early Christianity*, (Peabody, Mass: Hendrickson Publishers, 1995)

Casson, L. *Travel in the Ancient World*, (London: Allen & Unwin, 1974)

Chancey, M. and E.M. Meyers. "Spotlight on Sepphoris: How Jewish was Sepphoris in Jesus' Time?" *Biblical Archeology Review* 26 (July/August 2000).

Charlesworth, J.H. *The Old Testament Pseudepigrapha*, (London: Darton, Longman & Todd, 1983)

Clements, R.E. *God and Temple*, (Oxford: Blackwell, 1965)

Clines, D.J.A, and T.C. Eskenazi. *Telling Queen Michal's Story: An Experiment in Comparative Interpretation*, (Sheffield: Sheffield Academic Press, 1991)

Cogan, M. and H. Tadmor. *II Kings: A New Translation*, (Garden City: Doubleday, 1988)

Connolly, P. *Living in the Time of Jesus of Nazareth*, (Oxford: Oxford University Press, 1983)

Crossan, J.D. *The Historical Jesus: The Life of a Mediterranean Jewish Peasant*, (Edinburgh: Clark, 1993)

Cullmann, O. *Peter: Disciple, Apostle, Martyr*, (London: SCM, 1953)

Damerji, M.S.B., T. Takase, and Y. Okada. *The Development of the Architecture of Doors and Gates in Ancient Mesopotamia*, (Tokyo: Institute for Cultural Studies of Ancient Iraq, Kokushikan University, 1987)

Danby, H. *The Mishnah, Translated From the Hebrew*, (London: Oxford University Press, 1933)

Daniel-Rops, H. and P. O'Brian. *Daily Life in Palestine at the Time of Christ*, (London: Weidenfeld and Nicolson, 1962)

De Vries, S.J. *1 Kings*, (Waco: Word Books, 1985)

Dillard, R.B. *2 Chronicles*, (Waco: Word Books, 1987)

Dothan, T. "What We Know About the Philistines" *Biblical Archeology Review* 8 (July/August 1982)

Durham, J.I. *Exodus*, (Waco: Word Books, 1986)

Encyclopedia Judaica, (Jerusalem: Encyclopedia Judaica, 1971)

Eusebius, *The Ecclesiastical History and the Martyrs of Palestine*, trans. H.J. Lawlor and J.E.L. Oulton (London: SPCK, 1927)

Fillon, M. "The Real Face of Jesus" *Popular Mechanics* (2002)

Finegan, J. *Handbook of Biblical Chronology: Principles of Time Reckoning in the Ancient World and Problems of Chronology in the Bible*, (Peabody: Hendrickson Publishers, 1998)

Fitzmyer, J.A. "Did Jesus Speak Greek?" *Bibical Archeology Review* 18 (1992)

Foakes Jackson, F.J. "Evidence for the Martyrdom of Peter and Paul in Rome" *Journal of Biblical Literature* 46 (1927), 74–77

Freyne, S. *Galilee, From Alexander the Great to Hadrian, 323 B.C.E. To 135 C.E.: A Study of Second Temple Judaism*, (Edinburgh: T&T Clark, 1998)

Fritz, V. *The City in Ancient Israel*, (Sheffield: Sheffield Academic Press, 1995)

Fritz, V. and A.C. Hagedorn. *1 & 2 Kings: A Continental Commentary*, (Minneapolis: Fortress, 2003)

Frost, S.B. "The Death of Josiah: A Conspiracy of Silence", *Journal of Biblical Literature* 87 (1968), 369–382

Furfey, P.H. "Christ as Tekton", *Catholic Biblical Quarterly* 17 (1955), 204–215

Gamble, H.Y. *Books and Readers in the Early Church: A History of Early Christian Texts*, (New Haven: Yale University Press, 1995)

García, M.T. Florentino, and J. C. Eibert. *The Dead Sea Scrolls Study Edition*, (Leiden: Brill, 1997)

Gardner, J.F. *Women in Roman Law and Society*, (Bloomington: Indiana University Press, 1991)

Goodrick, E.W., J.R. Kohlenberger III, and J. A. Swanson. *Zondervan NIV Exhaustive Concordance*, (Grand Rapids: Zondervan, 1999)

Goodspeed, E.J. "Paul's Voyage to Italy", *The Biblical World* 34 (1909), 337–345

Gray, J. *I & II Kings: A Commentary*, (London: SCM, 1964)

Gregory, C.R. *Canon and Text of the New Testament*, (Edinburgh: T. & T. Clark, 1907)

Grierson, R. and S.C. Munro-Hay. *The Ark of the Covenant*, (London: Phoenix, 2000)

Grossman, D. *Lion's Honey: The Myth of Samson*, (Edinburgh: Canongate, 2006)

Guelich, R.A. *Mark 1–8:26*, (Dallas: Word Books, 1989)

Gundry, R.H. *Mark: A Commentary on His Apology for the Cross*, (Grand Rapids: Eerdmans, 1993)

Gunn, D.M. *Judges*, (Oxford: Blackwell, 2005)

Haas, N. "Anthropological Observations on the Skeletal Remains from Gi'vat ha-Mivtar" *Israel Exploration Journal* 20 (1970), 38–59

Hacker, B.C. "Greek Catapults and Catapult Technology: Science, Technology, and War in the Ancient World" *Technology and Culture* 9 (1968), 34–50

Halpern, B. *David's Secret Demons: Messiah, Murderer, Traitor, King*, (Grand Rapids: Eerdmans, 2001)

Hamilton, N.Q. "Temple Cleansing and Temple Bank" *Journal of Biblical Literature* 83 (1964), 365–372

Hamilton, V.P. *Handbook on the Historical Books: Joshua, Judges, Ruth, Samuel, Kings, Chronicles, Ezra-Nehemiah, Esther*, (Grand Rapids: Baker Academic, 2001)

— *Book of Genesis: Chapters 18–50 (New International Commentary on the Old Testament)*, (Grand Rapids: Eerdmans, 1995)

Hamm, D. "Luke 19:8 Once Again: Does Zacchaeus Defend or Resolve?" *Journal of Biblical Literature* 107 (1988), 431–437

Haran, M. "The Disappearance of the Ark" *Israel Exploration Journal* 13 (1963), 46–58

— *Temples and Temple-Service in Ancient Israel: An Inquiry Into the Character of Cult Phenomena and the Historical Setting of the Priestly School*, (Oxford: Clarendon Press, 1978)

Harrison, R.K. *Introduction to the Old Testament*, (London: Tyndale Press, 1970)

Harvey, K. *The Kiss in History*, (Manchester: Manchester University Press, 2005)

Hayes, J.H. and J.M. Miller. *Israelite and Judaean History*, (London: SCM, 1977)

Hazlett, I. *Early Christianity: Origins and Evolution to AD 600, in Honour of W.H.C. Frend*, (London: SPCK, 1991)

Hengel, M. *Crucifixion in the Ancient World and the Folly of the Message of the Cross*, (London: SCM, 1977)

— *Paul Between Damascus and Antioch: The Unknown Years*, (London: SCM, 1997)

Henry, M. *Matthew Henry's Commentary (Condensed)*. Hypertexted and formatted by OakTree Software, Inc.

Hirschfeld, N. "The Ship of Saint Paul: Historical Background" *The Biblical Archaeologist* 53 (1990), 25–30

Hoehner, H.W. *Herod Antipas*, (Cambridge: Cambridge University Press, 1972)

Honeyman, A.M. "The Evidence for Regnal Names among the Hebrews" *Journal of Biblical Literature* 67 (1948), 13–25

Horsley, R.A. *Archeology, History, and Society in Galilee: The Social Context of Jesus and the Rabbis*, (Valley Forge, PA: Trinity Press International, 1996)

— *Galilee: History, Politics, People*, (Pennsylvania: Trinity Press, 1995)

Hurtado, L.W. *The Earliest Christian Artifacts: Manuscripts and Christian Origins* (Grand Rapids: Eerdmans, 2006)

James, M.R. *The Apocryphal New Testament: Being the Apocryphal Gospels, Acts, Epistles and Apocalypses: With Other Narratives and Fragments*, (Oxford: Clarendon, 1924)

Japhet, S. *I & II Chronicles: A Commentary*, (London: SCM, 1993)

Jensen, E.E. "The First Century Controversy over Jesus as a Revolutionary Figure" *Journal of Biblical Literature* 60 (1941), 261–272

Jensen, M.H. *Herod Antipas in Galilee: The Literary and Archaeological Sources on the Reign of Herod Antipas and Its Socio-Economic Impact on Galilee*, (Tübingen: Mohr Siebeck, 2006)

Jensen, R.M. "Of Cherubim and Gospel Symbols" *Biblical Archeology Review* 21 (Jul/Aug 1995)

Jeremias, J. *Jerusalem in the Time of Jesus: An Investigation Into Economic and Social Conditions During the New Testament Period*, (London: SCM Press, 1974)

Jones, A.H.M. and M. Avi-Yonah, *The Cities of the Eastern Roman Provinces*, (Oxford: Clarendon Press, 1971)

Josephus, Flavius. *Antiquities*

— *The Jewish War*, (Harmondsworth: Penguin, 1981)

Keener, C.S. *The Gospel of John: A Commentary*, (Peabody: Hendrickson Publishers, 2003)

Kelm, G.L. and A. Mazar. "Excavating in Samson Country— Philistines and Israelites at Tel Batash" *Biblical Archeology Review* 15 (Jan/Feb 1989)

Kidner, D. *Genesis: An Introduction and Commentary*, (London: Tyndale Press, 1967)

King, P.J. and L.E. Stager. *Life in Biblical Israel*, (London: Westminster John Knox Press, 2001)

Kirsch, J. *The Harlot By the Side of the Road: Forbidden Tales of the Bible*, (London: Rider, 1997)

Klassen, W. "The Sacred Kiss in the New Testament: An Example of Social Boundary Lines" *New Testament Studies* 39 (1993), 122–135

Klein, R.W. *1 Samuel*, (Waco: Word Books, 1983)

Kraeling, C.H. "The Jewish Community at Antioch" *Journal of Biblical Literature* 51 (1932), 130–160

Kreider, A. *Worship and Evangelism in Pre-Christendom*, (Cambridge: Grove Books, 1995)

Kruse, C.G. *The Gospel According to John: An Introduction and Commentary*, (Leicester: Inter-Varsity Press, 2003)

Kutz, I. "Samson's complex: the compulsion to re-enact betrayal and rage" *British Journal of Medical Psychology* 62 (1989), 123–134

Landels, J.G. *Engineering in the Ancient World*, (London: Constable, 2000)

Lee, G.M. "The Books and the Parchments: Studies in Texts: 2 Timothy 4:13" *Theology* 74 (1971), 168–169

Levenson, J.D. and B. Halpern. "The Political Import of David's Marriages" *Journal of Biblical Literature* 99 (1980), 507–518

Levy, T.E. *The Archeology of Society in the Holy Land*, (London: Continuum, 2003)

Lightfoot, J.B. *The Apostolic Fathers*, (London: Macmillan, 1893)

Longenecker, R.N. *Galatians*, (Dallas: Word Books, 1990)

Lowrie, W. "The Kiss of Peace" *Theology Today* 12 (1955), 236–242

Lyons, W.J. "On the Life and Death of Joseph of Arimathea" *Journal for the Study of the Historical Jesus* 2 (2004), 29–53

Macmullen, R. *Paganism in the Roman Empire*, (New Haven: Yale University Press, 1981)

Malamat, A. *History of Biblical Israel: Major Problems and Minor Issues*, (Boston, Mass: Brill, 2004)

Margalith, O. "Samson's Foxes" *Vetus Testamentum* 35 (1985), 224–229

— "Samson's Riddle and Samson's Magic Locks" *Vetus Testamentum* 36 (1986), 225–234

Marshall, I.H. *The Acts of the Apostles: An Introduction and Commentary*, (Leicester: Inter-Varsity Press, 1980)

Maslen, M.W. and P.D. Mitchell, "Medical theories on the cause of death in crucifixion" *Journal of the Royal Society of Medicine* 99 (2006), 185–188

May, H.G. "The Ark. A Miniature Temple" *American Journal of Semitic Languages and Literatures* 52 (1936), 215–234

Mays, S. *The Archaeology of Human Bones*, (London: Routledge, 1997)

Mazar, B., M. Avi-Yonah, and A. Malamat, *Views of the Biblical World*, (Oxford: Oxford University Press, 1958)

McCown, C.C. "Codex and Roll in the New Testament" *Harvard Theological Review* 34 (1941), 219–249

Meier, J.P. *A Marginal Jew: Rethinking the Historical Jesus* (New York; London: Doubleday, 1991)

Meiggs, R. *Trees and Timber in the Ancient Mediterranean World*, (Oxford: Clarendon Press, 1982)

Messner, R.G. "Elisha and the Bears: A Critical Monograph on 2 Kings 2.23–25" *Grace Journal* 3 (1962), 12–24

Mitchell, T.C. *The Bible in the British Museum: Interpreting the Evidence*, (London: SCM, 1988)

Moldenke, H.N. and A.L. Moldenke. *Plants of the Bible*, (Waltham, Mass: Chronica Botanica, 1952)

Morris, L. *The Gospel According to John: The English Text With Introduction, Exposition and Notes*, (London: Marshall, Morgan & Scott, 1971)

Mowry, L. "The Early Circulation of Paul's Letters" *Journal of Biblical Literature* 63 (1944), 73–86

Muhly, J.D. "How Iron Technology Changed the Ancient World and Gave the Philistines a Military Edge" *Biblical Archaeology Review* 8 (Nov/Dec 1982)

Murphy-O'Connor, J. *The Holy Land: An Archaeological Guide from Earliest Times to 1700*, (Oxford: Oxford University Press, 1986)

Negev, A. and S. Gibson. *Archaeological Encyclopedia of the Holy Land*, (New York: Continuum, 2001)

Neil, W. *Acts: Based on the Revised Standard Version*, (London: Marshall, Morgan & Scott, 1981)

Neirynck, F.N. "The 'Other Disciple' in Jn 18.15–16" *Ephemerides Theologicae Lovanienses* 51 (1975), 113–141

Ober, J. "Early Artillery Towers: Messenia, Boiotia, Attica, Megarid" *American Journal of Archaeology* 91 (1987), 569–604

Oppenheim, A.L. "The Golden Garments of the Gods" *Journal of Near Eastern Studies* 8 (1949), 172–193

Osborne, R.E. "St. Paul's Silent Years" *Journal of Biblical Literature* 84 (1965), 59–65

Parsons, M.C. "Short in Stature: Luke's Physical Description of Zacchaeus" *New Testament Studies* 47 (2001), 50–57

Phillips, L.E. *The Ritual Kiss in Early Christian Worship*, (Alcuin/ Grove Liturgical Study, 36; Cambridge: Grove, 1996)

Porten, B. "Did the Ark Stop at Elephantine?" *Biblical Archaeology Review* 21(May/June 1995)

Potter, T.W. *Towns in Late Antiquity: Caesarea and Its Context*, (Oxford: Oxbow, 1995)

Pritchard, J.B. *The Ancient Near East in Pictures Relating to the Old Testament*, (Princeton: Princeton University Press, 1969)

Provan, I.W. *1 and 2 Kings*, (Carlisle: Paternoster, 1995)

Von Rad, G. *Genesis: A Commentary*, (London: SCM, 1972)

Ramsay, W.M. *St. Paul the Traveller and the Roman Citizen*, (London: Hodder and Stoughton, 1908)

— *The Church in the Roman Empire Before A.D. 170*, (London: Hodder and Stoughton, 1893)

— *A Historical Commentary on St. Paul's Epistle to the Galatians*, (London: Hodder and Stoughton, 1899)

Rapske, B. *The Book of Acts and Paul in Roman Custody*, (Carlisle: Paternoster Press, 1994)

Rauch, J. "Short guys finish last" *Economist* (23 Dec 1995)

Riesner, R. *Paul's Early Period: Chronology, Mission Strategy, Theology*, (Grand Rapids, Mich.: Eerdmans, 1998)

Robbins, F.E. "Review: Antike Technik by Hermann Diels" *Classical Philology* 11 (1916), 103–105

Roberts, A. and J. Donaldson, ed. *Church Fathers – The Ante-Nicene Fathers*. Edinburgh Edition, (Oak Tree Software)

Roberts, C.H. "Books in the Graeco-Roman World and the New Testament" in *Cambridge History of the Bible* (Cambridge: Cambridge University Press, 1970) I, 48–66

Roberts, C.H. and T.C. Skeat, *The Birth of the Codex*, (London: Oxford University Press for British Academy, 1983)

Robinson, D.F. "Where and When Did Peter Die?" *Journal of Biblical Literature* 64 (1945), 255–267

Roller, D.W. *The Building Program of Herod the Great*, (Berkeley: University of California Press, 1998)

Ryken, L., J. Wilhoit, T. Longman, C. Duriez, D. Penney and D. G. Reid. *Dictionary of Biblical Imagery*, (Leicester: Inter-Varsity Press, 1998)

Ryrie, C.C. "Especially the Parchments" *Bibliotheca sacra* 117 (1960), 242–248

Sanders, E.P. *The Historical Figure of Jesus*, (London: Penguin, 1995)
— *Jesus and Judaism*, (London: SCM, 1985)

Scobie, C.H.H. *John the Baptist*, (London: SCM Press, 1964)

Van Seters, J. "The Problem of Childlessness in near Eastern Law and the Patriarchs of Israel" *Journal of Biblical Literature* 87 (1968), 401–408

Shanks, H. *Understanding the Dead Sea Scrolls: A Reader From the Biblical Archaeology Review*, (London: SPCK, 1993)
— "Tom Crotser Has Found the Ark of the Covenant—Or Has He?" *Biblical Archaeology Review* 9 (May/June 1983)

Shanks, H. and B. Witherington III. *The Brother of Jesus: The Dramatic Story & Meaning of the First Archaeological Link to Jesus & His Family*, (London: Continuum, 2003)

Skeat, T.C. and J.K. Elliott. *The Collected Biblical Writings of T.C. Skeat*, (Leiden: Brill, 2004)

Smaltz, W.M. "Did Peter Die in Jerusalem?" *Journal of Biblical Literature* 71(1952), 211–216

Smith, G. *The Doctrine of the Cherubim: An Inquiry*, (London: Longman, Brown, Green and Longmans, 1850)

Smith, J.M.P. "The Character of King David" *Journal of Biblical Literature* 52 (1933), 1–11

Smith, J. and W.E. Smith, *The Voyage and Shipwreck of St. Paul: With Dissertations on the Life and Writings of St. Luke, and the Ships and Navigation of the Ancients*, (London: Longmans, Green, 1880)

Soggin, J.A. and J. Bowden, *Judges: A Commentary*, (London: SCM, 1981)

Speiser, E.A. *Genesis*, (Garden City: Doubleday, 1964)

Stambaugh, J.E. *The Ancient Roman City*, (Baltimore: John Hopkins University Press, 1988)

Stambaugh, J.E. and D.L. Balch, *The New Testament in Its Social Environment*, (Philadelphia: The Westminster Press, 1986)

Stanton, G. *The Gospels and Jesus*, (Oxford Bible Series, Oxford: Oxford University Press, 1989)

Stark, R. *The Rise of Christianity: How the Obscure, Marginal Jesus Movement became the Dominant Religious Force in the Western World in a Few Centuries*, (San Francisco: HarperSanFrancisco, 1997)

Still, T.D. "Did Paul Loathe Manual Labor? Revisiting the Work of Ronald F. Hock on the Apostle's Tentmaking and Social Class" *Journal of Biblical Literature* 124 (2006), 782–795

Strange, J.F. and Shanks, H. "Has the House Where Jesus Stayed in Capernaum Been Found?" *Biblical Archaeology Review* 8 (Nov/Dec 1982)

Taylor, J.E. *John the Baptist Within Second Temple Judaism*, (London: SPCK, 1997)

Theissen, G. and A. Merz. *The Historical Jesus: A Comprehensive Guide*, (London: SCM Press, 1998)

Thiede, C.P. *Simon Peter, From Galilee to Rome*, (Exeter: Paternoster Press, 1986)

— *The Cosmopolitan World of Jesus: New Findings From Archaeology*, (London: SPCK, 2004)

Tindall, E.A. *Expository Times* 28 (1916–17), 283–284

Van der Toorn, K., B. Becking, and P.W. Van der Horst. *Dictionary of Deities and Demons in the Bible*, (Grand Rapids:Eerdmans, 1999)

Van der Toorn, K. and C. Houtman. "David and the Ark" *Journal of Biblical Literature* 113 (1994), 209–231

Ubelaker, D.H. *Human Skeletal Remains: Excavation, Analysis, Interpretation*, (Washington: Taraxacum, 1978)

Vanderkam, J.C. *The Dead Sea Scrolls Today*, (London: SPCK, 1994)

Vermès, G. *The Changing Faces of Jesus*, (London: Penguin, 2000)

Walker Jr., W.O. "Jesus and the Tax Collectors" *Journal of Biblical Literature* 97 (1978) 221–238

Webb, R.L. *John the Baptizer and Prophet: A Socio-Historical Study*, (Sheffield: JSOT Press, 1991)

Wenham, G.J. *Genesis 16–50*, (Waco: Word Books, 1994)

Westermann, C. and J. Scullion, *Genesis 37–50: A Commentary*, (London: SPCK, 1987)

Whitehorn, J.N. "The Catapult and the Ballista" *Greece & Rome* 15 (1946), 49–60

Wilkinson, J. *Jerusalem as Jesus Knew It: Archaeology as Evidence*, (London: Thames and Hudson, 1978)

Wiseman, D.J. *1 and 2 Kings: An Introduction and Commentary*, (Leicester: Inter-Varsity Press 1993)

Witherington III, B. *Letters and Homilies for Hellenized Christians*, (Nottingham: IVP Academic, 2006)

— *The Acts of the Apostles: A Socio-Rhetorical Commentary*, (Grand Rapids: Eerdmans, 1998)

— *The Gospel of Mark: Socio-Rhetorical Commentary*, (Grand Rapids: Eerdmans, 2001)

Wolters, A.M. *The Copper Scroll: Overview, Text and Translation*, (Sheffield: Sheffield Academic Press, 1996)

Wright, G.R.H. *Ancient Building in South Syria and Palestine*, (Leiden: Brill, 1985)

Yadin, Y. "Goliath's Javelin and the מנור ארגים" *Palestine Exploration Quarterly* 86 (1955), 58–69

— *The Art of Warfare in Biblical Lands in the Light of Archaeological Discovery*, (London: Weidenfeld and Nicolson, 1963)

Zias J. and E. Sekeles. "The Crucified Man from Giv'at ha-Mivtar: A Reappraisal" *Israel Exploration Journal* 35 (1985), 22–27

Ziolkowski, E.J. "The Bad Boys of Bethel: Origin and Development of a Sacrilegious Type" *History of Religions* 30 (1991), 331–358

Zohary, M. *Plants of the Bible: A Complete Handbook to All the Plants with 200 Full-Colour Plates Taken in the Natural Habitat*, (Cambridge: Cambridge University Press, 1982)

INDEX

Abigail 29, 32 n.8
Abinadab 101
Achilles 57
Acts of Paul and Thecla 140
Acts of Peter 46-48
Adam 73, 174
Aeschylus 61, 67
Ahaziah 105
Ai 100, 102
Alexandria 138, 195
Altschuler, Dr. Eric 58
Amaziah 153–154
Amnon 175
Amon 104–105
Ananus 38
Andrew (apostle) 93, 124
Angels 69–71, 110
Anthony 65
Antioch 41–42, 44–45, 128, 135–143
Antonia fortress 38, 40
Aphek 102
Aphrodite 85
Arabia 137
Archimedes 156
Aretas, King of Arabia 20, 21 n.4, 63
Aristarchus 193–194, 198
Aristobulus 23
Ark of the Covenant 32, 71–73, 99–112, 131; construction of 100; mentions of in Old Testament 104–105
Artabanus 23
Ashdod 102, 130, 152
Asher 84
Asherah 105
Ashkelon 130, 152
Assyria 74, 156–157
Athaliah 105
Athens 196
Augustine 74 n.11
Azariah (see Uzziah)

Baal 105
Babylon, Babylonians 107–108, 110, 112
Balawat gates 55–56
Barnabas 135–143
Bartholomew 93
Baruch 110, 166
Bathsheba 29

Beth-shemesh 102
Bethany 35–36
Bethel 101, 102, 189, 191
Bethlehem 76–79, 81, 126, 159
Bethphage 35, 37
Bilhah 84, 171
Bithynia 44
Boaz 191
Bond, James 17, 130
Books – see *membranae*
Bronze technology 131–133
Brown, Dan 17

Caesarea Maritime 38–39, 44, 65, 193–194
Caiaphas 179, 180
Caligula 26
Cana 91
Canaan, Canaanites 31, 103, 130, 172, 174, 192
Capernaum 91, 107, 123–128, 159
Cappadocia 44, 139
Carmel, Mount 189
Carpus 165
Catapults 156
Cato the Elder 114
Cato the Younger 37 n.4
Cherubim 69–75, 100
Chuza 180
Cicero 145
Cilicia 139–142, 193
Clement of Alexandria 14 n.6
Clement of Rome 49, 51
Cleopatra 65
Clopas/Cleopas 95–97
Clothing, ancient 170, 171–176
Codex/codices 167–169
Cornelius 41
Corinth 44
Crassus 146
Crete 130
Crucifixion 51, 92, 145–151, 160
Cyprus 74, 135–136, 139, 142, 193
Cyrene 136, 142

Dagon 101
Damascus 67, 137–138, 142
Dan 84; (tribe) 130
Dancing 24

David 27–33, 77, 103, 105, 117–120, 160, 175–176
Dead Sea Scrolls 109–110
Decapolis 65
Delilah 58
Dinah 87
Disciples 180–182
Doctors 198–199
Donatello 70
Doors, in ancient near east 56
Doré, Gustav 53–55
Dyeing of fabric 173

Ebal, Mount 101, 102
Ebenezer 130
Eden 72, 73
Egypt, Egyptians 55, 112, 130, 159, 173, 174
Ekron 102, 130, 152
Elath 152, 154
Elhanan 118–121
Elijah 191–192
Elisha 189–192
Elizabeth 89
Ephesus 113, 128
Euripides 67
Eusebius 95
Eve 73, 78, 174
Ezekiel 71–75

Felix 193
Festus 67, 94, 193

Gabriel 70
Galatia 44, 141
Galilee 20, 61–65, 77, 92, 177, 180, 182
Gatehouses 55–56
Gath 56, 102, 121, 130
Gaza 53, 55, 130, 152
Gerazim, Mount 101–102
Gideon 31
Glory of the Kings 109
Golgotha 110, 146, 150
Goliath 111, 117–122, 129–130, 133
Gordon, General 110–111
Gospel of Hebrews 93 n.8

Hadrian 134
Haftara 166

Haran 87
Hebron 53, 152
Hegesippus 91, 93, 96, 98 n.16
Herod Agrippa I 41
Herod Agrippa II 193
Herod Antipas 19–26, 62–64, 123, 180; character of 22
Herod the Great 20, 21 n.2, 38–39, 42, 63, 65, 108
Herod's palace 39, 148
Herodias 19, 21, 22, 23, 24
Herodion 22 n.5
Herodotus 134
Hezekiah 157
Holmes, Sherlock 103
Holy Grail, non–existent 99
Horace 146
Houses, in first century 80–81, 125–128
Hushai 174

Iconium 142
Idols 30–31
Ignatius 44
Indiana Jones 73, 99, 107
Irenaus of Lyons 74 n.11
Iron production 131–133
Isaac 171, 175
Isaiah 74 n.12, 174

Jacob 70, 83–87, 171
James (apostle) 42, 92–93, 95, 97, 124
James, brother of Jesus 90–95, 97, 136, 160, 161; death of 93–94
James, son of Alphaeus 93
Javelins 121
Jehoram 105
Jehu 37 n.4
Jeremiah 106–109, 111
Jericho 15–16, 18, 36, 65, 100, 102, 152, 189; Herodian palace 22 n.5
Jeroboam 153
Jerome 74 n.11
Jerusalem 32, 34–42, 58, 65, 78, 92, 102, 104–105, 107–108, 110, 136, 139, 152, 154–157, 159, 177–179, 180–181, 193–194; church in 95–96; destruction of by Romans 43; population of 37–38

Jesus 14, 16–18, 25, 34–37, 39–40, 49, 52, 61–68, 113–116, 123–128, 135, 177–188, 200; appearance of 14–15; as tekton 61–63, 159; birth of 77–82; family of 89–98; arrest of 177; death of 145–151
Joanna, wife of Chuza 180
Joash 154
Job 174
John (apostle) 41, 93, 95, 97, 124, 183
John the Baptist 19–26, 89–90, 97, 183, 192
John the Elder 45, 183
John Mark see Mark
Jonathan 27, 132
Joppa 39, 44, 102
Jordan, river 101, 123
Joseph (patriarch) 171–176
Joseph of Arimathea 92, 150, 180, 184
Joseph, father of Jesus 62, 63, 77–81, 89–90, 96, 97, 159–163
Josephus, Flavius 22, 23, 26, 38, 63–64, 123, 148
Joses, brother of Jesus 90–94, 97, 161
Josiah 104–106
Jotham 153, 158
Judah (person) 84, 86
Judas Iscariot 113–116, 185–188
Judas, brother of Jesus (Jude) 90–94, 98 n.16, 160, 161
Judas, son of Ezekias 63
Judas, son of James 93

Karibu 74–75
Karnak 107
Kidron valley 40, 178
Kiriath–jearim 101, 102, 152
Kissing, in early Church 114–115; in Græco–Roman world 113–115

Laban 83–84, 87
Lachish 152, 154, 156
Lahmi, brother of Goliath 120
Last Supper 78
Lazarus 180
Leah 83–87
Leprosy 153, 158
Levi (tax–collector) 125
Levi 84

Levites 100, 106
Life expectancy, in Israel 162–163
Lucian 196
Luke (person) 165, 193–194, 196–200

Maccaabean revolt 160
Machaerus 21–22, 25
Manasseh 104–105, 109 n.22
Mandrakes 83–87
Mark (John Mark) 42, 43, 45–46, 142, 165, 177, 185, 197–198; as Peter's translator 45
Marriage, customs 24, 80
Mary Magdalene 94, 180
Mary, mother of Jesus 70, 77–81, 89–90, 93–95, 97, 159–163
Mary, wife of Clopas 94–97
Mary, mother of John Mark 42
Matthew (apostle) 93, 124
Megiddo 172, 174
Membranae 166–170, christian use of 167–169
Menelik 109
Michal 27–33
Mishnah 16, 108
Moses 100, 108
Mount of Olives 35, 40, 92, 126

Nabatea 21, 63
Naphthali 84, 123
Nazareth 62, 77, 88, 91, 123, 159, 161
Nebo, Mount 108
Nebuchadnezzar 107
Nero 48–49, 51, 146, 200
Nicodemus 180, 184

Obed–edom the Gittite 102–103
Octavius 65

Paetus 194
Palti/Paltiel 32
Papias 45, 183, 186
Parchments, see *membranae*
Passover 37, 78, 104–105, 159–161, 179
Paul 43–44, 51, 67, 89, 93, 113–115, 135–143, 147, 165–170, 193–195, 197–200; death of 49, 51
Persecution of early church 48–49, 200

Peter 41–52, 92–93, 113, 124–125,
    126–128, 135, 177–188, 200;
    appearances in Acts 41; death of 46–
    51; wife of 44; *Quo Vadis* story 46
Pharisees 15, 16 n.6, 68
Philip (apostle) 93
Philip the Tetrach 23, 123
Philistines 28, 29, 57–58, 101, 117–118,
    129–134, 154–155, 173; culture of
    130–131
Phoenicia 74, 135–136
Physiognomics 15, 17–18
Pilate, Pontius 38–39, 147
Pliny 194, 199
Pontus 44
Protevangelium of James 161
Putti 70

Queen of Sheba 109
Qumran 109–110

Rachel 83–87
Raiders of the Lost Ark 99
Rameses III 130
Raphael 70
Rehoboam 107
Reni, Guido 160
Rephaim 121
Reuben 84
Roman army 138; in Jerusalem 38–39
Rome 43–50, 128, 138, 165, 193, 194,
    197; church at 45

Salome (daughter of Herodias) 19–20,
    23–25
Salome (sister of Mary?) 94–95, 97
Samaria 44, 65, 189
Samson 53–59, 70; compulsive
    behaviour 57–59; Jewish folklore 57
Saul 27–33, 102, 131–132
Second Apocalypse of Baruch 110
Seneca 148
Sepphoris 62–65
Shalmaneser III 55
Shiloh 100, 102, 152
Ships and sailing 195–197
Shishak 99, 106–107
Sidon 65, 193, 195
Silas 142

Silvanus 43
Simeon 84
Simon the Zealot 93
Simon, brother of Jesus 90–94, 97, 160,
    162
Slavery in Roman empire 145–147,
    198–199
Solomon 31, 103–105, 109
Stephen 135
Symeon, son of Clopas 95–97
Syria 138, 140–142

Tabernacle 71, 73, 100, 103, 108, 111,
    173
Tacitus 146
Tamar 86, 175–176
Tanis 99
Tarsus 135, 137, 139, 140–142
Tax–collecting 15–16
Temple, Jerusalem 31, 71, 73, 80, 103–
    108, 154, 157, 183
Theater in Roman world 61; *hypokrites*
    in 65–66
Theophilus 199
Thomas 93
Tiberias 21, 159
Tiberius, emperor 23
Timothy 165
Torah 159, 165–166
Tosefta 107–108
Troas 165, 170, 198

Uzzah 102
Uzziah/Azariah 152–158

Vitellus 23

Wyatt, Ron 110–111

Zacchaeus 13–18, 180
Zebedee 94–95, 97, 124, 183
Zebulun 87, 123
Zechariah 36–37, 39
Zilpah 84, 171

ABOUT THE AUTHOR

Nick Page is the author of more than 50 books for both children and adults. His books include The Big Story, And Now Let's Move into a Time of Nonsense *and* The Bible Book. *He recently edited the* Collins Atlas of Bible History. *Along with many books on the Bible and Christianity, he has also written books on seventeenth-century history and English literature.*

A well-known teacher and speaker, he lives in Oxfordshire, England, with his wife and three daughters. He enjoys reading, cooking, travelling and supporting Watford FC (although with regard to the latter, 'enjoys' is not quite the right word).

THE BIG STORY

WHAT ACTUALLY

HAPPENS IN THE BIBLE

What actually happens in the Bible?
How do the individual stories fit in?
And how does the whole Bible come
together?

The Big Story is about what happens in God's amazing book.
From the creation of the universe to the end of the world, this
retells the whole biblical narrative in fifty bite-size chunks. This is
the ultimate family saga and the best of all blockbusters.

Fully illustrated, peppered with explanatory information and
written with Nick's trademark humour and insight, this is the Bible
as you have never read it before.

> *'Stimulating and original. Easy to read but highly*
> *thought-provoking. In one word - brilliant!'*
> Steve Chalke MBE, Oasis Global